EXPLORER

Also by Benedict Allen

Mad White Giant
Into the Crocodile Nest
Hunting the Gugu
The Proving Grounds
Through Jaguar Eyes
The Skeleton Coast
Edge of Blue Heaven
Last of the Medicine Men
The Faber Book of Exploration (ed.)
Into the Abyss

EXPLORER

The Quest for Adventure and the Great Unknown

Benedict Allen

CANONGATE

This paperback edition published in 2023 by Canongate Books

First published in Great Britain, the USA
and Canada in 2022 by Canongate Books Ltd,
14 High Street, Edinburgh EH1 1TE

Distributed in the USA by Publishers Group West
and in Canada by Publishers Group Canada

canongate.co.uk

1

British Library Cataloguing-in-Publication Data
A catalogue record for this book is available on
request from the British Library

ISBN 978 1 78689 626 1

Typeset in Garamond Premier Pro by Palimpsest Book Production
Ltd, Falkirk, Stirlingshire

Printed and bound in Great Britain by Clays Ltd, Elcograf S.p.A.

MIX
Paper from
responsible sources
FSC
www.fsc.org FSC® C018072

To Lenka, who kept the home fires burning.

'How much better it has been than lounging in comfort at home.'
Among his last surviving words, Robert Falcon Scott

'We travel thus, proceeding from valley to valley. The desolation is superb!'
Turkestan Solo, Ella Maillart

'I too for years past have been stirred by the sight of a solitary cloud drifting with the wind to ceaseless thoughts of roaming.'
Narrow Road to the Interior, Matsuo Bashō

CONTENTS

AUTHOR'S NOTE

This is the story of what led me, as a young man, to head off alone to the farthest reaches of our planet in an era when there were still valleys and ranges known well only to the isolated communities that inhabited them – and the story of why, thirty years on, I returned to a mountain in New Guinea and asked that no one come to find me should I not re-emerge.

It is an account, drawn from memories, rough field notes and diaries, about the urge we all share to explore, and what it means to be an 'explorer' in the twenty-first century. Above all, it's a book about friendship – the value of disconnecting from our own world and the importance of connecting with another.

Fiyawena Mission Station, Papua New Guinea,
17 November 2017

Last thoughts.
Outside, they're very kindly praying for me.

Normally the ladies at least wait till dawn – each day a little more fervent, and each day a little more high-pitched. The mist ascends, the birds of paradise open their wings in a shower of vanilla and gold, and up go the screeching pleas to heaven.

Last night Jokei lay on guard beside me, curled on his side, bush knife to hand. Now, though, my only companion is the moth that remains silent on the windowsill. Foxy brown and lightly furry, it lives on, like me. The difference is, all but the head, half a thorax and wings have been removed, gutted by the ants.

Time to say goodbye to my sanctuary, then: the dirtied window slats from which I hang my socks to dry, the motifs lovingly painted on the wall – 'Jesus Had Compassion On Them' – and the blue vinyl floor where American missionaries once held hands in prayer but where I sweat out my fevers.

On a separate page I have set out my intended route. I'm writing these last words here in case something else occurs.

Already I've checked the medicines and bandaged up my feet. I have thought through the usual protocols, everything that will help me stay alive over the next few days. There's little else to do now than study the map, tick off another checklist and say things to reassure myself. At such a moment it's hard not to think back – to times I might have died but didn't. To the life I've lived – and the life I haven't.

I will take up my rucksack at around 8 a.m.

PART ONE

A DANGEROUS YEARNING

I

I watched the progress of my father's aeroplanes, they say, even from my pram. Back and forth they flew, sleek birds that parted the grey clouds of Cheshire and laid their oily trails across my consciousness. Day after day through my earliest years my dad took the 'V bombers' to the brink – at first only the Valiant and Victor. Then there came into our lives a plane that was quite different.

This new one was far off when I first set eyes on it, aged four or five at most: no more than a black slit over Alderley Edge. Then, as if choosing to reveal itself, the aircraft banked, beginning a low run over Prestbury golf course. It was heading this way.

There was no forgetting the first sight of that silhouette (those gigantic delta wings, here at last the perfect paper dart), nor the commotion in its wake. We were watching from down by the stream, I remember. The cold water was spilling over the top of my gumboots. Stewart, my elder brother, held the half-filled bucket and I held a stick. We'd been collecting sticklebacks.

The sky roared and the garden shook. As we stood transfixed in the stream, the Vulcan bomber made its approach.

'Stew, isn't that plane a bit low?'

'It's low, all right!'

'Shouldn't we duck down?'

Such a screeching and howling – as if from a creature in pain. By way of reassurance, Dad gave us a signal. He dipped the Vulcan's left wing.

5

And, of course, looking back, I can't help but wonder if this precise moment – a father's salute from the sky – was the source of my restlessness. As youngsters we all dream of taking off, but now, the triangular shadow thrown fleetingly across my innocent, upturned face, my father seemed to be giving me permission.

———

In those days (this was the early 1960s) we had a red cotton kite. Here was our very own bird of prey, as it hovered, rattling in the wind. We paid out the line, running and shrieking through the sloping pastures, beyond the oak tree, across the stream. The Vulcan, though, was not like the kite. Blatant, unapologetic, possibly vindictive, the majestic harpy was only ever seen in passing. Each day, over at Woodford Aerodrome, the aircraft lifted heavily from the tarmac, being readied for the time it would be trusted with our nuclear deterrent. Initially in a coat of 'antiflash white' and in later years painted to mimic the birch forests and rich chernozem soils of somewhere beyond the Iron Curtain, the strategic bomber went about its grim duty.

Through the passage of my early childhood – by the age of six, my red kite snagged in the oak tree; by the age of seven, that tree a decorative feature of the new housing estate – I kept to myself, and sometimes I dreamed of these flights of freedom.

It troubled me not one iota that the Mark II being perfected by Avro over my blond curls was an executioner, that its high-altitude mission might one day be completed with a terrible finality. I looked up at those spread wings, a dark angel forever heading beyond Macclesfield: one day I too would go somewhere over the horizon, to the place where my father was always heading.

I lost myself in stories of others who, through the ages, had ventured to these faraway lands. First, as I understood it as a schoolboy, were the Phoenicians, who circumnavigated Africa, and then the Vikings happened upon America. We didn't know much about who they were, apart from Erik the Red, but we might guess that many met an interesting end.

Then came the Great Navigators, when the likes of the dashing privateer

Martin Frobisher, not to mention the Portuguese (Ferdinand Magellan, Vasco da Gama and Bartholomew Diaz) turned their thoughts to distant shores. Aboard their galleons and caravels, they traced the outlines of the continents and prayed for fair winds, making observations with their astrolabes and rash promises of landfall to their increasingly mutinous crews – just as they'd already made rash promises to their kings and queens – and many of these adventurers didn't come back either.

There followed the Golden Era of discovery, which saw Victorians penetrate the hinterlands often accompanied by a substantial number of retainers; they pinned specimens in cedarwood boxes, solved topographical riddles such as 'the Question of the Nile' and sought 'to Better the Lives of the Natives'. The most celebrated of all was the Scottish missionary Dr Livingstone, who, after thirty-two years of dedication to Africa, died in a mud hut, kneeling in prayer by his bed, having not quite managed to convert anyone.

Next, the Heroic Age, which appeared to be mostly about getting to one of the Poles before anyone else. At last, on 6 April 1909, Admiral Robert Peary beat his rival Frederick Cook to the North – or said he did, though later it turned out he hadn't quite either. The winner in the South was Roald Amundsen, who made light work of it, using just huskies and skis. Robert Scott, on the other hand, believed in the 'gentlemanly art of man-hauling' and was remembered because his end was so British, tragic and beautiful. As the blizzard swirled and the canvas of their little tent flapped, he extended his arm around his best friend, Edward Wilson, before that too froze solid.

True, the motivation of many was questionable – or so it increasingly seemed to me. Columbus, for one, was highly rewarded with gold (or, anyway, expected to be) and other notables weren't exactly averse to a little fame and glory. Peary, for instance, worked up detailed plans for an elaborate mausoleum in his own honour – as if a payment were now due from the public for his sacrifice.*

Few had time for the native populace (apart from James Cook, who,

---

* For more a detailed overview of many of the adventurers mentioned in this volume, the reader might wish to refer to *The Faber Book of Exploration*, which I happened to edit.

as the son of a farmhand, seemed to think them in a condition no worse than many of his countrymen, slogging away*). William Dampier, who had anchored off 'New Holland' in 1688, reported that the inhabitants of Australia were 'the miserablest People in the World . . . And setting aside their Humane Shape, they differ but little from Brutes.'

Regrettably, this somewhat set the tone for the next Europeans along, but in private, elsewhere and on better days, Dampier wrote in really quite respectful terms of the 'sagacity of the Indians', I felt. Another I had a particular affection for was Mary Kingsley, the indomitable self-taught lady who, hastening through the West African lowlands, fell into an elephant trap but was saved by her skirt. 'At first you see nothing but confused stupidity and crime,' she wrote of her travels in the 1890s, 'but when you get to see – well! As in the other forest you see things worth seeing.'† More often, explorers had a tendency to boss the locals about or just exterminate them – sometimes not even by accident. 'I am surrounded by savages,' lamented Henry Stanley, while noting in his private diary that he'd attacked and destroyed '28 large towns and three or four score villages', as he traversed the same region as Kingsley – his 'Dark Continent' – only twenty years before. Or else they pretended no one much lived in these lands – which was unfair because, if you thought about it, the forefathers of these 'savages' were also explorers. Besides, they knew in which direction through the thicket lay drinkable water.

The good thing was, none of these energetic people were daunted; they marched on while suffering. 'I believe we so forgot ourselves as to shake hands on it,' the crusty, moustachioed Bill Tilman said of his dignified arrival at the summit of Nanda Devi in the Garhwal Himalayas, and such mountaineers appeared to take with them little but their tweeds

---

* From Captain Cook's *Journal*: '. . . they may appear to some to be the most wretched people upon the Earth, but in reality they are far more happier than we Europeans; being wholy [sic] unacquainted not only with the superfluous but the necessary conveniences so much sought after in Europe, they are happy in not knowing the use of them'.

† With wit and irony, Kingsley enjoyed provoking her Victorian audience to rethink their prejudices. 'Human eye-balls, particularly of white men . . . are a great charm,' she informed readers with relish. Local cultures never ceased to engage and amaze – especially compared to the 'thin veneer of rubbishy white culture' that colonial officials and even missionaries were attempting to impose.

and haversacks. Fridtjof Nansen, the cold-eyed Norseman, wore a wolf hide and drifted sympathetically with the Arctic ice; Freya Stark rode without fear through the valleys of the Assassins; Douglas Mawson kept striding through the Antarctic even after the soles of his feet fell off.

And I became convinced that I too would join them – be one of these characters with their perpetual strivings and unquenchable flames. They seemed to feel it keenly: the sense that something in themselves or the world was missing.

But here's the truth of it. Whatever the ingredients – or lack thereof – that compel a child to head off, nothing might have come of it. Had I the talent, I might equally have been an antiques restorer like Stew or an editor like my sister Katie, but something in me would not listen. For my dad was a pioneer, and in delivering that Vulcan bomber into my life he had told me that it was possible for me to be a pioneer too.

—

Not a test pilot, though. Because, for all that I was a polite and earnest little boy, the sort who tries his best, there was an appalling streak of obstinacy about me. I didn't like to be told what to do. I didn't even like others being told what to do. To vent my frustration, I had to calm down in the garden with Toffee, our pet corgi. Gradually, I learned to go my own way.

And all the while, a sense of an era drawing to a close. When, in 1969, Wally Herbert completed his traverse of the Arctic via the Pole, a trudge of 3,800 miles over the ice, no one seemed to much notice. For that same year a test pilot who wasn't my father became the first to walk on the moon.

From down here on Planet Earth, how peaceful was the scene: that silvery disc so immaculate, placed unblemished by humanity in the heavens – and now within our reach. On this and succeeding Apollo missions I gazed up like every Cub Scout, hoping to spot the lunar module. Together we humans stood in awe, for somewhere up there the next chapter in the tale of exploration was unfolding.

There was just the one obvious problem.

'Mum, why did they plant that flag?'

'I expect because they're really proud. You see, the Americans got there before the Russians.'

'Seems a shame, that's all,' I said.

It was explained to me. This wasn't like the cowboy films on the telly. This wasn't the Wild West, and these weren't goldminers staking a claim.

My mum took me on her knee. 'You see, to hoist your flag is a perfectly natural way of celebrating your country – just a lovely thing to do.'

'Yes, lovely,' I said. 'And, Mummy, will they take it away with them?'

'Take what away?'

'That flag. When will they get rid of it?'

'I expect it'll stay put.'

Like a goldminer staking a claim, I thought.

What could anyone do with such a child? Throughout my life it would be a tussle: I was neither content to be the unflappable test pilot – obeying instructions, hands forever steady on the joystick – nor someone able to sit back.

I was ten before I told my father. By now he was flying from Heathrow, a captain with Zambia Airways. Already, he had brought back weaver bird nests, a stuffed baby crocodile, a night adder in a bottle of meths. I placed them carefully on my bedroom shelves, alongside my shark's teeth and ammonites.

'An explorer?' Dad said. 'I think that's a wonderful thing to want to be!'

I still recall standing by the door of what we called the drawing room – the brass handle like an apple in my hand, the carpet a mustard yellow, the thick linen curtains a burgundy red. And everywhere in that room the silence. At last I'd made my intent known.

'I expect he'll grow out of it,' my grannie said.

But my mum sighed, because she knew. Deep down, I think they all knew.

I went outdoors, pleased to have made my announcement. I strode back and forth along the herbaceous border, for the first time wondering about the practicalities of becoming 'an explorer'. Beside my mother's pastel blue delphiniums, I agonised with Toffee.

Slowly, my boyhood went by: Thor Heyerdahl sailed his boats of papyrus; Ranulph Fiennes led his 'Transglobe' team onward along the Greenwich meridian; Reinhold Messner and Peter Habeler climbed Everest without recourse to bottles of oxygen.

I took to collecting the picture postcards sent by my dad. From Nairobi, Nassau, Bangkok, Greenland, they arrived on the doorstep and I sello-taped them into my scrapbook, each one a depiction of somewhere where I wasn't. I would add images of the Garden of Eden – for that too was a land impossibly far off. I marvelled at the tree and its offer of knowledge, that blameless-looking girl and boy. Eve and Adam had the innocence of children – the wide-eyed innocence of me – and in due course, like me, their desire for that knowledge proved costly. But no matter. I peered at them, pre-temptation, carefree in alcoves and shampoo adverts. Rendered by the Flemish in oils, they wore their fig leaves, their glades populated by friendly lions, unharried peacocks and casually passing dromedaries.

I bided my time. Or, as Mr Laimbeer, my art teacher, put it, I wasted my time. 'Are you a dreamer, Allen?' he said once, viewing my artwork – repetitive scenes of Adam and/or Eve in prelapsarian bliss – with more than a hint of disgust. 'I rather think you are.'

A more impudent fifteen-year-old might have referred Mr Laimbeer to his own modest oeuvre, but I daresay he was right. Specifically, I was dreaming of what might qualify me for my first adventure. Already I'd set my sights on a degree in environmental science (it being obvious even in 1975 that humanity was making a mess of our spinning blue planet), while over in the school biology lab I was rearing exotic plants. Unable yet to go anywhere very far afield, I took solace in these humid mini kingdoms contained within a plastic cultivator box, the breath of sphagnum condensing and then peeling down the transparent sides. They purveyed the mystery of Sir Walter Raleigh's 'discoverie' of an empire in the wooded heartlands of the Orinoco, not to mention the 'Golden Citie of Manoa (which the Spanyards call El Dorado)'.

Each habitat was a land to investigate at my leisure, and in the centre of each I placed an insectivorous plant. A sundew, a butterwort, a Venus flytrap. Maybe even back then I sensed that trouble always awaited in Paradise.

And so onwards, towards the day of my father's retirement and the morning when my mother instead waved a first tearful goodbye to me.

II

When first I set eyes on it, a broken line of crimson on a map, I was studying for a Masters degree in ecology – though I wonder if I wasn't already going a little off the rails. I'd almost blown my first degree by joining, when I should have been swotting for my finals, expeditions to a volcano in Costa Rica and a ridge in Brunei. The same year I'd also led the university expedition to an Icelandic glacier and this didn't seem enough either. I paced about my student quarters, which were scattered with leaves to replicate a jungle floor. The walls were lined with charts depicting the Americas.

But now here it was, spread before me: an invitation. 'Perimetral Norte', the map stated above the unwavering line, which led onwards through the Amazon with all the confidence of a four-lane motorway – then petered out.

The road would, if completed, open the vast, uninterrupted forests of northernmost Brazil – and, you could safely bet, take little account of what might be encountered en route. (As an undergraduate I'd studied enough Environmental Impact Assessments to know that no one would have been dispatched across the four hundred miles of untrammelled vegetation to check.)

To the sort of student whose favourite sweatshirt lovingly depicted our planet – stamped with the words 'SAVE IT!' – the projected route looked like the line an underqualified surgeon might hastily dab in felt tip, before taking up the scalpel.

The Amazon needed no surgeon; it wasn't even a willing patient. I wondered what lay undisturbed there, as no doubt did the Brazilian surveyors presently perspiring at the road's end, staring into the greenery alongside their theodolites.

———

I don't suppose my mother was overly excited at the news that I had found my first major objective. It was bad enough that Rod, the son of her friend, Mrs Coatman, had gone down in the South Atlantic with Tilman, the same crusty and moustachioed mountaineer I'd admired as a boy.*

However, my own time was approaching now, and she, I suppose, accepted that I must be readied like one of Dad's planes for flight. I would take to the sky, a hastily-assembled prototype, and be tested to near destruction. And so it proved: I'd fare little better than the kite – reliant on favourable winds to clear that top branch. Again and again I'd return to the ground broken. It was she who would have to glue me back together.

'You must stay here as long as you need to prepare yourself,' my mother said, but had to turn her face away. She took a steadying breath before going to hang out the washing.

I needed funds; that was the worst of it. It was well known: every explorer took companions, what they called 'backup' – available through a reliable radio transmitter – copious tins of pilchards and, for the purpose of raising morale, daily rations of cocoa or Kendal Mint Cake. Without a plethora of obliging donors, expeditions didn't come cheap.

Time went by. I took it in my head to extend my journey yet further. If I could make it all the way from the Orinoco Mouth to the Amazon Mouth, this would take me through the land of El Dorado, the fantastical kingdom of gold that had already promised Raleigh and the 'Spanyard' so much and yielded so little.

———

* The *En Avant*, a converted steel tug, set sail from Rio de Janeiro in November 1977 for Port Stanley and foundered somewhere along the way. Tilman's biographer, Tim Madge, wondered if the sailor, now in his eightieth year, had known the Norse idea of old men on their final journey bringing with them young heroes to ensure a welcome in Valhalla.

As it transpired, no one wanted to sponsor my venture – or be loosely associated with it or any alternatives. But I dared say I'd manage somehow. Perhaps someone out there might lend a hand.

To pay for my return air ticket, I worked in a warehouse shifting books. (We were these days living in Hampshire, near Farnborough Airport, so that my dad could investigate aeroplane accidents – which, given the prospects of my own inaugural flight, was an irony not lost on anyone much.) The sweetness of my brother Stewart again stands out to me, thinking back. Gifted at all things practical – Meccano, the Airfix models – he patiently examined the plastic sheeting that I'd bought cheap for a tarpaulin and rivetted as best I could. This was a shoddy job and Stew must have known it. 'I'll be relying chiefly on the know-how of the Indians,' I told him, suddenly feeling a bit queasy.

Those 'Indians' have their work cut out, he must have thought, but was good enough to make no comment.

I stood in the hallway, about to cast off from the sibling who had always kept me safe. He handed me something to open on my birthday, and for a moment I felt immensely lonely. I looked at what he'd deftly swaddled in tape – 'To keep the contents intact in the heat,' he explained. In the event, the gift – a Penguin chocolate bar – exploded long before my birthday, succumbing to the unremitting swelter of the mangroves, but I wedged it into my overloaded rucksack and, as I did so, I listened to the slow tick-tock of the longcase clock, that I might recall it later.

'Now, you do have your survival kit?' my mother asked – for she had read somewhere that no explorer worth his salt left without one.

'Yes, Mum,' I said in the world-weary tone adopted by the young through the centuries as they take to their wings – and my mother smiled bravely, as mothers have done through the centuries watching them go. 'Don't you worry, I'll be fine,' I said, for I was twenty-two, and believed I was immortal.

She waited at the gate, unable to do much more for me now than hold back her tears and proffer a brief wave.

Dad drove me to the airport, and in the departure lounge I opened the bacon and egg sandwiches that my mum had wrapped in tin foil. They were still warm.

Only after take-off was I able to raise a smile. I played *Dígame!* – the BBC Spanish cassette course – and looked out of the window. At last I was away, my life stretching far beyond the scattered cumulus. Even after arrival in Caracas – this featured an attempted armed robbery at the bus station – it didn't seem to have occurred to me that I was taking it upon myself to cross arguably the least accessible reach of the whole of South America. Still ahead, the ranks of vegetation that seemed fixated on doing me in. The thorns, the vines, their ants.

By the time I crawled out from under that simmering green blanket of existence I'd completed a journey the likes of which, I dare say, those trees had never quite seen. Four hundred and thirty-seven miles in a matter of weeks. I was on my knees.

'You're safely back, that's the main thing,' said my mother.

I uttered nothing in response. I just hugged her again, and gazed about at familiar things, grateful to be spared an interrogation. Nonetheless she waited, hoping for a word of explanation.

But what was there to say? I'd met so many frustrated individuals out there. So many frustrated trees.

Yet I had been allowed to live. I'd come out into the daylight, trampling a corn crop, blinking in the sudden light. But why? I hadn't deserved to. A complete novice, I had attempted what might have been, had I recorded it properly, the last geographically significant Amazon crossing and got away with it.

I don't suppose anyone wanted me to die on their hands – not the goldminers, not the missionaries, not the people that in those days I called 'Indians'. I'd been handed onward like an unravelling parcel from one community to another. Day after endless day I thumped along in my German paratrooper boots – £7.50, from Laurence Corner, the army surplus shop in Camden – among species that smelt out the weak. Six months on from my departure, the forest had stripped me of everything, companions included. *It's up to you alone now*, I thought, hunched on the riverbank when my dugout capsized. Even today the memory is never far away – the water running off me while I looked about in shock. I was overshadowed by plant life, overshadowed by my helplessness, the full reality of a human's lonely state.

Three or so weeks I had stumbled on. No horizon or possessions to speak of. I was aged twenty-three, with two strains of malaria, and intent only on escape.

Yet once, as a student, I had loved the rainforest. In Central America and Borneo it had seemed enough just to look up at the interlaced canopy.*

I walked up the white, cast-iron staircase to my bedroom. I listened out across the house: the longcase clock in the hall, the forgiving parents passing through rooms. I knew the sounds of the door to each; they too were the voices of home – the slow, long sigh of the front door (the sweep of the draught excluder along the bottom, its black hairs like a cropped eyelash), the sharp clack of the old latch to the pantry (my mother withdrawing meat from the freezer), the cushioned thump of the glassed side-door (my dad coming in from the garden).

Quietly, I ran a bath.

And I looked about at my room: the snake in the bottle, the stuffed crocodile, the scrapbook. Faithfully standing guard above my bed, a poster of the mountaineer Doug Scott atop Everest. I sat on the bed, placed a hand on the clean cotton of my duvet cover. A relic of my childhood, it was patterned with poppies and issued the reassuring scent of Persil Automatic.

The pity was, I'd brought this on myself. It was as if I had provoked the trees – and these trees knew my sort well. For five hundred years they had faced the European and his arrogance. Now I too had been slapped around.

Be proud of your journey, I tried to tell myself. A phenomenal achievement – as a feat of stamina (and admittedly mind-boggling ignorance), it even brought to mind that of Gonzalo Pizarro, the conquistador who first descended into the Amazon Basin and was reduced to cooking a leaf soup in his helmet. But I could not be proud of it.

I eased my scrapbook from the shelf, opened it up. Coming loose from the cartridge paper was a print I'd once stuck in, with liberal squirts from

---

* From my diary of 1982: *So many trees gathered together and all left to their own devices. Here was the biotic climax – the dipterocarps, the 'walking' palms, the strangling figs, the kapok giants, all given the final say, these anchors of life with their considered, at times ponderous, way of managing the trials of life.*

my bottle of Gloy: the glorious, over-the-top rendition of Eden by John Millar Watt – lazing by the hideous waterlilies, more prominent than the kitsch lion and overcrowded omnivores, a squinting, jade-eyed tiger. There in the background I found them together as usual, Eve and her Adam.

A few pages on was a Renaissance fresco by Masaccio, and then the Delacroix, a distraught Adam post-expulsion, tearing at his face while his plump partner looked up, arms spread. Appealing for help, was she? Or forgiveness. Her first pang of guilt.

So many Adams and Eves, each expressing what we had without knowledge – an idyllic yet ultimately unsatisfactory state. They were waiting by that tree as if waiting for me. And always to hand, that crisp apple. They hung around their garden about to pierce the flesh, and then the dangerous longing and regret afterwards.

My mother came tiptoeing up the stairs. 'Just wanted to see you are all right.'

'I'm fine, Mum. Really, I am.'

'You can have a proper rest now,' she said. 'Later, I'll ask Dr Cubitt to give you a check over.'

We had roast lamb. 'Need to fatten you up!' Dad said, jollying me along. He raised a glass. 'Welcome home, Benny!'

I disappeared back to my room, thinking that what I'd feared all this time was true – that explorers weren't always what they should be. Even when we tried to do good, we plundered. What was the legacy of James Cook, that navigator of genius who, one might hope, brought the ideals of the Enlightenment to the South Seas? Seven hundred and fifty thousand* Aboriginals discovered themselves living in the Year of Our Lord 1770 and their home was *terra nullius*, nobody's land. There followed many more unfortunate encounters – though rarely were such encounters quite as unfortunate for the Europeans.

A familiar story, that of the tragic Burke and Wills expedition of 1860–61, well illustrates attitudes of superiority pervasive through the

---

* Source: Aboriginal Heritage Office, New South Wales – although estimates to be found elsewhere range from 500,000 to 2,000,000.

ensuring years. The fourteen-man party* set out from Melbourne to great fanfare though with no indigenous guide. But no matter. This was the best equipped expedition in Australian history and the outward journey – they were to explore a route north to the Gulf of Carpentaria – indeed proved relatively straightforward. On the tiring return leg, however, things became sticky: the four in the principal expedition party found their horses and camels fading, their supplies running dangerously low. Having already off-handedly refused generous offers of food from a people called the Yandruwandha, the Europeans were now reduced to copying them. Only, they failed to realise that nardoo, the seed of a fern, was toxic if not first soaked. 'It is a great consolation, at least, in this position of ours, to know that we have done all we could, and that our deaths will rather be the result of the mismanagement of others . . .' wrote Wills on 21 June, without any sense of irony. Three days later, weakening further, he wrote, 'We have but a slight chance of anything but starvation, unless we can get hold of some blacks.' The sole survivor, Irish soldier John King, was to live on by bagging crows until, among the red dust and gum trees, he located a group of Yandruwandha who kept him alive with fish and their nadoo cakes. On being shown Burke's remains, the Aboriginals who had saved him 'wept bitterly, and covered them with bushes'.

The same tale was to be told all around the world: an indigenous population retreated, the European advanced. Lost lives, lost lands, a lost sense of belonging.† We no longer sought El Dorado or La Candela, which was the elusive Kingdom of Cinnamon, but we still sought mastery, even those I loved the most, the Victorian specimen collectors

---

* After various farewell feasts and church services for the Victorian Exploring Expedition, fifteen thousand people assembled in the Royal Park on 20 August 1860 to send them off. A camel bolted through the excited crowd, resulting in a woman being thrown from her horse, and Burke dismissed his assistant Owen Cowan for being 'a little too hilarious through excess of beer.' From: Burke and Wills Web: the digital research archive. burkeandwills.net.au

† The formulation was repeated across North America, just as it had been in the South. Take Jacques Cartier, the sixteenth-century Breton who claimed Canada for France and the Florentine Giovanni da Varrazzano, first European into the Gulf of New York. Their legacy was the chance of a new life and prosperity for tens of thousands – the prosperity being for those whose land it hadn't been. For more on the catastrophic demise of the native Australian population, see, for example, Bruce Pascoe's *Convincing Ground: Learning to Fall in Love with Your Country*.

such as Richard Spruce, Henry Bates and Alfred Russel Wallace, or tire-less enquirers like Alexander von Humboldt.* They too advanced what was surely likely to be only our way of thinking. Such, it seemed, was the characteristic of our kind: even those with the best intent replaced mystery with our rationalising appreciation of the world. Or we didn't. Far from revealing what we saw as the truth, we generated myths of our own – of fearsome cannibals, of manly exploits, of piranhas.

And gradually what remained fell apart, and still we came and went, and always on our own terms.

Back at the warehouse stacking books, wracked not any more by malaria but bewilderment and shame, I wondered about the forest that nonetheless had spared me.

'I expect you were just trying to find yourself,' my mother said suddenly, one breakfast time.

'I expect so,' I said, and continued to tip the packet of Shreddies.

Kinder, I felt, to spare her. I hadn't been finding myself because I hadn't been lost. The act had been foolish but also deliberate, a clear mission like my dad's – and that was worse.

'Well,' my mum continued uneasily, 'It's all out of your system now . . .'

It wasn't, but to help the process along I put pen to paper.† I couldn't describe what had occurred with much accuracy, but I did remember that the people out there were meek and mild or else cranky, jealous and petty – in short, they were just like us, except they partook of life alongside rivers and among tall trees; they hadn't fenced them out. The Amazon wasn't the *Green Hell* that had so tormented Julian

---

* The former three were contemporaries. The botanist Spruce spent fifteen years exploring the Andes and Amazon Basin. Bates spent almost eleven years gathering an estimated fifteen thousand specimens; his *The Naturalist on the River Amazons* of 1863 remains one of the finest accounts of natural history collecting. Wallace, who initially travelled with Bates, lost his collection of almost the entire previous three years when he departed in the *Helen*; the brig caught fire and sank.

† This became *Mad White Giant*, at one level a rip-roaring tale of adventure, at another an angry attack on my own kind – 'the punk-rock book of exploration', according to one reviewer, Hugh Thomson. I had an opportunity to revisit the theme of the explorer as invader ten years later with my first venture into TV, the 1994 Amazon film *Raiders of the Lost Lake*.

Duguid, nor were these the last days of an Eden.* Not to the local residents.

No doubt the people who wandered the birch woods and icy tundra thought the same about their patch, too. These lands – so frightening or wondrous to us – seemed to me to be neither a threat to those who lived there nor an Acadia; they were just home. A resource, too: they provided food, medicine and shelter.

And so it was that my thoughts turned to the only people in the whole world I trusted to teach me the truth of it.

———

Obstinacy. Contrariness. Guilt, maybe.

Only now, all these years later, am I beginning to understand why I risked my life time and again as a young man, plunging deeper and deeper into the societies who seemed reasonably at ease with their surroundings. It was as if they knew what we refused to acknowledge – that trees, though annoyingly obstructive at times, are necessary on this planet; they might even be our saviours.

I headed to West Papua, rather than back to the Amazon that had almost finished me off, and there picked my way through the forests with a band of men armed with bows and arrows, led on by a ludicrous obsession with what I saw as my 'task'.

Once more, for weeks on end, no one from my world knew where I was. This was a frugal way of life – and, if you weren't alert, a short one. There were tree falls, deluges, festering bites. My jaw ached from the endless chewing – of birds, of bones, of snakes. I was helped with my rucksack, made payments in salt; I wrote, I photographed, I communicated with my hands. For almost half a year I sought to discover what I could – or anyway, some sort of reconciliation with the trees.

———

* I had in mind *Yanomamö: The Last Days of Eden* by Napoleon Chagnon. Though the primeval, 'natural' state is evoked in many such titles, other examples later joining my bookshelves were *Finding Eden* and *Adam with Plumes*. Duguid's less happy experience was of the 'mysterious jungles of Eastern Bolivia'.

But it was only across the border in Papua New Guinea that I found a place to settle down.

Kandengei village was then – as now – hidden away from the main slew of the Sepik river. Seek it out in summer time and along the waterfront you'll discover a parade of thatched dwellings interspersed by leaning coconut palms and handsome flowering trees. It's an agreeable leaf-scape, one further enhanced by the more daring children, who each morning can be seen gleefully leaping into the lagoon from higher branches. Overall, the impression is of a carefree, easy-going community. And, indeed, in my experience, carefree and easy-going the Kandengei people are, much of the time.

Not come high water, though. Then, the whole sleepy ox-bow is transformed – that agreeable waterfront made a disease-ridden mire. Each house is pitched high on stilts not for a better view of the pretty black surrounding waters but to safeguard its inhabitants through periods of inundation, when the rudimentary toilets (innovative constructions suggested by Catholic missionaries) spew their maggoty load. The wood piles also assist the Kandengeis in avoiding the attentions of the more malevolent water spirits – and offer a measure of protection from hostile human elements, too: for the village belongs to the Niowra confederation, comprising six major clans and seven communities, each more distrustful than the next. They are united by a series of complex marital relations, fear of the deceiving River Sepik and faith in the Avookwaark, or Ancient Crocodile, from which they traditionally hold they are descended. And, of course, one might say that this reptile usefully serves as a role model. Highly territorial, an apex predator, the crocodile defends its length of riverbank well.

There's much I've never felt able to say about my time in Kandengei.

Let me think back: it's March, which is towards the end of the high water season. I'm twenty-five years old, strawberry-blond, freckled, six foot four – a foot taller than nearly anyone else here. I'm sunburnt along the ridge of my nose, which is narrow and prone to peeling, and I am about to undergo the ceremony which is central to the Niowra's semi-aquatic existence. It is over, my childhood notion that the life of an explorer is a life of freedom. My focus has sharpened; my thoughts are no longer free-ranging. I understand how much more we all have to learn about such environments – and, at a personal level, how much more I must learn in order to endure in them.

All around me now, grandmothers, mothers and sisters begin crying because of what will shortly take place. This rite is secret but even the more clueless of the girls can guess it involves the most terrible hardship. The boys must now be made into men as strong as the crocodile.

I look on, with the other candidates, as a *banis*, or fence, is erected around the *geigo*, the spirit house;* this tall screen of encircling leaves is the perimeter of the *waarkdumba*, or Crocodile Nest, and this is where we, the *bandees*, will undergo our curious transformation.

Presently, we are having our heads shaved. The elders are putting on their shell anklets, their pig tusk earrings, their headdresses; Rom and Nau, guardians of the spirit house, ask the ancestors to forgive them, should they not have remembered the various tricky procedures. Next, they will call to the Avookwaark, asking Him to help make the next generation strong.

My own hair falls to the mud. Like the other *bandees*, I become absorbed in my own thoughts. Personally, I'm not bothered by the prospect of the discomfort that lies ahead – if nothing else, my misadventure in the Amazon has taught me I have exactly the pathological blinkeredness and unhealthily high pain threshold that so typifies the test pilot – but I am wondering whether getting involved in someone else's culture is such a brilliant idea.

For months I'd been telling myself so: that I will somehow do better, that I will find a way to explore our planet on terms dictated not by ourselves but by the aboriginal inhabitants. However, at this rather late juncture, my hair being hacked away with a blunt and probably unsanitary razor blade, I find myself asking whether this innovative approach to 'exploration' is quite as principled as I'd like to think. Not only does my presumption that I might usefully participate in someone else's

* The *geigo* (or *haus tambaran* in Tok Pisin, the lingua franca that's spoken across PNG) is a barn-like building forbidden to women and the uninitiated. Here the men sit on the two long, high benches and debate the concerns of the day. The culture of the Niowra, and my first experience of New Guinea, is outlined in *Into the Crocodile Nest*.

culture have a special impertinence of its own but I'm doubtless using these accommodating people's unusually violent rite to work through some sort of survivor's complex.

There's worse. The Niowra have surprisingly few qualms about letting me record what should be closely guarded secrets. No outsider has ever undergone this ceremony – why would they? – but the Kandengeis have yet even to ask my motivation for wanting to go through this bloody practice of theirs. I have an inkling why.

The welcome I've received here is not due to the friendly interest I've shown in documenting their rituals – and, more to the point, the use my white skin might serve, helping reinforce their ailing culture against the onslaught of Christian evangelicals and the increasingly ambivalent young. Not entirely, anyway. Nor any payment.* No, there is a lingering belief here, rarely articulated but all pervasive, that Europeans have – in some way that is not fully knowable – their origins in the spirit world.

As I proffer my head, listening to the ladies bawl their eyes out – for me, a perfect stranger – I'm beginning to understand that they are crying for someone who is, in some complicated way, regarded as one of their number. I might be useless at paddling a canoe while standing upright, as a man rightly should, but I must have a profound connection to them, be like a kind of quasi-Niowra, back from the dead.

It all makes a sort of sense: why else would I feel a need to involve myself here – of my free will to be inducted into their backwoods community through an act of such protracted agony? A month or two earlier, I'd turned up out of the blue. Jonny, from the Smaark clan, one with affiliations to eagles, herons and quite a few interfering spiritual entities, greeted me as I tied up the canoe. After untold years of searching, my spirit must have found its way home.

It's time. We are handed grass skirts, a couple of coconuts and a chicken. We step forward with our gifts, parting the leaves of the Crocodile Nest – only seventeen *bandees* just now, lest we do not find favour with the spirits and they kill us.†

---

* I did produce a case of beer – all I could manage.
† Thirteen more came to join us a few weeks later, when it seemed that all was well.

The thump of hand drums, the calls for us to be strong, and the sticks that rain down on those who protect us with their own backs on this first occasion. We see the welts on them, the shoulders now striated with bark and sap; we notice that the men don't cry – for they have learned to be brave, as we are about to learn to be brave.

We lie down, as instructed. They cut our chests and backs with blades. It takes time; we lose blood. After, we can barely stand up.

Then, later, the chill draught of the night as we lie naked. We rise before the dawn, totter to the lagoon. We savour its warmth – the soothing water on us like a brief, kindly embrace – then hurry to the Crocodile Nest, blowing whistles to warn the uninitiated to look away. The curtain of leaves part; we are back behind the *banis*. We dab each other with clay, the grey uniform of the dead. Together, we are being prepared for life – which turns out to mean we need five beatings a day. And for however long it takes.

It's as well I have made a friend here. Martin is gentle and sensitive – 'puny' would be harsh, but some of the bigger lads must have thought so. Along with Joel, Stens, Kennedy, Sebastian and Saun, he is a Smaark – the clan to which my spirit is thought to belong.

Dread occupies our time. And recovery from being thrashed – that occupies our time also. A month passes – and each day passes slowly when you are expecting any moment to be brought out into the sunshine for another round of pain.

'What will you do after, Martin?'

'Maybe I will live in Wewak, or maybe here in the village with you. We can travel to the fishing lake, where the birds have their little babies. It is very wonderful – you will see.'

'But Martin, I can't stay. Remember, I'm here only to record and understand the old men's traditions before they die off. I've got a life elsewhere.'

Joel says, looking up from where he rests, sprawled on the ground, 'You can marry a girl from the Yaargi clan, if you're lucky. They are fat and strong.'

A couple of other *bandees* join us. They wish me to buy them a wrist-watch or telly.

I don't mind. In fact, these days I would do almost anything for those being thumped alongside me. Also, I am obliged to. We are *wanbanis*, boys who were hatched in the same Crocodile Nest. There are thirty of us now and we're bound to each other for life.

'Be patient,' I tell myself, as the requests come in. This is a huge chance for them.

However, as I cannot – so it seems – conjure a wristwatch or TV right now, they ask for something else instead. They ask me what only I have the ability to reveal.

And, as the *bandees* gather closer to hear my words, I feel uncomfortable. 'It's not true,' I tell them. 'It just isn't.'

Joel says, 'You don't know what we are going to ask you.'

I do. I know exactly. We are standing together, bare except for the rope around our necks, and what everyone wants to know is how to access my wealth. For I am a white man, emanating from the land of the spirits (or so the oldest men keep stating), and possibly know the whereabouts of the keys – the ones that unlock the coffers in Paradise. The evidence, after all, is everywhere. You only need look at how rich Europeans are without having to hunt a single pig. Further clues: the rice, blankets, tins of this and that which are on sale in Wewak. Every single item has issued, like me, from somewhere over the seas.

My fellow inmates leave me alone, sad that I haven't felt able to be more honest. And it returns to me that as a child I collected images of the Garden of Eden. I wonder if we are all of us searchers for a Never Never Land.

Over the following days, they ask again.

'I wish I could change the facts, but I can't,' I tell them, blunter now.

The *bikmen* slip from their benches. They bring with them proof, a ten kina banknote.

'*Bandee*,' calls Rom, the senior elder, not stirring from his fireplace, 'you may tell the truth of it now.'

So, I tell the truth – and with a sinking feeling. Because the Niowra are right. My people did indeed create this money from out of nowhere. The bill says that it was printed by De La Rue Ltd – probably their outfit in Gateshead, up in the north of England. 'However,' I add, 'that's not to say money grows on trees.'

But it does! The banknote's made from paper! And I curl the money in my fingers, reeling from the thought that I am bound to these twenty-nine boys for the rest of my days, not to mention my obligation to everyone else in the village – and, for that matter, thousands of Niowra the length of the Middle Sepik, because they too are now my *wantoks*,* my relatives. Even though the Kandengeis look down on them.

'But you can't just keep printing more and more cash,' I explain. 'It doesn't work like that. You see what they've written here? Each small sheaf of paper becomes a promise to pay someone.'

'Yes! A promise to pay!'

The requests for a job in Gateshead come full and fast after that.

———

Did Martin understand? I did need him to. But two weeks on he too was telling me that Sebastian, son of Jonny and thus forever my 'brother', would be the one to thatch my house. 'Martin . . .' I tried to explain, but somehow I had lost him and perhaps that was the day he too lost me.

The next I remember, the elders were surrounding me, telling me to say goodbye to my fellows because a village elder called Anderloo was fading fast. I must go to his house and help.

None of the *bandees*, not even Martin, questioned the decision that one of their number was to be separated off. There was total obedience now.

But *I* questioned the decision, all right. Six weeks we'd spilt blood together, and how had this protracted effort of the community to unify their boys ended? One individual had been singled out because he was white-skinned. He alone might have the power to heal the sick.

The other *bandees* were lined up; I shook their hands in turn. I left my comrades there in a row and for the last time parted the bamboo leaves of the Crocodile Nest.

———

* *Wantok* literally means 'one-talk', or single-language group, and across Papua New Guinea it is to your *wantok* you have an allegiance. This is coupled to the payback system: if you do a favour for someone, that person is now equally obliged to you.

They beat them again, straight after. I walked off to tend to Anderloo, hearing the wails and feeling my betrayal. And all for nothing, because Anderloo – who anyway looked about ninety – had rallied.

I left Kandengei in a daze soon after, along with a girl whom I happened to very much like. In my diary, I see that I confided to myself 'she has a sophisticated grace and lips which readily part, revealing her delight and extremely neat white teeth'. Let me just say that she had an infectious smile. I know she missed Timbun, her home village, but she put a brave face on it among the women of Pagwi market and I loved seeing that animated smile – its resilience. She chattered incessantly as she tried to sell her (I'm afraid not very appealing) home-grown tobacco. Not daring to breathe a word about her even to Martin, I'd spent what seemed like every day of the incarceration thinking on that smile – imagining that I'd see it alight on her face again.

But no, she too was someone I was meant to save but couldn't. One day she fainted – and before anyone knew it had lapsed into a coma. It was cerebral malaria, at a guess. For a whole night I tried to spoon a weak sugar solution through those once-smiling lips, now clenched, while her mother and sisters wept around me. Towards daybreak the trees issued the sharp cries of frogs and to me they sounded like screams.

The next day, off I went from Kandengei with her nailed in a box beside me. My memory here is hazy, but I don't think I said a word of farewell to anyone, not even my 'father' Jonny. Perhaps I knew I'd be back before too long or perhaps I never said goodbye because the Niowra have no word for it. No one ever leaves.

III

I n the event, I stayed away a full two years, and for the life of me I'm not sure why I did finally board the canoe back from the roadhead at Pagwi. I told myself it was to understand better the customs I'd already so recklessly committed myself to.

Soon I was installed in Sebastian's bachelor hut and next taking my place in the spirit house. I discovered that I was no longer a *bandee*, like the dogs kept down on the mud, but a *g-eenjumboo*, a Junior Male, who must sit on the benches and rage about this or that injustice with the best of them.

However, this rank, like every other in Niowra society, had its own complications. The marriageable girls, for example. They were a complication.

From my notebook:

She arrived without notice. I hadn't invited her, yet here she was. One moment the tremble of the limbum palm floor, and then all was still, and she was breathing beside me – hot, nervous, smelling of river weed and also her apprehension. I smelt relief too. And no wonder: she must have wound her way three hundred metres through the village, evading the dogs and the old men as they potter.

At last her destination: Smaark territory. Now, for the next moment or two, till this liaison had followed its course, she was safe. 'Wumbunavan,' she began, using the name the Kandengeis have for me. 'So . . . I am come to see you tonight. My brother says me to make myself well known to you. "Do not be fright," he says. "Girl, you must familiarise yourself. Let the fingers do all the talking." But I AM too fright. But then I am not so fright because I looked at you in the canoe at Chambri and I like your backside and I think of being close-close with you.' She handed me some sort of shiny wallet to hold. 'Then I went for a hard look at your white skin when you digged for the bush eggs, and afterwards I am not losing thinking about you.'

In this way she talked on. She writhed a little as she eased down her denim skirt. She didn't give her name as she went about this thing she was obliged to do for her clan – but I had by now decided that she was the one they call the Typist.*

She's been to primary school – and briefly the secondary at Maprik, before she flunked her exams – and is better educated than most men around here. And now she's back, at dusk seen hanging around with the ne'er-do-wells, tantalising them with her sophisticated words, puce nail varnish and Chinese-manufactured perfume. She tells the fisherwomen they have voting rights and accosts even the bikmen if they hit their wives; she is seen as a problem. And now she was here beside me.

I listened: heard her lungs fill and un-fill with the moist air and I wondered what to do as she laid herself bare.

'Wumbunavan . . .' she said, and stretched her fingers to my Niowra scars – as if to reassure herself, touch something that belonged to her kin.

'For what it is worth, I too feel awkward about all of this,' I wanted to say. 'Though I can never really know what it's like to be you.'

I lay in the blackness contemplating this remarkable woman – this audacious, tireless spirit – shackled like so many of the female persuasion by her circumstance. Here in the Sepik, the instinct to search out new possibilities is curbed . . .

The girl waited, just as her clan waited; a young male and female

---

* 'The Typist' was excluded – with her rivals – almost entirely from the account that I wrote soon after, *The Proving Grounds*. For discretion's sake, I changed many names, most importantly that of Martin, who became 'Daniel'.

brought together by the forces of the river – which, though I've come here to document a 'dying culture', are proving SURPRISINGLY RESILIENT. I thought of my next move – me propped on my elbow and she flat on her back.

It was not to be. I handed the girl her shiny wallet. I reached out to Martin, who seemed extremely awake in the adjoining mosquito net. Even on a moonless night, a girl doesn't pass through a Niowra village without an awful lot of help.

Martin said, 'You must give her some time. Try her out.'

'I'm not so sure this is a good idea . . .'

'Oh, do not worry. You will learn each other.'

But I'd learned all that I needed to know.

Martin rose and leaned outside to whisper to Sebastian, or whoever it was in the shadows, and he in turn whistled like an owl to another. My guest wriggled back into her skirt and next she waited, holding her breath while crouching and listening. Suddenly, she lifted the net and was gone.

A voice said, 'You did not like her?'

'I'm sure she's lovely, Martin. But . . .'

'I do not understand,' he said. 'The girl is from the Yaargis. She's a good one.'

The next girl along was a Smaark – from my very own clan, which, from even a liberal interpretation of my notes, was tantamount to incest. Someone had decided even this was better than nothing.

Up the steps she came, hopeful feet all but silent on the rungs. She could hardly have been more than about fourteen. I patted her gently as I arranged another exit.

Martin had brought me his sister – or maybe she was a half-sister. And the remainder of that night I lay awake, all the requirements of the Sepik and its stymied waterways palpable in the heavy air. The entire riverine habitat seemed to close in on me – the floating weed, the half-dozing egrets and the fertility so openly expressed by the bubbling silt – a weave of processes and lives still so foreign to me.

Best to leave, I thought. *And not come back.*

IV

The elders had always said that the crocodile ceremony was only ever a preparation. For life, was it? Or for evading death? I should put myself to good use in New Guinea's heartlands, keep recording the perspective of others whose traditions were falling apart – but further inland.

It was as well that my 'father' Jonny was the principal representative of the Catholic Church; he seemed to have a measure of the white man and his disturbing ways – the wife-less priests, their cannibalistic rituals before the altar. He took me to the spirit house to break the news.

I needn't have worried. Even my sudden departure was celebrated as the act of a true Niowra. 'Wumbunavan is not so different from those Junior Men who've left us to work in Wewak,' the *bikmen* agreed, referring to those of my cohort presently hanging about with the wasters and *raskols* – criminal types – in the provincial capital. There they enjoyed the hospitality of the few unenviable Niowra people who were gainfully employed.

Sooner or later I too would be back, Rom said, and everyone nodded. And so it was with the blessing of the old men that I departed. I was again out there with the trees, this time beyond the Hunstein Range, working my way through the remote flood plains of the April, east towards another Sepik tributary known as the Korosameri. Helped by the more adventurous individuals of this or that hamlet, I sloshed through the wetlands and descended rivers on balsa rafts.

I grew in confidence. Thanks to the many small acts of kindness from those who helped me on my way, I was able to stay just the right side of being safe.* At last, time spent tramping through the quagmire became more compelling than spells of relative ease, when I rested up in villages. Like any climber pressed to a cliff-face, or seafarer whipped by the breeze, episodes of exposure made me feel more alive – and my very defenceless-ness forced me to be responsive to, and appreciative of, the domain I had thought to enter.

Sometimes I peered out and saw others of my kind – in the form of spirited Americans toiling for God.† It was touching to regard the evangelists and their efforts to be tolerably comfortable out here. To the north, like a street barricade, spread the first line of sago palms – in the wet season the whole clammy ecosystem transformed into a broth of dispossessed snakes and floundering, vindictive invertebrates – and to the south the grim, cloud-shrouded slopes of the 12,000-foot Central Range. Yet the churchmen had built themselves houses, each with an agreeable façade of weather boards, and up these they trained red roses – as if they thought they were still in New Jersey. Each day, while around them thrived the Anopheles mosquito and leeches, they took a bath, put on a freshly ironed shirt and solemnly placed their trust in the Good Lord and vitamin pills.

From time to time, the missionaries would call out to where I was camped in the underbrush. They knew well who I was: the crazy Brit whose company

* The realisation that a state of vulnerability in a visitor should be welcomed, not guarded against, was to evolve into my long-standing credo: 'To me personally,' I explained in *The Skeleton Coast*, 'exploration is not about planting flags or conquering Nature or going somewhere in order to make your mark. It's about opening yourself up, and allowing the place to make its mark on you.' As the radical essayist, but also farmer, Wendell Berry put it, albeit within a land-use context, 'the trouble was a familiar one: too much power, too little knowledge'. If an explorer was well supported, that might help the cause of scientific discovery, but arriving in a position of power might be disastrous to the local population – and to any attempt to appreciate their slant on the world. Better to be in a position of weakness and unknowing. 'For who but the ignorant would set out to extend their knowledge to the utmost.' See *The World-Ending Fire*, notably Berry's 1974 essay 'Damage'.
† Also Germans. Evangelists from the US at outposts such as Inaru and Niksek were supplemented by the (Lutheran) Liebenzell Evangelical Mission. The community of Bikaru, which I also visited, is even today classed by the above as 'engaged but unreached' – and is on many a church prayer list.

was their potential converts. 'Hey, you sure look like you could do with a glass of lemonade, Benedict! Come on over, we've just made a bunch of cookies.' My clothing still reeking from the malodorous backwaters, I'd linger at their picket fence to breathe in the scent of home. I'd fight back the tears, then. The laundry pegged on the clothesline reminded of what I'd foregone: safety, physical comfort, and my mum and dad.

A few months on, I came to Bisorio Mission, the outpost on the north bank of the Korosameri – posited far too near the coursing river, in my humble opinion, not to mention the inky waters of the local swamp. But I was fond of Bob and George, and their optimistic quest to draw the warring factions of hereabouts to live side-by-side as if in a tropical suburbia. They belonged to the New Tribes Mission and exhausted themselves each day translating Matthew, Mark, Luke or John.* Then supper time at last, and they would attempt to snatch a brief moment of peace around the table with their wives, the equally hard-pressed Harriett and Noby – but no hope of that because staring at them through the netted windows were those in unending queues awaiting treatment for real or imagined medical complaints.

For a while, all was well at the mission. These days, even the more hot-headed arrivals rarely discussed whether to chop the white people up, and many enjoyed the little box, nailed by Bob to the veranda, that explained the concept of capitalism. 'You fellas cut our lawn and you get one of THESE.' A round bit of metal. 'You want a T-shirt, like George? Well, you take that coin – called a kina, like your old shell currency – and you put it in the box. See? Like this: one coin IN, when

---

* 'By unflinching determination we hazard our lives and gamble all for Christ until we have reached the last tribe, regardless of where that tribe might be,' stated the first issue of *Brown Gold* magazine (1 May 1943). Founded in 1942, based in Sanford, Florida, the New Tribes Mission sends forth Christians 'to serve God among unreached peoples'. From time to time, the NTM – now officially re-branded 'Ethnos 360' – had been subject to negative publicity from a number of quarters, one direct assault being *Missionaries: God Against the Indians*, the 1988 book by Norman Lewis, whose emotive article 'GENOCIDE', published in February 1969 by the *Sunday Times*, had already led to the foundation of Survival International, an organisation that campaigns for the rights of indigenous peoples. Though Bob Kennell and George Walker were nothing other than generous to me, the stream of criticism had led to a general wariness at the NTM of those who might attract undue attention to their activities – something that I later feared might have serious repercussions for my own safety.

you've done a day on the airstrip. Another OUT, when you want to spend it at the mission store. But don't get your wives doing all the work for you – I'm not falling for that again.'

As I say, for the time being all was well. I would sit under a bread-fruit tree interviewing old men about the life they had abandoned, and George would sit under another, telling them what might lie ahead. When first approached, the Bisorios were 'isolated, fearful, a forgotten people', according to the missionary version of events.* All I knew for sure was that, singly or by the dozen, men wearing only a twirl of cane and leaves clumped in the front and back were beckoned forward. Gingerly, silently, they took their leave of the trees – and stepped into their first shorts. And, each new dawn, up and down the runway I ran with George as the clawing equatorial parasites worked on us and we strove to keep ourselves fit.

With the perspective of the years, of course, I can see that we were the same: united in our unflagging self-belief – and our naivety. The evangelists believed they were here to save the future of the 'natives'; I believed I was here to safeguard their past. I used the river to bathe in; they used it to baptise in. Each in our own fashion, curious and cour-teous, we did what we felt called in this life to do.

Except, maybe we weren't quite 'curious and courteous' enough because the Papuans, meanwhile, didn't believe the river was necessarily quite so cleansing. 'In that same water,' an old fellow one day informed me, drily, 'live the caring spirits who like to feed us, and in it also live many more who are spiteful and like to feed on us.' And I again had the sinking feeling that we, the worldly outsiders who knew so much, here knew nothing much at all.

Then came the news that would change everything.

For a while, there had been only stories. Up near Porgera, so it was said, there was to be seen a mound made of pure gold – lift any tuft of grass and nuggets dangled like peanuts from the roots. The schoolteachers had run off to dig; their pupils went with them. And now every village lay empty but for a few left-behind old lunatics and mangy dogs. 'Even if only a tenth of this is true . . .' said Bob – and went to pray that it wasn't.

---

* From the evangelical account *What's Going On Downriver?* by Rob Greenslade.

I can still remember it in my mind's eye – the first helicopters cutting through the heron-grey cloud to Malumata, just to the east. This told us gold was to be had down here in the lowlands too.

'Too bad,' said Bob, when a mining company announced they'd be needing the mission airstrip. 'Looks like we've all run out of time, Benedict. You, us, the Papuans.'

'I sure feel sorry for the Yaifos,' said George, referring to the last community on their outreach programme. 'Guess they'll never now know the change that the Lord may work in their lives . . .'

Bob said, 'They must be wondering what's about to hit them.'

We looked out to where the Yaifos were, somewhere up there in the mist.

It was a forbidding sight, the Central Range – at a guess. We couldn't see it. The foothills suggested, as they rose with their burden of trees unevenly to the immoveable cloud base, something massive, lumbering and untoward. In those days no outsider had been up there, and no human at all was likely to have tackled this portion of the ridge, crossing through the heavens and down the other side. Naturally, the very thought excited me. 'A lonely impulse of delight drove to this tumult in the clouds,' I said to myself, recalling a Yeats poem that was framed on my dad's oak desk. I pictured the smooth, giant knuckles of a cold escarpment, the stooped, black, tortured trees with arthritic fingers – everything up there soundless though dripping, and those dripping things unclassified, sleeved in hanks of moss and wiped by ceaseless winds. The only trusted map in 1987 was the yellow aeronautical chart meant for pilots: some bits were blank, as if the printing ink had sporadically run dry. Elsewhere, contours were overlaid with the disturbing pronouncement 'RELIEF DATA UNRELIABLE'. Yet up there, on the invisible mountain, were the Yaifo, located on my map where it said the elevation was 'believed not to exceed 9,300 feet'. They were alone; everyone else had left, descending to Bisorio to receive the Word of God, word of the Eternal Fires of Damnation they'd experience if they didn't accept Him, and medical handouts.

'Someone should go up,' I said. 'Reassure them. Explain what the helicopters are doing.'

'Benedict,' George explained, 'those Yaifo boys are what they call *man bilong pait*.'

'Meaning,' Bob said, 'they're not afraid to use their arrows. But they'll come down here to see what's happening – and anyway, they're not among our chief concerns this minute.'

Bob and George went to offer their chief concerns to Jesus.

There were a lot of these, just now. Already the mission was at a standstill and someone had stolen the tin box used to teach the virtues of a market economy. Perhaps it didn't matter; by this time, no one wanted to earn a few kina sawing planks or slashing grass, just as hardly anyone wanted to attend *lotu*, church. Why bother, when your prayers are anyway about to be answered?

'It's not the miners,' said George, visiting my hut one afternoon to see if I had picked up any news. 'It's what comes after. The drink, the women. No one here is ready to handle that stuff.' He looked up at those clustering on the airstrip, ready for the arrival of the mining company. 'It's only the Yaifos now,' George said. 'They're the last ones.'

'To hear about Jesus, or to hear about the gold?'

'Last ones to hear about anything.'

The thought struck me forcibly. Tomorrow, the next day, whenever the bemused Yaifo appeared out of the trees – as everyone agreed they would within days – we'd find ourselves witness to a closing epoch of humanity. Or so it seemed to me, aged twenty-seven, and I can see now that I was about right. There we were, positioned late in the twentieth century and deep within the world's largest tropical island, which thanks to the preponderance of cloud was less surveyed than the Amazon, and close at hand was a time when there'd be no more white patches on maps – not here, not anywhere. And definitely no permanent settlements without so much as a footpath to the wider world.

For a generation or so, the more nomadic bands would hold out – or hide out – in the South American tropics, the Sentinelese Islands, and here and there. They would duck and dive, evading all that we so voraciously consumed. But not so for settled peoples. For them it concluded here and now, in South-east Asia, this week with the Yaifo. This beleaguered hamlet of a hundred, perhaps two hundred men and women who had not opened a book, nor a car door or a can of Pepsi. They had not felt cloth against their skin, or known a shoe or sock or bike. The entire gamut of modern accomplishment had passed them by – from the advent of the plough to the despoiling of our own climate (the evidence was stacking up already*) – and just as well, many might say.

Only, they had no choice in the matter. The Outside World that was about to descend on us here at Bisorio would shortly descend on them. The Yaifo would not die from our everyday infections as others had done across the New World, but simply disappear, as so many communities had already disappeared.† Barely three years on and the people I'd known as the Obini, the most isolated of the lowlanders I'd encountered in West Papua, existed nowhere but in whatever I'd published or scribbled in notebooks, or hastily snapped with my Canon. The images included one of a clutch of ill-at-ease women in the shadows, pregnant and with ochre-coloured tassels in their hair; a youth staring incredulous as he examined with both hands my felt hat; a second man in the watchtower with one eye on me, bow half-drawn; a third man bent forward, working back and forth his stone adze. Otherwise, nothing remained.

Meanwhile, at Bisorio, each morning of this, our (at this rate quite brief) Anthropocene Age, began with longer than usual prayers. Out on the runway the Christian congregation prayed that their Paradise might hurry up and come, and Bob and George prayed that it would not.

It was the prayers of the congregation that were answered. The first plane unloaded crates stencilled with 'EXPLORATION PNG'. Next came a sizable Australian, who moved into my accommodation, told his cowering, right-hand man to wire up the generator and said I could call him Joe. 'I'll be seeing to the Pre-Wholesale Excavation Phase.'

---

* Something that I had been alerted to early, the Climatic Research Unit being based at my first university, the University of East Anglia. Soon evidence enough to act would be presented at the 1992 Rio Summit (the UN Conference on Environment and Development), but not in any meaningful way acted upon until the 2016 Paris Agreement, within the UN Framework Convention on Climate Change.

† The risk of infection that threatened many isolated people – and, for example, had emptied the Amazon of perhaps 95 per cent of its population – didn't apply in New Guinea, partly because of the mass contacts in the interior which had taken place from the 1930s onwards, but also because there had long since been well-established trade routes stretching from the coast, the universal wearing of kina, toea and cowrie shells by highlanders indicative of the continuous historic links with even the most inland peoples.

That was the day they brought the second-hand clothing. Out it flowed, disgorged along with wellington boots from the aircraft's belly, bale upon bale. The entire church congregation seemed to be possessed of the same need to extend their fingers to the merchandise – sized mainly 'XXL' and emblazoned with slogans such as 'MADE LIKE A MAN IN IDAHO' or 'HEY BABE, YOU LIKE WHAT YOU SEE?' They touched the trussed-up T-shirts with reverence, as if they were holy artefacts. Afterwards they went to the church and bowed their heads as they'd been taught to do before eating, thanking the Lord Jesus for what they were about to receive.

Except, they weren't receiving any T-shirts yet – not before they'd earned them. Soon, Joe was to be seen in his fold-up chair, negotiating wage rates and signing up willing hands.

But I should mention that at this time I'd fallen in with a certain youth called Tsogomoi. He was shy, with a very clever but serious face – a little too serious, I sometimes felt – and with a small hole through his nose, indicating a pagan upbringing away from here. Despite an occasional sheepish grin he had a melancholy streak and, as he helped me conduct interviews with the old-timers at a quiet spot down by the river, he was in the habit of gazing across the water and up into the deadweight of cloud. He did this even more than I did. And after a while of this companionable gazing I decided that I was good for Tsogomoi, and he was good for me. He restrained me from risking my neck (I had a mind to climb the mountain) – and in turn I snapped him out of his torpor. Put another way, whatever it was that drove the likes of me – let's employ that happy expression, a 'call of the wild' – he entirely lacked. Here, if you like, was the opposite of the 'explorer' – the itinerant with a set goal, the questing visionary in thrall of his feverish dream.*

'The Yaifo mens and womens,' he said once, using the rudimentary English he had somehow picked up. 'When they come one day, I worry for them. Bisorio it is hot and dirty too much.'

---

* Tsogomoi exhibited what, long ago, was termed acedia, a type of exhaustion or loss of life force – the condition which meant sufferers were in 'ill humour', unable to meditate or pray because they were under the baleful influence of Saturn – slow moving, blue, listless. Acedia was the early Christian precursor of that deadly sin called sloth. Today, we might say he suffered from bouts of depression.

I understood that Tsogomoi, who was in some distant manner related to the Yaifo people, missed the life he had once had up in the Central Range and I began floating the idea of us trekking up there together; we might record the community's last days. With their assistance we might even explore a way over the ridge, to whatever lay beyond.

Now, though, Exploration PNG had turned up. And such was the excitement engendered by Joe and the second-hand shirt merchandise that no one (apart from a grizzled character identified by George as a serial murderer) was interested in accompanying us. It didn't help our case that any potential recruits were distracted by Beni, an oily-faced character who took pleasure in agitating the crowds – 'Your birthright! Your gold!' – to extract a higher daily rate. Suspected by many to be a *glasman*, or sorcerer, Beni had for years been spoiling things for the missionaries; now was the turn of the goldminers.

There was nothing to do but see what transpired, and meanwhile ask Tsogomoi to assist me in interviewing the elders and invalids, as they too queued to get on the payroll. And we waited some more.*

What would the work entail? No one had the faintest idea. First Joe required his heavy equipment to be flown in – though 'bugger all sign of that yet', he confided. 'This might just have to be a bucket 'n' spade job.' For a while, Joe sat it out, his eyes shut to avoid the hopeful faces of the dilapidated old codgers – still queuing – and the grinning visage of Beni.

Days passed. Tsogomoi looked up into the emptied forests, at what seemed to him to be a happier place. And I expect I deliberated on what the Polish philosopher Henryk Skolimowski had to say: 'The first act of awe, when man was struck with the beauty or wonder of Nature, was the first spiritual experience.' But that word 'nature' seemed to me to only exist as an idea among those whose societies

---

* Also at this time there were reports of a few Yaifo men having turned up at the exploration pits around Malumata; they were bewildered and asking for food. I sent a message up there with one of the helicopters that were now visiting Bisorio to recruit workers, asking if any Yaifo might escort me to their elders. In the event, it was to this request that two Yaifo men chose to respond.

are separated from it, and I wondered, as I had at Kandengei, whether we are all at heart wishing to cross that metaphorical river.*

Sometimes, Joe could be heard indoors telling 'Cookie', his diminutive chef, to extract another Coke from the cooler. Otherwise there was only the occasional burp. Later, Joe took to curating his album of what he called Papuan Boobs. They had been snapped for, I think, one kina a go – as his schedule and the availability of agreeable ladies allowed – from mining sites up and down PNG. Thus the redoutable Australian passed the quieter hours in the company of his pornography – assembling the bosoms in size order, wistfully poring over them with the dedication of a Victorian ethnographer to his 'type specimens'.

During those last days at Bisorio we all seemed to be waiting. The Bisorio congregation waited for their Paradise, the missionaries waited for their goldmining hell. Joe waited for word of his mechanical excavators, and Tsogomoi and I waited for the Yaifo, who might or might not come down the mountain.

We were waiting – for another chapter, another future.

Ahead of us all was the Information Revolution – the next leap for mankind. This would allow humans the first mass harvest, as it were, of the notional Tree of Knowledge. It would be a free-for-all – no fruit remained unplucked. Soon, shortly into the next millennium, even a child would be able to look up whatever information they wanted – and do this on what they would learn to call a 'search engine', one of the most predominant being Google – a company not even to be founded for another ten years. Likewise, that child might, with a little parental supervision, navigate with a convenient, handheld device through what remained of the verdant forest to where a relict people called the Yaifo

---

* At around that time, I pondered a lot on this subject – one laden with complicated historical issues. As Alex Hutchinson discusses in his essay 'Why We Wish for the Wilderness', the soubriquet 'wilderness', like 'nature' and 'wild', becomes problematic when we consider that so many of these natural-seeming landscapes, like the Central Range, were occupied at one time or other. This was much like referring to the depths of the Amazon as 'Virgin Forest', as adventurers even now are wont to do, when these habitats were once – before catastrophic population loss through diseases introduced by us – more akin to informal orchards, and furthermore have been modified by fire, vegetable plots and so on. In calling these places 'natural', we were in danger of denying the existence of those who once lived there.

had once lived. Furthermore, thanks to a constellation of satellites in geostationary orbit 12,500 miles above, that child might determine his or her position to within a few metres – and not by skilled use of a sextant and logarithmic tables, but at a glance. Likewise, the most hardy lone mariners of the future, though described as 'solo' adventurers, would think nothing of downloading a weather chart mid-Pacific, of consulting their dentist about a loose filling. If homesick, they might ask their little ones back home to sing them 'Happy Birthday'.

And into this fast, unimaginable, interconnected future the Yaifo now stepped.

V

The two figures appeared on the far bank. They peeled open the sun-blanched leaves as if parting a curtain, then moved forward. They left the shade warily, extending into the sunshine a leg at a time, along with their bows and arrows. They blinked at their destiny across the Korosameri.

A canoe must then have been sent to fetch them over; my next memory is of them being suddenly with us here, showing themselves like an apparition on our river side. They wore leafy bustles and aprons, their foreheads were dressed in black paint, and from all about their heads sprang the white and crimson feathers of eagles and parrots. But mainly I remember that the two men always seemed to be running.

They sprinted about like felons not wanting to be caught. First they ran to the airstrip to see where the ground had been cleared of trees and lain flat. Next to the red tractor in its shed and at last to the shop where you could buy, if you had earned it, a comb, mirror or soap. The two men spoke only a little as they rushed about – and nothing at all to me. Once, I thought I saw something like panic in their eyes.

That same day – which was the very one on which Joe announced he'd be initiating the Pre-Wholesale Excavation Phase first thing the next morning – our Yaifo visitors announced that they had already seen enough. They would be leaving for home, also early tomorrow, though were happy to take the two of us along. Tsogomoi and I might explain to their community what was happening down here.

We gathered the few provisions that we had. The four bags, once weighed and readied on the grass, looked very inadequate. Even given that both of us were at that time young and hardened to a life out in the forest, we were about to stride off the only decent map in existence, guided by men who might abandon us anywhere along the trail. Except, there was no trail.

'Are you sure you have every eventuality covered?' asked George, looking aghast at our four sorry packs. He was clutching his brow as he sweated; perhaps he had a migraine. 'I know you are well versed in this kinda thing, but Tsogomoi says you might even press on over the Central Range, if you can find a way . . .'

'It must be extraordinary up there,' I said.

'That's for sure,' said George, again wincing.

'But we'll see. First we have to see if we even reach the Yaifo.'

'Seems to me this trek is a risk way, way too far. I mean, isn't there anyone else who will accompany you?'

But there wasn't – just as there was no one very willing now to work for him.

This was how we ended up taking along George's temporary kitchen hand. I suppose Namoleeyo must have been fifteen years old at that time; he had recently been baptised 'Michael' and was presently stuffing his face with rice leftovers at the sink. He had a well-padded belly – the well-padded belly of a white man. 'He's the only kid here interested in food,' explained George, as Michael moved on to the nut roast, 'rather than becoming a tycoon a few days hence. Expect he'll stick with you if you keep him well fed.'

The following morning I thanked George and Bob, and they watched us cross the river with sadness – either because they felt we were going to our death, or because I too was forsaking their mission to pursue my own.

———

Of the trek itself, I recall little. I do remember swearing never to do such a thing again. The Yaifo men walked off uphill through the trees quickly;

I remember that much. They wanted to put distance behind them before the afternoon rains, but also – it strikes me now – to put space between them and all that was erupting at Bisorio. Below us, Day One of the Pre-Wholesale Excavation Phase: first job, to create a five-by-five-metre pit without the mechanical digger.

We stopped to look down as, shovel by shovel, the alluvial sediments were exposed. Joe was overlooking proceedings, face hidden to us beneath his hat, big pink hands on his hips. Trees were lopped down, branches hacked back; straighter limbs were picked out – they would do for poles – and whacked into parent soil. Everywhere hook-billed birds – fig parrots, Sepik lorikeets – were jabbering as they circled, not sure any more where was safe to settle.

This was to be the last I saw of the Korosameri riverside for thirty years: the unsettled birds feathered in scarlet, lime green and sunflower yellow, and Bob and George's parishioners stripped to their underpants and getting in the way of each other. As we made our way upslope, one or two workers watched us disappear; they gazed, all the while scraping the mud off their arms and legs with their bush knives, incredulous that we should leave now, at this time of good fortune. Then their heads dropped back down again. They worked on; at any moment they might sight the first grains of the precious metal – a precious metal entirely absent, as it turned out.

The Yaifo youth leading us was called Kaibayoo, and he had acquired a sponge from the mission station. With this he wiped away perspiration, and then, good-naturedly sticking out his pink tongue to express his satisfaction, tucked it between his spine and baggage and resumed the climb.

We hopped over streams, dipped through long-tipped, acuminate leaves. The air fizzed, the silent ants walked by. No one spoke much. 'We must not break either one leg or the other,' Tsogomoi said, as he puffed along. 'Or it is finished for all of us.'

More than once that first morning we lost the Yaifos entirely – only to find them patiently waiting for us to catch up, having tucked their decorative hind leaves beneath them as a cushion. Before moving on, I would orientate the map to true north and assess our progress relative to Bisorio, Inaru and Malumata, none of which were marked, but which we must limp to, if things went wrong.

Each day the sun rose, warming the air till it had the sickly tang of rotted fruit, and then we might hear the lesser birds of paradise chirping and burbling their melodies in the treetops. Sometimes we saw them too – an explosion of gold, a flurry of burnt umber – but only ever a glimpse. On we went. Periodically, Michael looked glumly upslope, asking me how far there was to go while dousing himself with the water from his wellies.

And so it was for four or five days, the Yaifos darting up ahead, their hind leaves like the tail feathers of the cassowary. Until one day – the lowlands curtained off by a drifting fog, the air up here cold and odourless – when quite suddenly the slopes fell away to both sides and we made our way along a level wooded ridge to where the trees were fastened to the main looming body of the mountain. Here the Yaifos began singing out, calling in turn.

WHAP!

Whoop!

WHAP!

Whoop!

Before much longer, we came upon a loose blue mist. We smelt wood smoke and, only a few paces on, the trees parted. From memory, to the right and left were heaped rows of tilled soil, and further off stands of sugar cane and plantain. Just ahead, as if confronting us, was a large, windowless wood house and all around an eerie stillness.

I remember so well that stillness – and Kaibayoo depositing his pack gently, as if not to disturb a single ant. After a moment's thought, though, he called out – that same song. WHAP! WHAP!

Nothing – as if the forest itself was holding its breath.

'They've gone? Everyone's packed up and left for Malumata?'

Tsogomoi said nothing; he curled out his lower lip, thinking about it. Michael came laboriously up the slope, clumping along in his gumboots. Tsogomoi and I listened again – but could now only hear Michael gasping.

Kaibayoo called once more. And this time an answer, like a dim echo – the trees calling back.

I don't think any of us were prepared for what happened next. First, just visible among the diffuse cloud, came bright feathers, fluttering and flapping. And then the shouting: out into the space ahead of us sprang a party of extremely athletic figures wearing black face paint, forehand straps of cowrie shells, arm bands of wicker, and leaf tufts front and back. The air was suddenly full – of the slowly twirling mist and of the Yaifo men, their yells and the slap of hands against arrow strings.

Michael issued a doom-laden moan.

There was nothing now to say or do. More men piled in; there were twenty-five or so circling around us in a throng, and the bow of each was ready with its arrow. *This could end badly*, I thought, *and in the next few seconds*.

'We do not move,' said Tsogomoi, slowly. 'I think.'

'Tsogomoi, you must calmly tell them – you may need to shout – that we aren't goldminers. That we're not here to take their land. And we're not missionaries either.'

Tsogomoi was unable to calmly tell anyone anything. His eyes were locked on a boy, aged about fourteen, who had snatched his bush knife; the boy was thrashing the ground at his feet and each wound in the clay spoke of his anger and fear. But the sound of each blow was lost in the yelping, the smacking of bow strings and everyone's confusion at the collision between two worlds.

VI

There is, I suppose, only so long such a defensive display can last, and when it became apparent that there were only the three of us, and that we were not launching an assault, the clattering of the men died away softly, like applause.

The community had made its statement and wished for our reply. The men leant on tree stumps; they rested their legs. Their arms were folded, their shoulders raised and tense.

'I think you had better say something, Tsogomoi . . .'

'Me? You are the boss!'

'I don't even speak their language!'

In the end, there was nothing for it but to hand Tsogomoi my camera and go forward myself. 'Just keep clicking . . .' I said. 'Whatever happens next, get what you can.'

The photo that Tsogomoi took, just a few seconds later, shows a figure who is skirted in leaves, decked in feathers and hunched on a log beside his fellows. He gapes, hardly able to believe what he sees. Towering before him is someone implausibly pallid and fatigued, as soft-skinned as a maggot. This lean giant, sheathed in his alien materials and into whose grey-blue eyes he is staring, doesn't know what to do other than compliment him on his arrows – in Tok Pisin, a language he has never before heard.

I did my best, passing a series of friendly nods to those catching their breath around me. *Advertise your innocence*, I thought, *in case your ridiculousness in slogging up this mountain isn't obvious enough*.

One of the group, his forehead adorned by the creamy-white pelt of a cuscus, laid his bow to the side. Encouraged by what seemed to be a gesture of friendship, I moved along to him and offered my hand. This he looked at for a moment, confused. Then he gave me a nervous half-smile and gently took hold of my fingers. Fear among the Yaifo had given way to wonder: this colossal weakling, an off-white-coloured boy, had made it up through the dank greenery to see them – and evidently he meant no harm.

The women were brought out of hiding. They came forward from the bushes, and some from the house, with hands uniformly placed on their heads and escorted by yet more armed youths; furtively, chests painted with white stripes, they journeyed with their eyes around all that was unknown to them – the boots, the socks, the laces, the buttons. Here it was, then: the first sample of the industrialised world about to engulf them.

But not today. Plainly, I was helpless. I couldn't have been more so.

Tsogomoi put down my blue rucksack – it had been on his back all this time – and in his own tongue explained that we wanted nothing more than to record what we could, before going on our way. If they liked, we could also tell them about all the helicopters that they'd have noticed coming and going.

The man whom I would later know as Sawi – the same individual whose arrows I'd inspected – looked up, bemused, at the sky. 'The metal birds?'

Another said, 'He is welcome to stay. But we are not important. Why is he interested in studying our habits?'

And another: 'He has been sent by someone more powerful to trick us?'

For a while, we addressed the men's concerns as they sat arrayed in their finery along the tree trunk. Tsogomoi helped me explain who we were, and how and why things around them were fast changing. However, even at this delicate stage, I was also aware of the need to quickly establish the feasibility of crossing the mountain. I had dragged Tsogomoi and Michael all the way up here and it was important from the outset that I knew our options for getting out safely.

'I have asked them already,' said Tsogomoi. 'There is no way over the ridge. There is only cloud up there.'

'No hope at all?'

'None at all,' added Michael firmly, from where he was spread on the ground, gumboots off and wheezing.

'If you walk up there, your lives will end!' exclaimed Sawi. And we laughed together – then saw that our hosts weren't laughing. Mainly, they were staring into the branches uphill, through the soft, mist-filtered light. Some twigs shifted in the breeze, but most did not; with the lichens wrapped around them like crusty skins, they looked half dead. Every upper surface appeared to have been settled by sedges, mosses, orchids and filmy ferns. Fed steadily by the fog, they heaped as best they could wherever they could, creating extravagant bolsters.

Tsogomoi said, 'These Yaifo people will leave anyway in a few days, I think. So we will go down together to Bisorio.'

'Fair enough,' I said. It was no less than I had expected, and I should be pleased to have got this far up the mountain.

———

The Yaifos grew better acquainted with us. They learned that I didn't mind if they examined my skin – 'he is like a soft pig' – or cautiously picked through my few belongings. 'This is his food,' the women said, scratching at my lemon soap. 'This is what they eat that makes them white.' The men took the soap, giggled at the way it jumped from their hands. They took it on themselves to smooth the yellow bar over me as I tried to find privacy, washing in the brook.

They studied Tsogomoi too, told the boys to pick the lice from his hair and noted the poor condition of Michael's skin – which was better than most down in Bisorio, where those brought together in the name of Jesus were readily colonised by a pernicious scaly fungus.

In turn, I became better acquainted with those here – only seventy-two men, women and children. In particular, I remember a boy called Feefee – aged perhaps nine or ten, with wonderfully quick, inquisitive eyes – crouched with the men, peeping at my notebook. Later, he would run his fingernails over the pages to experience their smoothness, tracing the indentations of my words as might a gramophone needle.

Alone up on their mountain – the women with earrings of looped cassowary quills, and the men's noses projecting stripped-away, foot-long parrot feathers – the Yaifos' existence seemed defined as much by the obscured sky as the obscure forest. They sheltered from the chill in a single dwelling, that amounted to a fort: five feet off the ground, fashioned with stout timber, the only means of access was a narrow, low door, reached – if you were nimble enough to ascend it – via a notched pole. In times of attack, the pole could be discarded with one kick.

But there was no one to attack the Yaifos any more – not with knives and arrows. Their neighbours were gone, and that left only the massed forces of the late twentieth century, which the settlement was already making moves to accommodate. Both Yaifo men and women were exhausting themselves by clearing trees, even in their last days up here.

'Brr, brr!' Those hacking with their bush knives tried to explain, drawing an arc over their heads.

'They think the helicopters are birds,' Tsogomoi said. 'Or bees. They are making a nest for them.'

'Time has run out for this backward place,' declared Michael, rather less sympathetically. 'They can stop chopping – and we can leave.'

Through each day, as I wrote my notes, I could hear the men working around me: the squeak, chop, squeak of their blades labouring into the flesh of another tree. I recorded the Yaifo names, their food, all that I could think of – thankful to be here, sad that no one else could be here to write down more. And throughout these few days Feefee always seemed to be observing me – in many ways a wholly unrepresentative specimen of what was shortly coming his way: someone with a two-metre arm-span, no less than two fathers now, and an inclination to push himself to the margins of oblivion. Why had I bothered coming up here, when the Yaifos I wished to document were due to come down? No wonder my every movement as I boiled the rice pot or brushed my teeth was a fascination.

Such poignant scenes: the women for the last time in their communal home patting the carbon off a taro extracted from the embers, or the men chiselling sharp their arrow blades with a rat's tooth. I watched as, each night, they tucked forward their antennae-like nose feathers before lying on their sides – no pillow, no blanket – and each morning searched through the cinders for a glow, then nurtured it tenderly, as if a much-prized butterfly, or sawed a rattan across a split cane to catch hot dust on the bark cloth and start the fire afresh.

Once upon a time, the time of the Great Flooding, the Yaifo had lived far from here, in the heat of the plains – so their story went. One man and one woman escaped the rising waters, transforming themselves into mosquitoes and hiding in the fur of a rodent as it scampered up the slope. They came here, to this very fold in the mountain, and among these harbouring trees and skies they had stayed until today. Or until tomorrow, or perhaps the next day.

When precisely would they leave? No one was quite decided. Some of the older men felt they might hack down more trees; others wished to depart immediately. A couple more days went by. Feefee and a grumpy eight-year-old called Ashkai tossed a pig's bladder back and forth. The women, heads protected from the rain by flat pandanus leaf umbrellas, hoed the gardens with sticks. Small girls hauled about small boys, and these girls wore a dainty swatch of leaves and the boys a single cockle shell. By night we choked in the fire smoke as I wrote my notes, and throughout Feefee sat cross-legged, with a straight back, eyes still on me.

So when, late one afternoon, a hunter returned with a lesser bird of paradise – it hung from him like the Ancient Mariner's albatross, ruddy breast punctured by an arrow – it seemed to me like a confirmation of the end. The Yaifo were done for. And the plants and animals that shared their slopes – silent, creaking and groaning, or bickering and croaking – they were done for too. This was the way of the white man, so it seemed: first they came for your soul, then they came for what lay beneath your land, and finally they came for the land itself.

And thus passed the last moments – or so I thought – of the Yaifo, the last of the people who stood alone.

—

'They go from here tomorrow, I think,' said Tsogomoi, one evening when we were indoors. Sawi had come over to show me his hand drum – he was pleased with the quality of its tree kangaroo skin. 'They want to sing and dance for themselves.'

Various men rose, built a fire to shed more light, then inserted in their armbands spindles fashioned from seeds, beeswax and the plumage of parrots, eagles and birds of paradise.

Sawi tapped the drumskin, applying little blobs of beeswax to tune it. Then, happy with its tone, he and ten or more men began stomping and twirling about – their feather ornaments swaying around them, the leaves that skirted them billowing.

Through that last night they danced, fanning the smoke, raising the dust. The fire burned lower and yet lower, but still the men strutted and spun around. Tsogomoi, Michael and I were perched alone up here with the Yaifos, a people who were for only a few hours longer subject to no one but themselves. And, as they whirled, they chanted the names of the entities with which they shared their mountain – the lonesome cuscus, the drowsy fruit bat, the spinning waters of the brook. They named them, these their companions, as they stamped their floorboards. And they were defiant and they were joyful.

Later, they might discover they were worshippers of entirely the wrong god – for so the white men had it in Bisorio – and later it might be said of them they lived in fear, for they would burn in hell.* But that night I saw only rejoicing. The Yaifo celebrated – for the forest, for their own Almighty God (the one called Dinaiya) or for themselves, calling this final time like the courting birds they lived amongst. And they were content with that.

Remember this, I told myself. *If you survive to have children, tell them about this.*

Here were the last flickers of a flame. Next would be the guttering, the plume of smoke from the cooling wick. I had already seen it in West Papua among the Obini: a people cornered, looking about anxiously,

---

* 'Death is ever stalking us,' earlier arrivals from the Central Range said, according to Rob Greenslade in *What's Going On Downriver?*. 'It is our bitter food day and night!'

just like their dogs. Perhaps, after all, it was better the Yaifo left, and of their own initiative, tomorrow.

I woke the next morning, like everyone, with a cough and sore throat – all that trapped indoor dust and bitter, clogging smoke. Tsogomoi and I packed up, then we all sat together, the whole surviving community, passing around and sipping mugs of sugary tea – for the Yaifo had taken quite a fancy to it. The birds sang on around us, but we drank together in complete silence.

We were leaving shortly – and all of us together, I assumed. I asked Tsogomoi if anyone here might spare a feather ornament for me to remember my time here. Someone stepped forward, plucked out a cluster of feathers – a bouquet of maple yellow with a filigree of white. Sawi then timidly presented me with a neat little bag. Woven from the bark of the tulip tree, it bore an extravagant fibrous cuff, this deftly pinned on with the wing bone of a flying fox. In return, I gave Sawi what he most wanted – he couldn't take his eyes off it – my plastic toothbrush bag.

And then something odd. Once I had prepared my load and was all set, Sawi lifted my blue rucksack and handed it to an unlikely, reticent character who had large, friendly but rather vague, wondering eyes and whose name, according to my notes, was Gorsai or Korsai. This fellow called Korsai or Gorsai gave a short, reassuring nod to me, then invited the three of us to accompany him, along with a small lad called Yado. They were heading not down the mountain but up.

There followed some discussion – because Michael made it known he wasn't thrilled at the prospect of crossing a mountain range, let alone one that the Yaifo had said was uncrossable. 'This Benedik has already almost killed me off!' he said to Tsogomoi, and refused to put on his wellies. Finally, it was agreed: Michael would head downslope with the rest of the community a little later.

I didn't look back as we walked off. Seeing these people, the Yaifo, abandon their home – all these drenched trees which had, I couldn't help but feel, imbued them with such courage – could only ever be a matter of terrible sadness. For a while, though, Feefee and Ashkai accompanied us; soon they had discovered a bird's nest. They ran alongside, holding the eggs in a leaf package. Then, an hour or two on, the boys fell away; the trail had dissipated to nothing and now we were alone.

Korsai led, stepping quietly, tentatively, up and up. He spoke rarely, except to chuckle '*Bee-ale!*' – Goodbye! – whenever I slipped. Soon, though, it was obvious that he worried for me – just as I worried for him. Even that first day his face thinned and stiffened in the chill. The mist snagged in his eyebrows; the soot gathered in the creases of his arms and legs.

Higher and higher. We parted the moss with our feet, the trailing lichens with our hair. The trees shrank. They appeared to twist in agony. We sheltered in caves, made big fires to heat their walls. Each night, Korsai stayed apart, clinging to himself beside the embers. He used the blanket I'd given him but only as a pillow. He hated to wake with a cold head.

It was perhaps four days' climb to the main ridge, and much of that time Korsai's feet were in front of my face, his toes rasping at the stones, squeezing the sludge. I was so tired now I could hardly take my surroundings in. Sometimes, all I wanted was to keel forward, sink my face into the sphagnum. Other times I had to stop, light a fire to bring feeling back to the Yaifos' extremities – 'The ends of our legs have died!' – and in the cold before sunrise I cooked porridge to share with Tsogomoi – who increasingly took to staring morosely into the understorey, as if for companionship in the gloom.

Finally, it was done. We were across the divide and picking our way downslope. The trees gathered in numbers and strength. Crested lizards ran along the logs; they rattled the leaves. Unwieldy beetles took to the wing.

We came to the first human signs: a sliced branch, a scored trunk. We had reached a fly-blown settlement in Hewa territory – only a handful of famished-looking inhabitants, but in comparative terms here was safety, the beginnings of the ever-hungry world to which I belonged. Two disgruntled youths, less broken than the rest, agreed to take me from here.

It was time for me to part from the others; already the two Yaifos were proffering a hand each to be shaken, as they knew I liked to do with them. '*Bee-ale*,' farewell, they said softly and took my fingers in theirs. Then Yado and Korsai turned sharply and sped off, as if scared of being infected by all that was awaiting here. Tsogomoi went with them, smiling his furtive, tight smile and waving back as I called out my thanks.

The end of our journey had been all too quick. And the last I saw of the three was Korsai, this good man who had done this good deed for a stranger. He paused, one leg raised mid stride, to check I was happy to be left. Then he rejoined the others, walking back up into the spinning clouds with his light, tiptoeing gait, his rump of worn-out leaves merging into the nothingness.

They were gone, and I was left to ponder what they had achieved for me: navigating a way across a mountain with inadaquate clothing for such cold, and with very limited food. For the defeated people I had known as the Yaifo, this had been their penultimate act.

On I went, through the messy interface with my own kind. Here, the future had already arrived. There was gold up ahead – and lots of it. We were approaching Porgera, destined to be one of the most productive mines the world has seen. For, at last, it had been found – not in the heartlands of the Orinoco or Amazon, but in the very depths of New Guinea. Here was El Dorado.

But there was no joy that I ever saw, just disorientation as the young ran off for their share. Working through the trees were mud streams created by a torrent of bare feet. These joined with others – and all running the same way. Later, there were ladies raking the soil with their fingers and, from what I can recall, an aeroplane unloading only spades and a frozen chicken. I believe I took that same plane out, and from the sky I looked about, trying to trace the route presently being taken by the Yaifo downhill to what lay waiting for them at Bisorio.

All so long ago now. I've tried to recollect a whole era, a brief chapter in a young person's life, lost forever.

VII

I should add that before heading home I called in one last time at Kandengei village. I owed it to the elders, to Martin, and probably to myself. I needed to tell them I wouldn't be back.

'Not until the summer?'

Martin and I were ambling along the shaded path that led through Yaargi territory.

'Not even in the summer.'

My best friend said nothing for a while. He showed not the slightest emotion. 'The Typist would like to say hello to you,' he then informed me, brightly. 'She is pretending to be sickly, in her little mosquito net.' Martin raised his chin to point at the large house through the coconut palms ahead. 'She says she likes you many times. I think she likes you too badly!'

'Martin,' I said, 'I'm feeling torn apart. Do I belong here – or back in my own country? I hardly know any more.'

Yet even Martin, this dear, tender soul, someone who'd been with me through hell, seemed unable to hear.

'Remember,' he said, seeking to reassure me, 'that you are one of us. You are Wumbunavan. The *bikmen* still only ever like us to say this name when we talk about you.'

'I have my family in the UK. A mother, a father, sister and brother. I can't keep doing this, seesawing back and forward. I'll crack up.'

'You have your father Jonny *here*. And you have me, and Kennedy and Stens and Saun. And there is Sebastian, your nice brother.'

I could only repeat what I'd already told him, however hurtful it might be. I'm not sure it ever really sank in.

'During the *banis*,' Martin said, a thought occurring to him, 'I told you how good the summer is. I said to you that we would look at the fishing birds high in the trees with their eggs. And I did indeed take you to see these things.' We stopped where we were, and Martin smiled as he remembered.

'And it was wonderful,' I said. 'Quite a sight!' Overhead, hundreds upon hundreds of bickering fledglings, while down below a mattress of belligerent roots splattered with guano and stinking of the fish that the more clumsy parents had dropped.

'The *bikmen*,' continued Martin, sounding lonelier now, 'have told us that probably the spirits of white men are not born here on the ground, but like those fishing birds out of our reach.'

I remember nothing more of my last conversation with Martin.

As a canoe took me away, he didn't linger. 'Sebastian needs help with the making of his pretty new roof,' he said, or something along those lines. Still he didn't believe I'd be gone forever.

I tried to take it all in a last time: the clay that was malleable and cold beneath my toes; the duckweed odours that lifted around us as *bandees* when we washed, quiet under the starlight; the lame and yet always sprightly elder called Kumbui, 'fruit bat', dressed in his faithful red *laplap* (which is a waist cloth), taking the time to answer my questions about clan lore even as he steered his troublesome pig with a stick; the children giggling at me with fingers in their mouths.

And Martin turned away, and that was how I left the Niowra – a people to whom I was Wumbunavan, a boy they had made into a man as strong as a crocodile.

———

For twenty years, I went elsewhere. I was always likely to be the sort who had to find his own path, and my specific job, as I saw it, remained the same: learn about people and places that are remote from our lives – be a reliable witness for those without the privilege, ability or frankly the inclination to take on these journeys with their associated risks. A generation before, the author Jan Morris – I think it was – said that I'd have been killed by the people whose customs I was attempting to understand. A generation after and their customs would not exist.

The technique remained unchanged too. Go alone and place your life in the hands of those we once called primitive. Do this, and they might trust you. Do this, and you might live to go home.

Things did not always go smoothly. I was shot at, sometimes I was robbed – though never by indigenous communities, I noticed, just as I never seemed to fall victim to anacondas, tarantulas or those invasive fish that smell out your urine and that had populated the tales (along with Eskimos in igloos and fleet-of-foot Amazons) that I'd adored as a child.

In those days, I had been drawn to these powerful notions of the exotic, but now the more I looked, the more I seemed to find only similarities. After a while I became suspicious of our use of the word 'tribal' to denote the kind of people I'd lived with – were their underlying needs, strictures and emotions really so very different from ours? – and I drove myself on, from time to time venting the same old frustrations. 'Imperialism is the life-blood of exploration,' I pronounced on stage at the Royal Geographical Society – a sweeping condemnation greeted very graciously, all things considered. 'Trust to your map,' I added for good measure, 'and all you'll come back with is a better version of that same map.'

The Niowra, the Iban, the Yupik, the Martu, the Nenet, and so many more. So many closing windows I'd been allowed to glimpse through, with the help of those who had made their lives among buttress trees, or with camels shifting over clay pans, or guiding beloved cattle among rocks, or their reindeer herds across silver lichen fields.

I was pushing myself further and further to extremes – from rain-forests to wind-strewn sands to unrelenting ice – as if my main need was the struggle itself. And perhaps it was.

At last there came a day when, out on the pack ice, separated from my dog team, I knew that one way or other this, my pursuit, was at an end. Alone in the Bering Strait, trained by Chukchi sledge-men but now fending off frostbite and the temptation to sleep, I was forced to reflect. 'Man cannot discover new oceans unless he has the courage to lose sight of the shore,' as André Gide said, but I was in danger of losing sight of the boat as well – and my compulsion showed no sign of abating. Sooner or later I'd end up like Livingstone, writing his concluding thoughts with berry juice, or Ludwig Leichhardt, last seen cheerfully making for Australia's interior.

It was a long night before I was reunited with my dog team, and during that night it became obvious even to me that I was seeking something that lay beyond an ever-receding horizon. I was just one more of the delusional. 'You need have no fear of any failure,' wrote Colonel Percy Fawcett in the Mato Grosso before he, too, marched off to his demise.

But out there in the screaming wind, among the ice-blocks of what passed for no-man's-land, halfway between Russia and America, the Old World and the New, I was made to reflect.

I had reason, I now saw, to be extremely grateful for the opportunities my life had given me. Though I wasn't sure what all this effort amounted to, I don't suppose anyone yet born had lived in such isolation with such an array of remote peoples – nor would anyone again – and, though that might not be a cause of celebration, this must count for something. It comforted me that, with the help of several publishers and a handful of people at the BBC, I had been able to share what otherwise no one might ever see or hear.*

Despite myself, but with the help of numerous falling-apart cultures, and not to forget my tolerant friends and family, I had fulfilled my unlikely childhood dream, more or less stuck to the values I held dear, and I should be thankful for that too. Year on year, accountable only to my uncomplaining hosts, I had repeatedly been out of all contact with my own kind for months at a time – something unthinkable today.

Things would never be this way again. At a more practical level, my

---

* I'd been allowed to make six series for BBC 2, thanks largely to the bravery of Bob Long at the Community Programmes Unit, using a technological innovation of the time, the camcorder, to dispense with a camera crew. This allowed the sharing of a complete experience of immersion in extreme environments for the first time.

luck would surely run out. Next time, like Vitus Bering himself, I really wouldn't make it back.

There and then, having delivered myself and sledge-dogs from the pack ice, I decided I must go home and settle down.

This I now did. I married. I had two children, became heavily weighed down with a mortgage – and was pleased to be. I had devoted my adult years to conducting my expeditions alone, without the support of – and therefore obligation to – any scientific institution or commercial sponsor. This had seemed the right thing to do – and, of course, that was my choice. But now I paid the price. So long stubbornly pursuing my vision of how things should be done had, in turn, done for me. I needed to stay put, go gently about a more normal existence.

With time I became a family man in a neighbourhood described by Dave the chirpy estate agent as 'pleasantly suburban'. I enjoyed hearing about the others still out there, and felt for the Arctic man Pen Hadow, measuring his sea ice with aching fingers, shuffling along with sledge through the unending white-out*, and each morning I held the little hands of my children as they trotted to school – Orleans Primary, near Twickenham. There in south-west London I began to nurture their dreams instead of mine. Only occasionally did I think back to the people who'd helped me understand their take on our planet. The Iban, the Matsés, the Mentawai . . . so many confedera-tions and mini-nations whose best days were done. And my best days, they were done too. Which was fine.

Only, I couldn't help remembering the Yaifo – more doomed even than the rest. We should never have regrets in this life, but I did regret having left them there on that mountain in their dying days. In particular, there was that gentle man called Korsai; he must have been about my own age, now I thought about it.

He had been quietly spoken – we'd hardly exchanged a word – but

---

* Hadow led the Catlin Arctic Survey of 2007–12, measuring ice thickness, ocean currents and acidification. While the formidable lone expeditions of the Norwegian Børge Ousland across the Arctic and Antarctic have established him as 'the leading polar explorer of our time', as observed elsewhere in this book it seems fair to suggest that to traverse a landscape is not necessarily to explore it.

at great risk to himself he'd helped a stranger on his way. I could still remember the prints of his markedly elegant feet: a dry compression of the moss, a wet impression on rock.

But all in the past. And he'd have remained so, if I hadn't – two and a half decades later – gone along to an unlikely event organised by the Traveller's Club, a much-cherished pillar of the establishment located in Pall Mall.

PART TWO

A MOMENT LOST FOREVER

I

As I remember it, the evening was to be an 'informal gathering of like-minded adventurers' and the year was 2010. I chained my bike to a convenient lamppost, then ran my thumb over the embossed lettering of the invitation, asking myself why I'd come.

But now fast approaching was a fellow guest – Frank Gardner, the distinguished security correspondent severely wounded by terrorists some years before.* He had on the dapper charcoal suit he wears on the telly and, speeding along the pavement towards me in his wheelchair, his face broke into a friendly smile.

Gratifying, I thought. *He remembers me from my books, all that time ago.*

'Ben Fogle!' he said, seizing my hand. 'Always been a fan.'

I took the rear of the wheelchair, helping him up the steps. 'Actually,' I said faintly, 'you're thinking of someone else.'

Bump, bump, bump. Together we made it to the top.

'Forgotten our jacket and tie, have we, sir?' said the doorman, placing a thin arm in the air between us. He waved the BBC man on through.

'See you later,' Frank said cheerily. 'With any luck.' He accelerated

---

* Gardner was shot while reporting in Riyadh, Saudi Arabia, in 2004 by Al-Qaeda, along with Irish cameraman Simon Cumbers. Gardner alone survived.

away, and I was left fishing through my rucksack inside the austere portals – and all within the disapproving gaze of Wilfred Thesiger, KBE, DSO, whose severe, sculptured head stood beyond another set of doors.*

I headed up the wide stairs, pondering on this rarefied male hideaway, memorizing what I could for any 'field notes' that I might write up, concerning the inhabitants of this unfamiliar land, and regretting my red socks. There were drinks with HRH in the library – my worst work prominently on display – and then we were arranged around a dining table.

Aside from Frank Gardner ('muscled hands', I later recorded in my unsparing notebook, 'solid wide shoulders; eyes gunmetal grey and discerning'), we had Col. John Blashford-Snell – affectionately known as 'Blashers' and rumoured even now to favour a pith helmet when venturing to the Tropics. ('He's stiff and compact. Gaze steady. Toys with his glass.') Around the table was HRH ('hair of course thinning; courteous, impeccably turned out') to the right the desert veteran Charles Blackmore ('sandy and tanned, forceful, decent, clearheaded'). Otherwise, there was only me – a character whose days of derring-do were long gone.

Together we eyed the menu, wondering if our royal companion might generously be thinking of footing the bill.

'And what do you do?' HRH said, turning to me. 'When not off in the jungle?'

The man from the royal protection detail looked up. He eyed me with suspicion – the cheap shiny suit, the unforgivable socks.

'These days I'm afraid not very much,' I said. 'Apart from have more and more children. Mainly, I hide in the garden shed.'

'Ha-ha! Oh, very good, very good.'

But it was true.

---

* Another severed head accompanied that of Thesiger: this belonged to Patrick Leigh Fermor – Paddy, to his friends. In *Travellers' Century*, the BBC TV series I made with Icon Films, we chose three travellers to represent the different strands of that very British occupation, that of the travel writer. There was Eric Newby, the amateur who sets off with his suitcase, revelling in his very lack of preparedness, for the rewards of his journey were to be found not in achieving the end goal but in the spirit with which you face adversity; the wandering minstrel (Laurie Lee); and the Byronic man of intellect and daring combined (Patrick Leigh Fermor).

'And do you ever go adventuring yourself?' I asked. 'I mean, in your . . . line of work?'

'Sadly, not as much as I would like.'

I opted for the fish soup and a promising-sounding duck.

An atmosphere of genteel reverie now pervaded the well-proportioned rooms of the establishment. Old spies fondly remembered prep school days, former ambassadors recalled sojourns long ago in Foreign Parts, and I too couldn't help but think back through the years.

Our 1950s brick house in Cheshire, with its highly innovative (and largely dysfunctional) central heating system came to mind, and then my unassuming father – a surprisingly absent-minded character for someone who tested aircraft of mass destruction. I could only suppose that, like me, he somehow or other found what was necessary within himself when called upon. Soon I was thinking back to my very earliest adventures – and, before I knew it, I was recalling the veering rivers and soaring uplands of New Guinea, and Korsai was again ahead of me as we scaled the Central Range.

There was the boy called Feefee. Ten years old, perhaps a little less. Unlike his grouchy pal Ashkai, he was always at the ready – eyes excited by the mossy tree world he was getting to know. Once, as we rested in a patch of sunshine, he leapt at a friendly looking rodent. It had pretty eyes and smoky grey fur. Feefee took that rodent in his hands and treasured it as it seemed to me he treasured his future.

My duck, when it arrived, was found to be swimming in a strange yellow sauce.

'Blashers,' HRH said, peering closer, 'I expect you have to eat all sorts of disagreeable things on your travels?'

'Sorry, what's that?' Blashford-Snell cupped a hand to an ear. 'Too long on the shooting ranges. Bisley.'

'Eaten any horrible creatures on your wanderings?'

Blashers told of his time negotiating the Darién Gap, and afterwards Charles Blackmore of the waterless tracts of the Taklamakan. Frank and I exchanged memories of Thesiger, the renowned traveller of Arabia – the one whose sculptured head was displayed in all its severity downstairs. Frank first met him as a sixteen-year-old, when he went round for tea at his Chelsea flat. Thesiger, who was somewhat Old School (Eton, a boxing Blue at Oxford, couldn't change a tyre), had worn a three-piece suit and pocket watch, and along with his curved daggers and camel saddles had left an immense impression on the young Gardner. He'd gone on to study Arabic himself. *

We talked, we ate. We ate some more. From time to time the royal protection detail looked over longingly. The subject turned to future expedition plans – of which I had none. 'And you, Frank?'

'I told the surgeons, after I was shot. It's just such a shame I'll never now see birds of paradise. For the most part, they live deep in New Guinea.'

I smiled, remembering the plume that I'd retrieved myself from the highlands.

'I'd give a lot to get out there.'

'Expect we all would,' said HRH. 'The Papuans are a delightful lot, I hear. And, of course, mile upon mile of unspoilt forest.'

Before my eyes, the whole tableau passed by – the stewing marshlands, the gleeful smiles of roadside women, the powerful dances with *kundu* drums. People I shouldn't have involved myself with, people I should have involved myself with more. What now of the Yaifo? And what now of those I'd known over in West Papua?

HRH suggested we retired downstairs.

We did as suggested. Thus far the evening had been most enjoyable, but also, like Thesiger, peculiarly old-fashioned – just the sort of evening that explorers, in the public imagination, always had.

And it was perfectly true. In Britain, if you assembled a room of what were commonly today called 'explorers', you'd find yourself surrounded by types who looked and sounded oddly like me: a rippling pool of

---

* Thesiger had also left an impression on me – wearing a Harris tweed jacket while ensconced with Samburu herders in the thorny scrub of Northern Kenya. The man had twice crossed the Empty Quarter – 'that bitter, desiccated land which knows nothing of gentleness or ease' – in the company of Bedouins and till the very end harboured a resentment of what he called 'modern inventions', reserving particular dislike for the internal combustion engine. 'The harder the way,' he wrote in *Arabian Sands*, 'the more worthwhile the journey.'

white individuals, nearly all of them male and looking to overcome adversity.

For the larger part, they were a competitive lot – 'full of themselves', the harsher critic might say. 'Robust' is the word my grandmother would have favoured – for though born two generations earlier, she too was brought up to be an Edwardian; although in her case, because she actually was one. Like Ernest Shackleton or Lawrence Oates, they were educated at often very distinguished schools to uphold the empire – now gone. On playing fields, they were still taught to show 'character'. They knew the words of Kipling's 'If'.

However, it would be a mistake to think that they – by which I suppose I mean we – really were all the same.* There was what one might usefully call the Military Wing – the subset of those paratroopers, marines and so on for whom a perilous exploit was routinely defined as 'a bit hairy'. These lads talked of 'sucking up the pain' and 'giving it 110 per cent'.

They pitted themselves against fast water and vertical spreads of crumbling granite, seeking enemies wherever they could. 'To strive, to seek, to find, and not to yield!' they muttered, quoting Tennyson's 'Ulysses' – then pressed onward with gritted teeth. Their physical accomplishments, though no longer strictly necessary, were astounding – more so when you consider that many of the environs they found so inhospitable were merrily harvested by people who had lived there. Where nomads in seal-skin boots had once harpooned the walrus, or in warmer climes where womenfolk chatted as they plucked berries and scooped fish, our own crawled onward and made TV programmes about how only the toughest might survive.

The Poles, though, were genuinely home to no one and, like mountain peaks, offered a more measurable and marketable challenge. With great aplomb, our modern gladiators took to the ice.

---

* The concept of the modern-day 'explorer' is for the Antipodeans and North Americans less laden with social distinctions. In the US, for example, time in the Yellowstone National Park might be understood as simply 'a wilderness experience' in the backwoods, as once investigated by the early pioneers. For the French, a hike becomes a philosophical sortie, or *flâneur*, the Enlightenment idea that any individual might just stroll about purposefully observing. For the Germans, there is the concept of *Fernweh*, far-sickness – or indeed that word we borrowed, 'wanderlust'.

Many of the more humble souls shied away from these great natural arenas. They – the hill walkers, fell runners, scramblers, rock-climbers, weekenders with yachts kept at Littlehampton – were not in the classic explorer mould, if only because they slipped into the blue without a fuss. They climbed, they paddled, they put one foot in front of another only 'to get away from it all', 'to clear the cobwebs', or just for the 'sheer hell of it'.*

But whatever the motive, whatever the social background, not many were at ease with what we might call 'the establishment' – though this was assumed by many to be so. A large proportion were outsiders, willing or unwilling outcasts. These were more complicated cases – individuals in search of a home or escaping one, those seeking hope in an apparently hopeless cosmos and those seeking punishment. They wrestled with each other, or else measured themselves, finding relief and sometimes meaning for their lives, no different from Raleigh four hundred years before in the Orinoco – 'Fain would I climb, yet fear I to fall.'

As a youngster, this thought had given me much comfort. I smiled to see the pictures of Edmund Hillary and Tenzing Norgay in the Western Cym, enamel mugs in blackened hands, before or after having 'knocked the bastard off'. Their wind-burnt faces were not self-satisfied, but satisfied. 'It is not the mountain that we conquer but ourselves.'†

---

* To recap: we had had the Age of Pre-Historic Migration, next the Great Navigators – Chinese, Phoenician, Maori, a plethora of people besides the European – then the Golden Age of Victorians, and so to modern times. Now, concurrently with the Heroic Era of high-latitude explorers (Nansen, Shackleton, et al., but also others less prominent, such as the Scot William Speirs Bruce and Russian Eduard von Toll) was fast evolving a more individualist approach. These were the specialist Modern Adventurers (the American Amelia Earhart, the first female solo aviator across the Atlantic, and the Italian Umberto Nobile, one of the first to fly over the North Pole) and more whimsical Independent Travellers. 'Exploration' was becoming experiential. Whatever their upbringing or background, the adventurous were freer than ever to 'sally forth', assisted by looser social constraints and the rise of steamships, and increasingly these were female. They included such notables as Ella Maillart, Gertrude Bell, Kate Marsden, Aleksandra Potanina and the missionary trio Mildred Cable and sisters Evangeline and Francesca French. Specialisms began to develop. In *Scrambles Amongst the Alps*, published 1871, Edward Whymper expresses his devotion to the sheer thrill of bagging peaks. The 'sport' of mountaineering was born.

† 'My feeling was essentially one of considerable satisfaction,' Hillary later said of the moment he reached the summit just ahead of Tenzing, having led the final stage. He did not jump around

Put another way, a great many of these pioneers were, for all their extraordinary mental and physical powers, needy. They needed to exorcise their demons, to show off, run away, enact a penance, or do what had been drilled into them at school. Sometimes it hardly mattered where they went – but it did matter how far from the everyday they took themselves. Tilman found a rare contentment exposed on a crag with his hob-nailed boots and pipe – but also on the high seas; Francis Chichester exchanged his Gypsy Moth de Havilland bi-plane for his *Gypsy Moth III* yawl, then *Gipsy Moth IV* ketch. The protagonists were absorbed by the challenge of achieving their final objective and this meant absorption in the threats to be negotiated along the way– the devastating swell, the crushing avalanche. So, too, the turbaned Lady Hester Stanhope – disappointed in love, digging through the ruins of the Holy Land with her entourage, the Swiss male-dressing Isabelle Eberhardt. There was Freya Stark, her hair caught in a loom. Gertrude Bell in Syria, who sought inspiration and, we sense, ease in the abrasive sands 'glittering in raw sunlight, an unanswered question and an unanswerable doubt hidden in the fold of every hill'. All had abnormally itchy feet – and in *The Springs of Adventure*, the mountaineer Wilfrid Noyce came up with quite a few explanations – The Hair Shirt, The Escape Simple, The Escape Becomes Lodestone, The Cult of Danger, The Scientific Man, The Doers of Good, The Machine Loving Man.

In the smoking room, a gentleman was sleeping fitfully between the outstretched pages of *The Telegraph*, with the fire well stoked. The royal protection officer found a chair in the corner. He played with his phone, fiddling with it joylessly, as if needing his revolver.

The conversation again returned to Frank's elusive birds. HRH learned there were thirty-nine species of the passerine, each as splendid as the next. They were known for their outlandish courtship behaviour, lavish colours, intricate ornamentation. Feathers sprouted like antennae from

---

and throw his hands in the air. 'The whole of my life has been a battle against boredom,' he said. He attributed his drive to the hardships of his childhood. His father, a 'very firm man', would take him to the woodshed for a good beating every now and then. Hillary was stubborn too. 'It didn't matter how much I was beaten, I never agreed that what I'd done was wrong.' *Outside* magazine, 1999, Allison Chase and Gordon Brown.

heads, others like wires from tails, or they were in bunches like arrange-ments of flowers.

'They are essentially a crow,' I offered. 'A primitive crow.' They tasted like that, too.

'It seems,' Frank continued, 'the island is free of the more usual pred-ators, such as cats.' There was an abundance of fruit trees, and this freed up time for the males to display and for females to be entranced. The earliest foreign visitors, too, were entranced; they examined dried speci-mens, wondered at their lack of feet – which, for convenience, had been chopped off by the various 'natives' tasked with ferrying them from the island's (for now) inpregnable interior. The Europeans imagined the foot-less birds in their secluded realm, forever flittering in the clouds.*

'Well, let's hope you see them yourself one day,' said HRH, kindly. 'Where there's a will, there's a way.'

'Very true,' said Frank. 'Must put my mind to it.'

Together we eyed the bill.

'And do you have an interest in birds, sir?' I said, satisfied I'd at last found a safe line of conversation.

'I'm ashamed to say not really,' said HRH. 'Beyond bagging the odd woodcock.'

It might have been a joke. We weren't quite sure.

Frank said, in the ensuing silence, 'Come to think of it, you've been to PNG, haven't you, Benedict?'

---

* '[T]hese birds . . . flie, as it is said, alwaies into the Sunne, and keepe themselves continually in the ayre, without lighting on the earth, for they have neither feet nor wings . . .' From Jan Huygen van Linschoten's *Itinerario* of 1596.

II

After that first encounter with Frank, I wrote in my diary:

All being equal, I'd love to make it happen – take him off to see his birds. But to lug someone with that many internal injuries through the interior of PNG would be lunacy. Nor am I enthusiastic about contracting malaria again. Four times is plenty.*

Still, I can't help thinking back to when I too was shot at. Frank was hit by six bullets, which is about the same number that passed me by.†

For Frank, though, no such escape. Simon Cumbers [the cameraman] killed outright, and for Frank month after month prostrate in a hospital bed. The surgeon, a relative stranger – just one of those who has been fighting to save him – is no stranger to the

---

* I had succumbed to, and recovered from, strains of malaria in the Amazon (twice), PNG and Tanzania (respectively, *Plasmodium falciparum* and *P. vivax*, then *P. vivax* again, then *P. falciparum*)..
† My own 'shooting' nowadays had been reduced to no more than a faintly amusing anecdote. I could afford to laugh – even though the incident was considerably more serious than the single shot I once used to tell everyone about – because Pablo Escobar, in charge of an empire worth $3 billion a year, had evidently hired two bodyguards who were incompetent. Crossing the Amazon Basin at its widest – north-west to south-east – in the early '90s, I passed a camp where Escobar was thought to be briefly hiding out. Two armed men anyway gave chase. I paddled my canoe for all I was worth, they shot at me for all they were worth. Together we sped up a creek off the Putumayo river. Then I took my chance, jumping for the forest bank. I ducked behind a curtain of riverside leaves and was safe.

*contents of Frank's body. He has seen his organs, his guts, the hospital
pea soup as it pulsates through. He knows that some patients will fight,
some will not. He has seen what Frank is made of – in a sense, he has
seen what lies within us all.*

*Sure enough, Frank gathers himself. He re-equips himself. He will
not let this life pass him by.*

The fact of the matter was that to get Frank anywhere remote would
cost a small fortune and carry a considerable risk to his health; nonetheless, I wondered whether the BBC might stump up the cost – for such
an uplifting spectacle must surely speak to this or that neglected sector
of the demographic.

I put the idea to a TV production company based in Bristol. With
lavish illustrations and amid much excitement, they sent it off – though
personally I wasn't sure the corporation would be especially thrilled at
the prospect of their esteemed employee, a national treasure already beset
with life-threatening injuries obtained while on assignment, launching
off on a 'jolly' through the murderous foliage and rank heat.

In the event, the commissioners were faster than even I expected in
coming to a decision. 'So sorry to be the bearer of bad tidings,' said Dick
Colthurst, ringing on behalf of Tigress Productions. 'They say it's just
not the right climate for this sort of programme. Inexplicable, really.'

The escapade was forgotten. I continued my existence as before, not
venturing anywhere much. More years went by. It was a shame, in a way:
I'd been granted views of our planet now lost to us all – even to those
as keen to get off the beaten track as Gardner. I was especially haunted
by the purity of his dream to see a bird.

My retirement from the world at large continued. I sat in the shed
with my second-hand travel books, remembering how as a boy I'd sought
them out, these marvellous tales of corseted and hatted travellers who
were misfits like me.* Together through my university years, these

---

* The 'gypsy-eyed' Richard Francis Burton; the unrepentant, spirited and capricious (in the
end totally unrestrainable) females such as Isabella Bird – draped in her Manchurian silks – and
Alexandra David-Néel – yak boots, loose llama robes. They came from as far afield as Arabia,
the most acclaimed Muslim being the early fourteenth-century Ibn Battuta ('I have indeed –

turbulent souls had stood close by like allies. Most people would never know what it was to feel this degree of yearning – 'because it's there' – or so it had felt to me. The 'true explorer', I told myself, travelled not for the sake of mere pleasure, the simple joy that Robert Louis Stevenson gained by passing through the unfamiliar – 'I travel not to go anywhere, but to go. The great affair is to move.' Movement in itself did not suffice. These wanderers seemed in want of a resolution, a peaceful destination – their baobab, their fig tree, their Eden. 'Life, which you look for, you will never find,' the poet says in the *Epic of Gilgamesh*, dated 2000 BC, but that did not stop them trying. Off they, the unstoppable, went. There were two paths to knowledge, so the ancient Greeks had it: *mythos* (fables, allegories, a poetic context for our lives) or *logos* (the rational, the logical) – but this mattered not. Each in their own way, they grappled with the tree that grew the bittersweet fruit.

And now, all these years on? These books, like my adventures, were behind me. Nor did I feel any nostalgia for those days. I had a wealth of memories to treasure and pass on, and the truth was that so many years adhering to my idiosyncratic 'philosophy' – if I might call it that – had not been without an emotional cost. I'd almost died nine times on my expeditions, so it was said – and this might well be true. Undoubtedly, I'd been selfish to many who were dear to me, especially my mother waiting back home. So the arrows I'd hunted with were not displayed on the wall – as is traditional among the travelling fraternity upon retirement – but shoved in the corner, along with a quiver of poisoned arrows, a spear once allegedly owned by Fawcett and two New Guinea war shields, still with their Air Niugini baggage tags.

In quiet moments, though, just every now and then, I sought out the woven bag given by that kind-hearted man called Sawi, or checked the Yaifo feathers to make sure they were safe from mites. And through the shed window I watched my own children play. I warmed to the thought that they too were exploring.

---

praise be to God – attained my desire in this world, which was to travel through the earth'), and Japan. 'To strengthen my legs for the journey I had mugwort burned on my shins,' wrote the seventeenth-century poet Matsuo Bashō, before patching his trousers, donning his bamboo hat and plodding his way into the northern interior.

Then, one wintertime is must have been, I attended a service at St Paul's marking the centenary of Robert Scott's fateful Terra Nova expedition. 'We shall stick it out to the end,' he scrawled on 29 March 1912, 'but we are getting weaker, of course, and the end cannot be far.'

I found myself queuing around the back of the cathedral alongside a bright-eyed child who was buttoned up against the chill. Proudly, he stated that his name was Crean – and I knew then that he must be a relative of Thomas Crean, the burly seaman who was a companion both to Scott and Shackleton in Antarctica.

I was reminded of myself at the boy's age, born in Macclesfield because my father needed to be a short drive from Woodford Aerodrome. Such impressionable years, the passage of so many planes across the cloudy wide skies of my childhood.

The weak sun shone softly off the hairless round head of William Hague, the then Foreign Secretary, as he marched up the aisle. He spoke stirring words. We were invited to think of Scott's spirit of patriotism, the expedition's unstinting dedication and sacrifice. The national anthem was sung, and during this I again thought of Crean, the Irishman so neglected by history, and of Scott, beleaguered in his tent with 'Uncle Bill' Wilson and 'Birdie' Bowers. I thought of Amundsen, one of the first of the truly modern adventurers. This journey south was nothing more than a contest, he decided, and he saw what winning would take. The man he outmanoeuvred – first pretending to head to the North Pole – was commonly depicted as a rigid man of empire who extolled the values of a lost age, though the truth was more complicated, for Scott was to have the greater legacy. Two years of important scientific research the British Antarctic Expedition bequeathed us; the defeated Southern Party, needing something to fight for, dragged thirty-five pounds of rock samples to the very end.

As the service of thanksgiving drew to its solemn close, I pictured the harsh magnificence of the white continent – the Beardmore Glacier, Scott struggling onward through 'a scene of whirling drift', and suddenly I felt that I shouldn't have given up either.

Everywhere – in Indonesia, Malaysia, Peru and Brazil – trees that I'd once slept among were gone, and with them people I'd once held as friends. 'Benedict,' I said to myself as I filed out with the great and good, 'you need to pull yourself together.'

Even so, that might have been it, had I not met a writer friend at the Turk's Head, a Twickenham pub with large TV screens and hardly any chairs, a convenient watering hole for rugby fans making their way to the stadium.

John Perry had been a rock musician, the editor of *Loaded* and a journalist on the *NME*; he was streetwise and stylish, and I wasn't. But we were both born in the vicinity of Manchester, and had sheds at the end of the garden where we tried our utmost to write. Today, he'd brought along a book inscribed by Ranulph Fiennes, the man traditionally referred to as the World's Greatest Living Explorer.*

'It's about how his ancestors won the battle of Agincourt,' said John, laconically. 'No mention of yours . . .'

Flicking through the volume, I noticed that Ran had scribbled a brief message: 'For Benedict,' he had written in a permanent marker pen. 'Get Again Into The Amazon!'

I put the book down. I swigged my pint.

'Get again to ANYWHERE,' said John. 'That's what he means. Don't just sit in Twickenham.'

I reminded John that he too just sat in Twickenham. No one told *him* to go off to the jungle.

We talked it over for a while and finally I told him there were more important things to do in the twenty-first century than burn fossil fuel on unnecessary journeys. And that was that.

---

* A title bestowed by *The Guinness Book of Records*. Sir Ranulph Twisleton-Wykeham-Fiennes, baronet, stood firmly at the opposite end of the 'explorer' arc from me. Though he too was keen to follow in the wake of his father, in his case to be commander of the Royal Scots Greys cavalry regiment, his approach has been deliberately impactful, rather than immersive. He had served eight years in the military before being 'forced', as he puts it, 'to become a civilian', then looked to 'expedition-leading' as a means of earning a living. 'Fate, army training and a lack of A levels led me to do what I seemed to be best at doing.' From then on, he maintains, his career has been compelled onwards principally by the requirements of his bank manager. Just as the modern professional adventurer is advanced by having the three key words 'Summiteer of Everest' on their CV, business logic dictated that he make as big a splash as possible – obtaining 'firsts' on mainly polar ventures by thwarting equally combative rivals – for greatest impression on sponsors and public. 'Priority was the key,' he writes in *Beyond the Limits*. 'To be second was of no value to us.'

Only, there seemed to be a horrible inevitability about this. Next thing, I found myself invited to yet another get-together of adventurers, this one at Buckingham Palace. Once more, I dug out my moth-eaten suit, took out my bike and prepared to tackle the murderous traffic of Hyde Park Corner.

Reinhold Messner, Chris Bonington, many of the most significant climbers of the day were there, and such a throng of rowers, kayakers and yachtspersons that I couldn't properly view the oil paintings.*

The Queen wore lilac gloves; they were very warm. *Good circulation*, I thought, accepting a glass of champagne. *She'd do well in the Arctic.* Ray Mears, the bush craftsman, tried to engage her with small talk about campfires but she was having none of it.

Perhaps Her Majesty is a bit burnt out, I thought, rapidly depleting my glass. *Like me. Or, more likely, she suspects, deep in her royal heart, that the time of the stout-hearted explorer is gone. She's very polite about it, but thinks they should move over, make room for the boffins – the botanists, arachnologists, herpetologists and volcanologists.*

And I was inclined to agree – this was several years ago now. You need no further example than Mark Hassall, a former tutor of mine. His life work was the terrestrial woodlouse. What, Dr Hassall sought to discover, were this humble isopod's allies? What is its role in the greater scheme of things? Hassall must be retired now and would have put it differently – 'phenotypic variation in the breeding phenology of the woodlouse *Armadillidium vulgare . . .*' etc. – but I was pretty sure he was nowhere near a complete understanding of his small grey subjects. In the UK there were some thirty-five species of the armoured crustacean – this left about ten million other kinds

---

* Reinhold Messner and Chris Bonington were leaders among the post-war generation of mountaineers who, with the help of commercial backers and slide lectures, effectively made their passion a career. And so to the present day, the Era of Ubiquitous Travel, when the rise of a more stable world order, wider prosperity, cheap plane flights and more leisure time permitted endeavours undertaken by everyone from the packaged tourist to the casual, impecunious backpacker, to the dedicated sub-class known as the Professional Adventurer. By the turn of the new millennium, almost the whole surface of the planet had become readily visitable.

of living things we'd not got around to.* Yet, with the best will in the world, not many of those here assembled were adding substantially to the stock of human knowledge.

It was no one's fault, really. Our emissaries have long since been expected to report back with something that is a little at odds with what might more conventionally have been described as the truth. Essential to the drama was the landscape, our overwhelming backdrop. For centuries, these displays of valour and perseverance had reassured us of the success of our species – and relative success of our race. We had learned of societies we might look down on because they grubbed about in bogs – and conversely our explorers also told us of folk we might aspire to, perfect people – 'naked and painted', as the historian Bartolomé de las Casas put it, chronicling Columbus's encounter with what he thought were the Indies – who enjoyed simple, inoffensive lives and knew eternal truths that we had long forgotten.

For, around twelve thousand years ago, somewhere in the Fertile Crescent, our Neolithic ancestors chose not to be hunter-gatherers but count ourselves among the civilised by ploughing the land. In biblical terms, Adam had been banished to earn his living 'in the sweat of [his] face'.

And we are still trying to get over it. Through the millennia we in the West had looked to our adventurers to re-enact for us the perennial struggle, help us heal the trauma of our separation from what we now called 'wilderness'. Off our champions ventured into it, and the relation-ship we had with these wild lands was adversarial: us against Nature. Whether our protagonists were historical – Alexander MacKenzie, first European across the Northern Americas (major travels from 1788) – or contemporary – Les Hiddins, Australia's beloved 'Bush Tucker Man' (major broadcasts from 1988) – here was Robinson Crusoe time and again: the more enlightened sort of human, now bereft. He discovers the tools to persevere, not be a savage but constructive, moral. These

---

* Give or take 1.3 million – the probable figure in 2011 was 8.7 million. Of these, 86 per cent of land species and 91 per cent of marine species have not been named, studied or described. Figures quoted from 2011 *Census of Marine Life*.

days we might watch our champions endure night after night on the telly – they drink urine, they swallow maggots, they pretend to be attacked by a wolf and they win. The human is validated; he has triumphed.

To those left at home, it didn't matter that their heroes were governed these days not by the harsh strictures of Godforsaken Lands, but Health and Safety procedures, nor that they didn't much write their books, or on the telly rendered the humdrum lives of indigenous peoples into entertaining spectacles.* Here was the version of reality that we had always most valued, a condition of transcendence that the discovery of new worlds might provide for us – the *wonderstrands* that Leif Eríksson encountered, steering ever westward in his longship at the turn of the eleventh century.

And so, I thought, taking another unwise swig and warming yet further to my theme, *even today we send them out, these our seekers, desiring to know our place in the firmament. They transported us to the cliff ledge, as it were, that we too might test our grip, there inspiring us to believe the well-nigh impossible. And it was always thus.* 'I shall perform the deeds of a hero,' proclaimed Beowulf in the Old English epic, as he set to sea 'fierce in war' against the monster giant. 'I, alone, will fulfil the wish of the people . . . or die in the foe's grasp.'

Like shamans they departed, entered realms of the immortals forbidden to most of us and returned proffering their marvels and their hope. So we indulged them – their vainglorious acts, their tales of dragons. They made us feel better about ourselves. And some sought to conquer and others to be conquered. They sought kudos, or just a thrill, and many were insufferable – but deep down we loved them because we too were needy.

Personally, I had a soft spot for the yachtsman Bernard Moitessier – the 'fastest vagabond' – who practised yoga on his deck and lost interest in the race he was winning, defiantly speeding on east past Plymouth,

---

* Just as Marco Polo's *Il Milione* told of the marvels apparently to be encountered beyond medieval Europe – ensuring a wide circulation by including men with tails, unicorns and lands where, enticingly, 'no man would ever on any account take a virgin to wife'.

the finishing point, to Tahiti.* For him, too, it was never quite what Bonington dubbed a 'quest for adventure' – though there was plenty of that involved. 'At its finest moments,' commented Doug Scott, the figure standing upon Everest in my bedroom, 'climbing allows me to step out of ordinary existence into something extraordinary, stripping me of my sense of self-importance'. Here was a sentiment I recognised, and this was why – for all that I'd been an obdurate youth who'd thought he could do it differently, and for all that the mountaineer standing on that peak looked *exactly* like a conqueror – I kept his poster over my bed.†

I looked around at the explorers of today here present. Many were by now slightly the worse for wear, like me. Unaccountably I had two empty glasses in my hand, the renowned travel writer Colin Thubron was dashing by in his much-loved tweed jacket, and for reasons I couldn't comprehend Bear Grylls, the chief scout, had just pinched my bum. The Duke of Edinburgh was saying, 'I know why *you* became an explorer, Benedict! You missed out on doing your DofE at school!'‡

I bumped into television producer Dick Colthurst. 'Have you heard? "Authenticity" is back in vogue at the BBC!'

'Really?'

'Well, to a degree. So give me a call sometime. We ought to get you on the telly again!'

'Yes, I suppose we should,' I said doubtfully. 'Why are we here, do you know?'

'A birthday of someone? Here comes another tray of nibbles. Quick, cut him off before the mountaineers get them.'

———

* The Frenchman was competing in the 1968–9 *Sunday Times* Golden Globe Race, the first non-stop, single-handed race around the world. The prize and a knighthood was given to the British outsider Robin Knox-Johnston.

† 'Hope it didn't give you nightmares,' I recall him saying to me, much later. And in a sense the poster did exactly that, though it gave me dreams as well.

‡ The Duke of Edinburgh Award is the 'world's leading youth achievement scheme'. I had occasionally met HRH Prince Philip, along with Premier League footballers and other interesting celebrities, while presenting DofE gold medals.

I agreed to meet Dick at the Westfield Shopping Centre, a mall of fashionable brands and tinted glass, just off Shepherd's Bush. The sparkling water cost £3.50; we both opted for tea.

Dick got to the point. 'I always thought that idea of taking Frank Gardner off to PNG had particular merit.'

'Yes, pity about that. Never mind.'

'You think he's up for it still?'

'Well, that was ages ago, Dick. I'm sure Frank's thought better of it.'

'Thing is, the idea is so beautifully simple. You go back to your crocodile tribe and they show you a way through the trackless jungle. At last, the pay-off: in the heart of Paradise, Frank glimpses his bird and is moved to copious tears.'

'I've had no contact with the Niowra for thirty years, Dick.'

'You and Frank together in the fecund wilderness,' mused Dick, playing happily with his tea bag. 'A sort of bromance.'

'Nor will they take kindly to me turning up after three decades of neglect, I should think.'

'I'll draft a treatment.'

The TV treatment when it emerged looked to me exactly like the one of years before. The nation's much-loved security correspondent would be assisted, the premise went, by the Last of the Old Time Explorers, 'who will have an emotional reunion with his blood-brothers' – presumably, the very same who'd once put me through their unimaginably painful rite – 'and together seek out the glorious birds that the naturalist Wallace called "the most beautiful and wonderful of living things".'*

Dick submitted the proposal to Kim Shillinglaw, head of BBC 2.

Rather a long silence followed. Then Dick rang excitedly to say there'd been a 'positive update'. He arranged a conference call, so that we could together hear more from Frank first-hand. Apparently, he had conversed with Ms Shillinglaw – the scarily powerful executive whom

---

* From *The Malay Archipelago* of 1869. Recovering from the horror of losing his Amazon specimens when his ship went down, Alfred Russel Wallace moved his attention to South-east Asia, his observations bringing about a theory of evolution independently from Darwin.

Frank, Dick noticed, now proceeded to refer to in terms you'd normally reserve for a dear family friend.

'Well,' reported Frank, 'I was waiting at the lift at the Beeb and bumped right into the lovely Kim. And Kim – so sweet of her – said, "Are you sure you want to do this, Frank?"'

'Love the way it sounds like she's doing you a favour!' exclaimed Dick. 'Go on.'

'Well, seems she happens to be a fan!'

I said, 'I'm amazed she even remembers me. I was dropped from the BBC's Christmas card list years ago.'

'A fan of mine, I meant,' said Frank.

'Ah.'

Frank explained that he'd chatted to the lovely Kim as they ascended together from ground floor to fifth. 'The upshot is, we are actually commissioned.'

Oh God, I thought.

As it happened, Kim Shillinglaw mysteriously vacated her job two days later. Even that didn't stop the project.

Not long after, Frank came over to my house for a bite of lunch. We'd both agreed it would be a good idea for us to get to know each other better – 'before we're stranded forever in the swamp and it's too late', as we said at the time, jokingly.

I wrote the following in my diary:

Pursued by [my six-year-old boy] *Freddie, I led Frank to the garden shed. Perhaps that's the difference between us, I thought. The six bullets meant for me missed and the six bullets meant for him did not.*

From the doorway, Frank peered in. I showed him the carved arrows, wooden shields, the hand-drum that I used to dance with: 'Incredible,' he commented pensively, as if surveying a recess of the Pitt Rivers Museum. 'Can't wait to get out there.' He's imagining, I suppose, that I'll receive a rousing welcome on my return to Kandengei – though it's anyone's guess.

We ate spaghetti, and while Baby Beatrice was chuckling in her IKEA high chair, plastering her face with pasta strings, Frank enthused about the 'Bs of Ps', as he calls them, and their competitive displays known as 'lekking'. The King B. of P., said Frank, is small, 'a gem' – as if he's wearing a Napoleonic tunic. Another, the Superb, entertains mates with his bouncing dance and his tar black cape of feathers, from which radiates an iridescent breast plate. The King of Saxony even has two scalloped blue plumes or 'head wires' that he can erect at will.

Frank stopped himself. There seemed to be something on his mind. 'You should know,' he said abruptly, 'that I've done with pain . . .'

I reassured him. 'We're not going to PNG to test ourselves to the limit. Not as far as I'm concerned.'

'What I was doing when I was injured was totally different, Benedict. I wasn't doing anything crazy, like you. We were just standing in the road.'

It came to me then that Frank had driven all the way over from New Broadcasting House just to say these words: I have done with pain.

He left, Freddie still wondering how many bullets he had stuck in him.

'Your friend looks a bit poorly,' Natalya [my eight-year-old] said as Frank lifted himself from his wheelchair, folded it away and then drove off. 'He's all red around his eyes.'

'I know,' I said. 'Worries me too.'

I told Dick. As ever, he brushed my concerns away. 'Just a lot of late nights in the newsroom.' And, of course, Dick was a veteran of taking hapless TV presenters into uncomfortable places. He laughed and said, 'But I do wonder if he really knows what's ahead of him!'

'So do I,' I said, and told Dick what he needed to know: that the Niowras were not to be underestimated. 'There are factions, there are jealousies. For all I know, someone might try to do me in.'

Dick chuckled, indulging me.

'Remember, they beat the hell out of their own children – and for a month or two. Their wives get not much better treatment the rest of the time.'

The twentieth century saw the end of the classic explorer figure – the specialist who sought out and investigated for their people uncharted realms – and rise of the spirited, independent traveller. 'Curiosity is the one thing invincible in Nature,' wrote Freya Stark. Hulton Archive/Archive Photos/Getty Images

We undertake these ventures in order to conquer what is out there – or to conquer what is to be found within ourselves? Doug Scott having summited Everest 'the hard way', via the south-west route. Copyright © The Estate of Doug Scott

Highly driven, idealistic – and often hopelessly naive. The aspiring 'explorer' wearing his SAVE IT! sweatshirt while on his first expedition to a volcano in Costa Rica in 1979. Copyright © Richard Baker

The prime duty of any explorer through the ages: to report back. In this family snap I'm eagerly showing my insect specimens to my patient cousins on my return from Brunei as a student. As it turned out, among the collection were quite a few fig wasps unknown to science.

An awfully big adventure: self-portrait from my first, almost impossibly ambitious, independent expedition (1983) as I climbed up to the summit of Mt Roraima alone, needing to gather myself for whatever lay ahead in the Amazon.

Another window closes: I took these photos and just a few others, aware that that year (1985) I was the first, and most probably last, outside witness to the independence, condition and culture of the Obini. Today, nothing much else remains.

Trying it a new way. Kandengei, a village hidden within a mosquito-blighted swampland, in 1985 became my new home and a route into a world barely documented by my own kind.

Attempting to raise morale with members of the Smaark Clan while inside the *waarkdumba* or Crocodile Nest. This rare photo was one of few allowed by the Niowra elders, who safeguarded the traditions of the exacting ceremony with considerable vigilance and pride.

A second safe return: my arrival at Heathrow Airport after six months in New Guinea's lowland forests is caught by my relieved parents. I'm dressed up in my prized tropical suit – bought at a jumble sale – and, though I'm carrying my hunting arrows, there's little to suggest the extent of what I've seen or been through.

What next? Alone in my bedroom – the poster of Doug Scott atop Everest just visible above my second-hand travel books and my childhood poppy duvet cover.

Evangelist George Walker busily baptising in the River Korosameri.

Trusting to the unconverted instead. The expedition as we were about to set out from Bisorio Mission with our few provisions – Michael to the left, Tsogomoi in mining helmet and Kaibayoo closest to me, behind.

The Yaifo 'settlement' – a single, fortified structure that was hidden away on a northern slope of the Central Range.

'The yelping, the smacking of bow strings and everyone's confusion at the collision between two worlds.'

The terrifying view through my camera lens on our arrival – Yaifo bows at the ready, and Tsogomoi's stolen bush knife being whacked into the ground.

Unsure how to reassure the Yaifo community, I was reduced to admiring their arrows for quite some time. Sawi keeps watch (rear right) while Tsogomoi (behind the camera) is eyed with suspicion by a young Ashkai – from where he is seated with Feefee, who clutches our confiscated bush knife.

The Yaifo women under armed escort as they emerge from cover. Leading them is Ba-lei-ya – later the mother of Koi-ak-kei, who a generation later would accompany me over the Range.

Feefee and his friend Lei-yai (left) with a pig's bladder for a ball.

Sawi, father of my key future ally Samwell, experimenting with my backpack before deciding the community would help us over the mountain. Tsogomoi looks on, from below.

Showing me a way. Sawi discussing the best chance of a route to safety, up through the mists of the Central Range.

My view looking back, soon after our departure. We were tracing the course of a river to assist with navigation and for now were accompanied by Kenowa, father of Feefee, and Sawi, Feefee (standing, centre) and Ashkai (to his left) at the rear.

Tsogomoi, in a cliff-side camp we fashioned while negotiating a way across the Central Range.

'Steven knows his stuff,' Dick said easily. 'Steven' was Steven Ballantyne, who had the title of location supervisor for our project and knew PNG backwards. 'He's even been kidnapped, held for a couple of weeks!'

I waited. Was this meant to be reassuring?

There would be a 'full recce' by Steven, Dick continued, then another recce. We would even have along a medic – one of those discreet, brawny types that, for reasons of insurance, are deployed off-camera to keep our more audacious TV adventurers from harm.

The weeks went by, and the nearer the prospect of a return to New Guinea loomed, the less my experience of it remained secure in my past. It was as if I had unlocked a forbidden door. All manner of unwanted memories tumbled out.

Once again, the Sepik was sliding by – quiet and powerful, as it licked at the reeds. *It's evening here*, I thought, *but on the other side of the world my one ally is waking up*. Dreamily, Martin potters on his skinny legs down to the waterside, there to have a little dip. Maybe he finds Jonny up early, at work on another canoe before the sun bears down. 'Wumbunavan is coming back,' Jonny tells him – because the news is already out. 'At last. So long he's been gone, and not one kina in that time for his father – or for his brother. Or everyone else.'

What a horrible can of worms lay as yet unopened. All these voices and more, percolating up as if through the sediments from somewhere back in time.

I asked myself again why this journey was important. 'I'm not sure that it is,' I remember answering aloud. 'Not for me.'

It seemed enough that it was important to Frank. I had come through unscathed and he had not.

I began preparing for my return – acting, I began to realise, as if this was a full-on expedition, whereas this was just a film shoot. However, preparing for a proper expedition was the only way I knew – checking my water bottles for leaky tops, my boots for weak stitching.

I went shopping for Jonny, Martin, Sebastian and the rest of my twenty-nine *wanbanis*. Wristwatches? It's what they wanted back in 1985

– but in those days it didn't matter if the watches worked, they just had to look good as bracelets.

As I packed my rucksack, Freddie said, 'Daddy, are we going camping?'

'No, just me. I'm off to the jungle.'

'But Daddy, you never go *anywhere*.'

'Well, now I'm going with Frank. The one in a wheelchair.'

'He's so cool!' Natalya said.

'Yes, he is, rather, isn't he?'

'Except,' said Freddie, 'he didn't answer my question about why he's going in a wheelchair. Why doesn't he just walk?'

III

The next days took place as if in a dream. Everything I encountered coming back to Papua New Guinea was only vaguely familiar. Yet once upon a time I'd known something of this land – the women who were shoving their sweet potatoes, babies and washing-up bowls in their string *bilum* bags, even as they disembarked the plane, and the scary-looking men who delivered the softest of leathery handshakes – it was as if they were wearing gardening gloves – and the pavements they had adorned with ruddy splashes of betel nut juice.

Steven was ready at Arrivals. He wore sandals. He had eyes that were strong but very tired from what he termed 'the set-up'. You got the feeling – his leanness, his ash-coloured beard – that he was an Old Testament prophet, especially when he strode onward, parting the crowds. He kept going – early signs showed – on a diet of mainly coffee.

I found I was monitoring him as I used to my expedition companions: noting their weak points, quietly keeping an eye on what they were eating and how much. Presently he was listening to Simon, our slightly out-of-shape, thoroughly overstretched director, who was telling him we needed more time to sort out the gear, which was in 'a right old state'.

'Always a thousand solutions,' said Steven, smoothly. He led us on like Moses: me, a man haunted; Simon, who hadn't slept on the plane and looked like death; Frank, zooming about in his chair – 'I'm all fired up about this!' – and Mark Roberts, the silent soundman, immaculately turned out in uniform grey. Finally, David Osborne, known as 'Os'. He was a 'remote trauma specialist' and had the unenviable responsibility of getting Frank home in one piece. A rugby player, he had a chunky, muscular neck and shoulders – 'Just fat in all the right places,' he said modestly – and, with no discernible effort, placed on his huge back a colossal red medical bag.

Very soon, Simon looked even worse than before. Given this assignment hot off the back of another, his head, sat-upon by a loose cap of gingery, corkscrewing hair, was tinged with crimson, and as he wrote his bedraggled-looking notes in felt tip there was always a sense of something momentous coming – that he'd explode or faint.

At the hotel we left Simon to put his legs up. Frank and I went to tea with Simon Tonge, the High Commissioner, on his veranda,* Frank with binoculars to his eyes much of the time ('Masked lapwing! See its yellow wattle?').

We travelled onward by plane to Wewak, the capital of East Sepik Province – where once, I dimly recalled, I used to come on outings with Joel, Martin and my 'brother' Sebastian. But, of course, thirty years on everything would be radically changed.

Except, it wasn't. As the plane descended, Simon handed me a small camera – 'Just say a few words about your excitement and so forth' – and I saw that the forest was still there: an unbroken green-hued canopy was laid like baize inland over the coastal hills. Instead of speaking to the lens I looked on in amazement. Below now should be the shanty town – the mess that you see around Ulaanbaatar, Mombasa or any number of cities that have spread ruinously in the intervening years. But no. All was as it once was. And I began to understand that I'd been fooling myself. That I hadn't come back for the sake of Frank; I'd come back because I had unfinished business here.

Os took one side of the wheelchair, I took the other, and we heaved Frank down the steps of the plane. 'Someone should be filming this,' he said as he descended lopsidedly from the Fokker. 'In case we don't get very much further.' We looked out across the warm tarmac, which was

---

* Simon and a lot of others in his team were good enough to facilitate the search for me two years later.

steaming from a recent downpour. Beyond the runway were the trees. Arrayed in heavy veils of silver rain, the forest looked dark but patient, as if biding its time.

Men with large bare feet lugged the baggage over to a rack and we picked out our kit among a mob of betel nut-chewing onlookers – or maybe they were fellow passengers. Some were ancient Papuan soldiers wearing ill-fitting fatigues, others Australian aid workers or skinny white nuns in black habits.

Then, rising from the chaos, a stray cry from an old fellow with two prominent black teeth: 'Oh, is that you, Benedik Wumbunvan? *Yu kam bak!*'

Or was this my imagination? Perhaps it was the sighing of the rain.

Steven was trying to keep us together – our sound man Mark (grey attire still immaculate) was lost among the nuns, our poor old director Simon was in need of another burst of nicotine. Frank was heading off towards the runway with his binoculars and our camera kit was scattered about everywhere, looking very desirable in smart metal cases. We were shepherded to the exit by burly Papuans who waved eagerly, grabbed everything that we were carrying, and might or might not have been working for Steven.

Finally, having been whisked away in an air-conditioned minibus, we were deposited in a simple hotel, where we tried to sleep but couldn't. By the time we rose the next morning, Steven's helpers had already dived into what he called a 'boy's breakfast'.

'What's in it?' Frank asked, wheeling up. 'Feeling peckish myself.'

'Sheep's knuckles, or something. Everything we would throw away, plus rice.'

Our own breakfast – a steak, Nescafé and soggy bread – was thumped down by a resentful-looking cook who had varnished his toe nails. 'He looks badly in need of love,' said Os, sympathetically. But we all had jet lag and none of us right now could summon it ourselves.

There was to be a production meeting. 'It'll be on the veranda in five minutes,' Simon said and disappeared for another cigarette. Frank sped off again with his bird book and the rest of us sat around a table, waiting.

Simon rejoined us. His nerves were still on edge. He admitted to not sleeping in Moresby – or much the previous weeks – and outlined what lay ahead: today just a few 'establishing shots', with Frank and Benedict looking from a hilltop into the forbidding interior, then tomorrow (Official Day One) the picturesque journey by vehicle to the Sepik river. Days Two, Three and Four: the reunion of Benedict with his old friends – at what Simon calls 'KanDENgy'. Days Five and onwards will be 'into the heart of Paradise, etc.'

Frank listened intently, as if at a news briefing. I noticed that he favoured combat trousers – thigh pockets for easy access to his notebook – and that he conducted himself with the neat, self-contained operation that I hadn't seen since among the Himba of the Namib or walking with the Gabbra 'shepherds of the desert' in the Chalbi. A simple zipped holdall on his knees contained all that he needed.

The meeting ended with an address by Os. 'If I could run over a few medical issues . . .' he began. 'We are about to head into a harsh environment. It's humid, it's wet. Perfect conditions for some of the nasty stuff. We can expect infected insect bites, diarrhoea, skin fungus . . . So don't be a hero. Be strict with yourself – and each other. If in doubt, flag any issues up to me.'

And I found myself thinking that this didn't sound like a journey 'into the heart of Paradise, etc.' From what I could recall, the Kandengei villagers thought Paradise was the place from which we'd come.

But all in all, it was good to be back in this colourful and welcoming country. I knew the physical hazards of old – no concerns there – and was beginning to feel that my sense of foreboding was altogether misplaced.

IV

That night the hotel almost went up in flames. The black noxious fumes were found to be issuing from Os's room – specifically, an electrical outlet unequal to the challenge of topping up our stock of camera batteries.

Finally, already a day behind schedule, we boarded two old Land Cruisers and trundled south towards the Sepik with our police escort – three men with pot bellies and a tendency to chatter on their walkie-talkies about whatever came to mind. A lorry with a caved-in windscreen carried our gear.

Occasionally, vague memories were aroused by the shading breadfruit trees from under which enthusiastic women waved vigorously at every passer-by.

In a couple of days, I'd be feeling more settled. I'd be chatting away with Martin – and Joel, too. A relaxed, lugubrious sort, Joel was the Smaark whose crocodile scars came out the best, in splendid curving tracks over his wide shoulders. There was my honorary brother Sebastian as well. Only fifteen or sixteen years old during the *banis*, he was always the most sensible of us.

On the whole, the people of Kandengei would be forgiving, I decided. Or else they would not.*

---

* Before departure I'd received a very considerate message from one James Skinner, who explained that he'd been attached to a VSO education programme and had visited the Middle

Near Maprik, we pulled up at a roadside market, having mislaid our police escort – they were still insisting on their walkie-talkie 'call sign' being Papa 1, not Papa 3. Once out of the Land Cruiser, Frank fitted an extra front wheel to give his chair more stability and soon was ingratiating himself with the ladies sitting cross-legged in the dirt; they wore tea-cosy hats, kept their cash in their bras, and their produce was laid out in tidy little stacks, each judged worth a kina – ten betel nuts, say, or five taro. '*Nem bilong me* Frank' – my name is Frank – he said to each woman, as I'd taught him, and they squirted betel juice from their lips and tittered. The camera crew pursued him as best they could.

More memories were coming back. The musty scent of vendors, the sticky, oily reek of the home-grown tobacco. I should buy an enormous branch of betel nuts to lay before the village *bikmen*, I remembered. To them, the gift was much the same as a handshake.

'Benedik,' called a soft female voice to my left.

Was I hearing things again? We were still four hours from the Sepik and no one could possibly know me around here. I bent, handed over a few notes.

'Benedik . . .' That voice again, more insistent.

I turned. The woman who had addressed me was about forty years old, with nervous, fidgety fingers and worn knees. Before her was spread a grubby plastic sheet and on this lay rows of dried fish.

'Did you say my name?'

A dozen or two flies rose and then settled as the woman stirred the air with a plaited leaf. 'Benedik, you knew my father.'

'Your father?'

'Maans. He brought you to Kandengei the first time. That was in his old canoe, that one which leaked too much.'

Sepik only months before. He thought I should know that the Niowras were very much aware I was on my way – and they had a number of grievances. James ended, 'I wanted to share everything as soon as possible, as I would hope that folk would do the same if I was in the same situation.' The news, though, wasn't any more than I had feared. The trouble would stem from Korogo, a Niowra village populated by ruffians, so the Kandengeis had it. Personally, more worrying to me was that James had heard that someone in the village called Martin had died; however, 'Martin' was a common name and James agreed that he might well not be one and the same Martin who was my friend. Personally, I thought it unlikely.

'That's extraordinary! You're right, Maans did bring me. But how did you recognise my face?'

She jutted her head forward, a little surprised that I should ask.

I said, 'You must have been a child, back then.'

'His best wife called Emma came along,' the woman said, slightly irritated now. I was meant to know all this. 'She's alive yet. Lame now – because she's too fat. Like a fat elephant.' Mechanically, as if reciting some prose that she'd been made to learn at school, she began the story. 'Maans, Emma and you came from Mindimbit village, up in the Blackwater neck of the woods, and then to Timbunmeri, where you stopped a while, and then over the Chambri Lake to where you finished up your journey with those rowdy people at Kandengei. You parked outside Jonny Gowi's house. That's Smaark land – and he's a Smaark.'

The woman began turning her fish over, sorting through them. She flicked her impatient eyes towards the camera crew, who were packing up their gear. 'Those white men with you want to buy a couple?'

I paid for the two nearest fish and then said, 'I'm afraid I don't quite remember you . . .'

'Because you are old now.'

'Only in my fifties!' I corrected her, cheerily.

She counted out the change, unenthusiastically. 'That's right,' she replied. 'You are fifty-six.'

There our intriguing little conversation had to end. Steven had found the police escort and Simon was reminding one and all to finish their packed lunches because we were running late. On we drove, and I was left to speculate on how a market lady who lived out here in the dry, infertile grass plains could possibly recognise me, let alone know my exact age.

'Don't forget, you are part of their cultural history,' said Steven. 'Amazing, when you think about it!'

I thought about it: how Maans had steered the canoe to the shallows and Emma then grasped my hand and said to me tenderly, 'You need to explain your purpose, Benedik. These backward people will see your skin and think you are rich.'

The shore had been empty but for a furious-eyed young man fashioning a canoe. The old fellow beside him was feeding woodchips to a fire. The sweet smell of sap drifted around us.

I'd offered a greeting, '*Apinun!*'

'*Apinun*,' replied the youth guardedly. This was the first word that I think Jonny Gowi, or 'Eagle', ever said to me. I hopped ashore with the mooring rope and the man who was to be my father laid down his adze as he assessed me with practised eyes. 'I am, so to speak,' he said, switching to English, 'the Catholic presence around here. The head of our church that is so badly needing funds.'

—

Slowly our convoy made its way, jolting through dun and beige hills to the road's end at Pagwi. Frank was now looking like someone liberated – no longer the readily identifiable TV reporter lodged in a wheelchair ('my boring platform') but the latest guest in a land of marvels, someone excited by the prospect of the River Sepik flood plains, their multiple folds and creases. He peered from the window at the beauties steadily revealed: a whistling kite spiralling through the late afternoon haze and, ornamenting the roadside foliage now, the enflamed red livery of eclectus parrots and a bird that may or may not be – 'Slow down a sec!' cried Frank – a Pinon's imperial pigeon.

I wasn't feeling liberated in the slightest. Rather, as we neared the impenetrable reedbeds, I felt like an inmate in a prison van. I could see it before me, there through the foliage at the end of the track, the collision between two irreconcilable worlds: the European and the Niowra, the past and present, the youthful man setting out, the older one coming back. Damage was inevitable; I saw that too. The well-meaning idealist who'd gone to such lengths to document another people's customs was about to meet another – the later version of himself, the weary one who'd sought so long to leave those customs behind.

The river came into sight – as silent and troubling as ever it was. And across the sleek flow the forest was looking on, as tenacious as it ever was.

—

'Right,' said Simon. We had halted beside the riverbank. 'Turn the engine off. Mark, put a mic on Benedict. He's going to say a few words.'

I unbuttoned my shirt, looked at the reeds – a single species from the genus *Phragmites*, but once I'd known them only as *pit-pit*, their long seed heads like plumage, my *wanbanis* used to say – and Mark fed the microphone lead in. I noticed three or four egrets half rise, hoping not to have to surrender their perch.

We used to watch them fly, I remembered. *During the initiation ceremony, week after week. They passed sedately over our heads, dawn and dusk, to and from their own nests at will. We longed for just one white feather to drop down.*

'Is he mic-ed up yet? Benedict, you stay in the car. In a minute, give us a few upbeat thoughts to camera. What it's like to be back in your old stamping ground? Thrilled, curious, nostalgic, whatever comes to mind, but be quick.'

I unwound the window, needing fresh air. *I've always made a point of looking only forward*, I thought. *Now I'm being made to look back.*

'Stay put, Benedict!' Simon said, because I was becoming agitated. 'Wait till we've set up the main camera.'

Over in that breadfruit tree, I thought, *Sebastian once spotted a couple of fruit bats – sleepy after a night's feed. We teased them with sticks. Martin, too. Or maybe that was another time.*

I began to feel it now – the impact, the coming together of my two incompatible lives. As in a car accident: no feeling of pain at first, just the confusion as time becomes fluid and you seek to break free of the wreckage.

'Can somebody give me a hand with the tripod?' Simon was saying. 'Mark, you all set? At this rate we'll lose light at the next stop – Yenchy-wagamama or whatever it's called . . .'

I was grappling with the door handle, attempting to free myself.

'Benedict? Benedict, where are you going?'

Down by the water's edge, the market women were loading their unsold produce, stacking their baskets. Among them once would have been the tobacco seller, the girl who had smiled so readily at life.

A gruff voice said, 'Welcome home, brother.'

Another said, 'Ah, Wumbunavan, *Man bilong Kandengei . . .*'

Those addressing me were shirtless men who gestured at me with large, intimidating hands and bore, all over their upper bodies, a horrific number of scars.

'Benedik, you have come back then . . .'

'Yes,' I said. 'Yes, I have.' I couldn't yet take it in.

'Remember me?'

Standing there on the bank, reunited with the Sepik mud, I looked at the river. It slinked; it churned. 'You're Jimmi Maik,' I said slowly, it coming to me. 'You delivered a message to the post office.' I'd wanted my mum and dad to know I was still OK.

'I assisted you in your hour of need,' Jimmi said, happily.

Physically, Jimmi hadn't much changed. His head sat firmer into his shoulders and his eyes, bedded deeper in their sockets, glinted as before beneath a baseball cap. His lips still smacked as he chewed his betel nut. And my obligations to him, they hadn't changed either.

'You have a little gift for me, *wantok*?' Jimmi smiled a pleasant smile. 'Like a laptop or something?'

I felt the crushing weight of the word *wantok* – the thirty years of duty that had stacked up among my 'relatives'. The only person who wouldn't ask for anything was Martin.

'Or a thousand dollars cash. Whatever is easiest for you.'

I backed away, rejoined the film crew – another lot of people I was obliged to.

'Well, that was a dog's breakfast,' Simon was saying. The tripod was lifted, the sound boom lowered.

'Sorry. So very sorry.'

Simon ran his hands through his sweat-soaked hair, spread his fingers and plied them repeatedly across his scalp like a rake. He seemed to be having an outbreak of eczema.

'Baggage all transferred to the canoes,' said Steven, striding up. 'Need to press on.'

Simon said, despairingly, 'Frank, are you able to say a quick word to camera?'

We all turned to Frank, presently watching the herons stream to their roosts in orderly fashion across the violet sunset. 'How long do you need? Say, thirty, thirty-five seconds?'

He proceeded to speak with erudition for thirty to thirty-five seconds. It was just the professionalism that Simon needed – but on this occasion from the wrong man.

Os, here to tend to someone shot in the spine, instead saw to me. He began squeezing my shoulders, administering treatment as if to a patient in trauma – which I perhaps was. And I wondered what on earth I was thinking, bringing Frank here. He was expecting something quite lovely from this adventure but was instead going to get the truth of the sublime, dangerous, convoluted Sepik and my own unresolved issues.

Steven brought forward the Papuan helper who only ever liked to wear his yellow and green striped rugby shirt. 'You've met Felix? He'll be making sure you get safely in and out of canoes, Frank.'

'Sir, are you ready for the lift?' Felix said, then noticed Frank's Timberland boots. Camel suede, they were totally pristine – and they would remain so; their tread would never wear down, never know mud.

'Do call me "Frank", please. And *you* are the boss, Felix. You take charge.'

'I take charge?' Felix squeezed his rugby shirt and looked about, worried.

'If you drop him,' Os said. 'It's game over.'

However, a dozen men had already decided to lend a hand. They piled in, transporting Frank unevenly over the silty waters to a dugout wide enough to accommodate a wheelchair.

———

Did I say anything to Frank, as the large Yamaha outboard powered us downriver? I suspect not. I was lost in my own thoughts and Frank in his. Onward we charged through the fading light, Frank marvelling at the birds – 'Blue-black kingfisher! And, oh look, monarch flycatcher!' – and me hoping we'd sink.

We didn't sink. We pulled into Yenchenmangua – one of the more decadent of the Niowra villages, we always thought – and there Felix rallied his team, manhandling Frank and chair unceremoniously through the riverside ooze and up the rickety steps of a thatched house on stilts. He was shadowed every step of the way by Os with his red medical kit.

'Let's give them a bit of a show,' said Frank, once safely up – and alarmed the local children by waving madly.

'Mr Frank, here they have a pet birdie,' said Felix, and pointed out a cormorant attached to a long black ribbon.

'Not interested,' murmured Frank. 'Can't stand it when birds are tethered.'

Tethered like you, I said to myself. Then I thought: *no, tethered like me.*

Steven noticed me standing apart, as Wendy our cook assembled tuna and spam and then vaguely toasted white bread on a fold-up table. 'Must be quite a lot to take in, Benedict,' he said, gently. 'You need some space to decompress. I know I would.'

I'll always be grateful to Steven for that. He led me to another house and Felix looked at me pityingly as he rigged my mosquito net. 'You try to be joyous, brother. The Kandengeis are very rough, but maybe they will welcome you back nicely.'

Alone, I got out the present that I'd give Martin tomorrow. I turned the wristwatch over in my fingers, examined its clear, smooth face, a capsule that marked out a white man's time and was water resistant to a hundred metres. Dear old Martin, I thought. 'Do not fear,' I remembered him saying on the eve of the ceremony, 'I'm coming to the Crocodile's Nest with you!'

I hadn't been afraid. But I saw the fear around me – and among the *bikmen* as well as the women and boys.*

In the neighbouring house the film crew were chatting.

'So, tomorrow we arrive at KanDENgy . . .'

'KANDengei,' Frank said. 'I think it is.'

I looked out of the window and noticed the cormorant in silhouette against the river as it ran from the west, a spillage of mercury from where

---

* The *banis* hadn't been performed for about ten years. Such was the concern among the elders that they'd angered the spirits through this neglect that at first many gave up only one son for the ceremony, just in case.

lay dying the sun. 'Maans' was what we called a cormorant in Niowra, and I remembered again that it was the name of the man who first brought me to Kandengei.

Nearby, a baby began crying frenetically.

'Someone tell Benedict to quieten down!' Frank said, and everyone laughed.

'Right, guys,' Os said. 'A word on safety. Tomorrow, it's going to get tougher . . .'

The cormorant opened its mouth and no sound came out.

—

Through that night my memories ran rampant – of Martin never saying goodbye, of girls (I've only mentioned a couple) who were to me forbidden fruit. And, oddly, of a small cooking pot in which I brewed my tea: how scared I had been of losing that pot and everything associated with it – the dropping in of tea bags, the stirring of the powdered milk. These simple rituals were mine alone: they reminded me of who I really was.

There were other recollections too; whole unwelcome scenes came back to me. Like the girls, I hadn't invited them.

V

Instead of joining the film crew for breakfast, I went to be alone by the river – this conduit to somewhere back in time.

'Welcome,' said a newly arrived teacher, stopping me on the path. 'I come from Lae. You heard about these people's customs?' He laughed, thinking about them. 'They worship the crocodile! They cut up their boys to make them lose their female blood!'

Which would seem to amount to about two pints, I thought.

I paced up and down the Sepik and wished it would drain away. Then, around seven in the morning, the last of the sunrise pink on the water, along came Caspar, Steven's right-hand man. A highlander with a side-line in bartering betel nuts, he had a shambling gait and a weathered, floppy hat. He stopped, offered me a smile. Like Felix, he knew what it was to belong to one of the country's tight-knit communities; he seemed to feel for me. 'Brother,' he said, and handed me a betel nut. After a moment he said what he had come to say. 'You know, I heard a rumour that your father is coming by to pick you up.'

I nodded, trying to assess the significance of this. 'Actually, he's not my real father,' was all I wanted to say. 'My real father was a test pilot. He died in Cheltenham Hospital – a public ward with the curtains drawn around. I failed to be there for him.' But Caspar was only trying his best.

I went to the riverside, there to brace myself for the arrival of Jonny Gowi – not someone of whom you'd want to get on the wrong side.

Sometimes, just from the corner of my eye, I was aware of our long-suffering director, Simon, weighing up whether he might brave the ooze with our only big camera and persuade me to offer an insight into my steadily unravelling mind.

After a while of staring at the grey water – so laden with the debris of the past – I reminded myself that Jonny no less than me had his duties. He was my father and, when push came to shove, must support me – which among the Niowra meant with a bush knife, if necessary. Jonny was an ally in this.

I waited for the seemingly inescapable while the bats headed home and wader birds headed out – and gradually my worry became that I wouldn't recognise Jonny, or that we wouldn't have anything to say. In other words, I worried about all the things any child might worry about on being reunited with his dad.

There was, in the end, little doubting it was him. Jonny appeared from the south bank in a voluminous dugout, standing bolt upright in the prow and looking ahead – this man, who was meant to be my father, for his own cultural reasons acting as the very embodiment of the expressionless crocodile. I studied his face, trying my best to read it for signs of anger or resentment. But nothing, not even as he drew near. Just occasionally, though, you got the impression he was watching – watching me, the river, Mark the soundman in his spotless outfit and Simon barefoot in the foreshore slime, sinking ever deeper. All these people evaluating him, but the crocodile doesn't so much as blink.

Jonny stepped from the shallows and we embraced awkwardly.

'Hold it there,' said Simon. 'I need to get the reverse angle. Err . . . Jonny, your footprints are EVERYwhere. This is actually creating quite a problem.'

Jonny said, 'Benedik, I thought you were dead and now here you are with us.'

'Yes, here I am,' I said. We looked at each other in silence, cross-checking our memories, assessing what we were dealing with. For my part, I appeared to be dealing with two strong and proprietary eyes, well emphasised by a thickened, permanently furrowed brow.

'So, hello.'

'Not exactly a bundle of emotion,' I heard Simon mutter, lowering the camera. 'Not exactly a father ecstatic at the return of his prodigal child.' He kicked off the mud.

However, it seemed to me that Jonny was behaving like this only because among the Niowra a father was an aloof figure. If you wanted a hug you went not to him but to your *wau*, your uncle – who was another person I needed to provide with a wristwatch.

I took Jonny up the frail steps of the crew's house to introduce Frank – for safety's sake, he'd been left up there with the cormorant. 'I AM VERY PLEASED TO MEET YOU,' Frank said in loud, plain English, and pressed his hands to his heart. 'A GREAT HONOUR.'

'Yes,' said Jonny.

I felt it was only fair to make clear my intentions straight away, so I informed Jonny that I wouldn't be staying long at Kandengei. 'Frank and I are heading further south, to find a few birds of paradise.'

'And so?' Jonny said. 'I will go with you.'

'You'll leave the village and come with me?'

'Why not?' said Jonny, indignant now. 'I am your father! It is my right and my solemn duty.' He relieved me of my substantial branch of betel nuts. This he'd enjoy at his leisure rather than share around with the *bikmen*. That too was his right – though not exactly duty.

Before long, the crew were swigging their 3-in-1 coffee to keep them going and then we were across the main river, winding through the creeks.

Had I really made a home here – breathed this stagnant air, cleaned myself each nightfall in this mucky soup? I sat in silence with Jonny, even now trying to fix myself in this sultry habitat that apparently had such a claim on me. I watched Felix punting his way through the reeds as I once did, working the three-metre pole – blade shaped like a crocodile's webbed foot – plying the murk.

The grasses encroached further. They stood high around us, the breeze faltering, the fenced-in air stale. Frank handed over his binoculars and said, staring ahead, 'Benedict, you really do need to see this . . .'

They stood at the end of a further water corridor, as unwavering as the reeds. Quiet, unaware of us, as yet, they were steadying themselves by the forest edge, preening and adjusting their decorative feathers in the low morning light: twenty, perhaps twenty-five men aboard two vast dugouts, each figure adorned with a headdress of cassowary feathers, a dense quiff of charcoal that splayed stiffly upward. On their arms were bound pig's tusks and from their waists dripped slick vermilion tongues of foliage. For now the crowd stood passively, content to blend with the deadwood and tree shadows. Their facial features were obscured by shells, rendered unearthly by grim swirls of bone-white chalk, but there was no mistaking the impression they wished to give. For all that they held dance-drums or else palm wands, this was a body of men who would be willing, with very little provocation, to fight.*

'Your *wanbanis*,' said Jonny, nodding approvingly. 'It is right they do this for you.'

'Looks more like a war party than a welcome party,' observed Simon. Yet there'd been a time when I must have known each of these individuals about to confront us – their whitened, skull faces implying aggressive intent, the gaudy cordyline leaves suggestive of spilt blood, the wands suggestive of spears.

The first dull notes of the hand-drums passed along the channel towards us, each stroke strident and muscular as it journeyed over the warm, peaty water – slap, slap, like the tail of a crocodile on mud. To this steady thump were added the bass voices of the men. And the song being sung was the song I'd once sung with them.

I had no interest in singing it again. *You don't belong here*, I reminded myself. *You never did and never will*. Nonetheless, I was on my feet. I was swaying.

'This is FANtastic,' said Frank. 'I so envy you this.'

Frank, I thought. *We sang this tune while being beaten. We sang harder to hide the screams.*

The *wanbanis* were near at hand now, raising high their drums, saluting

---

* 'Temper tantrums are applauded as the way in which action can be initiated,' commented the anthropologist Margaret Mead. 'Among the Iatmul [language group of Middle Sepik peoples] rage is good.' See also Gregory Bateson, *Naven*.

with their yellow wands. *I used to do this*, I kept thinking. *I used to be seen as one of these proud men.*

I studied those at the prow of the nearer canoe. Oddly, thus far there was not a sign of Martin or Sebastian. The man leading proceedings was a portly fellow swathed in cowries. Norbet, was it? Or Noah. No, more likely Fredalin, the boy who wouldn't stop bleeding. For a week or two, I tried to plug the worse leaks with clay. It never did much good.

We were up close now, right among them: their clattering anklets of shells, their flapping leaves, their acrid cloud of betel nut and sweat.

But now Jonny and I must have transferred canoes because I found we were standing with them, all about me faces which I couldn't identify because they were overlain with crude bands of blackboard chalk and soot.

Round the river bend now, and before us across the lagoon was Kandengei – exactly as I'd left it. Like the rest of the country it lay as if still waiting, immutable – the tatty thatched houses on their ironwood stilts, the palm trees tilting, the lesser-used canoes along the foreshore half-drowned by rainwater.

Hearing us, children now sprinted along the waterfront. They yelled, they scampered for a vantage point. Jonny rose beside me. Before the whole community, he was bringing back his lost son.

'Thoughts, Benedict?' asked Simon from the crew's boat. His camera was pointed to my face.

I tried to speak. Like the tethered cormorant, I opened wide my mouth and nothing came out.

I was grateful to be greeted in this way by my *wanbanis* – of course I was. Grateful to Simon and his patience with me, too. But there seemed to be nothing to do about it. Perhaps I was too scared to accept the embrace of an alien culture all over again, or perhaps I was beginning to remember that it wasn't appropriate to cavort at this moment for a TV camera or even to smile – it wasn't my place. I felt it strongly, in the eyes of the Niowras, all of them on me: I was no longer a *bandee*. I wasn't even any more a *g-eenjumboo*, a Junior Male. I was a *jinbungee*, a Senior Man.

The crowds were massing, the community readying itself to receive me – the men with quiet, dignified smiles, the women wriggling their hands delightedly, trilling and beaming and shrieking.

But not a sign of Martin. He hadn't been among the *wanbanis* to welcome me, and now, where he might have been standing on the shoreside among Jonny's wood chippings, awaiting his friend while quietly appreciating the pageantry, was a space on Smaark territory occupied by a freshly constructed archway of palm leaves.

'You are ready?' said Jonny.

'Yes, ready.'

I'll be expected to pass through the arch, I thought. *Women will come forward, do their skipping dance in their sago fibre skirts. They'll chant their screechy words and swing their arms and backsides loosely before me.*

Be solemn, I told myself. *As is fitting. Do not prance around to amuse them, as you did in the old days.*

Three women separated from the crowd, flicking up dust, provocatively shifting their bums, the way they do. This would be the official Smaark contingent, their female greeting party.

'The sister of your *wau*,' said Jonny. 'And Rhonda. And Imelda. You remember?'

Martin's dead, I thought. *My only friend here is dead because otherwise he'd be standing on the bank for me.*

'You must get out of the canoe first,' Jonny said. 'It is expected.'

I stepped forward. I bowed. I accepted in turn the decorated bags that must be passed over my head and hung from me. I ducked through the leaf arch.

'You must say something to the crowd,' said Jonny. 'They are happy to see you.'

The drumming stopped. I rustled up a few words in Tok Pisin.

'And now you come inside my house,' said Jonny. He waved his hand dismissively at the villagers swarming around us. 'Away from these noisy types of people.'

A moment later we were out of the sun and away from all the eyes. Alone in Jonny's house, it was cool, very dark – a merciful relief. 'And so you are back,' said Jonny, and pulled up a stool.

We sat facing each other. Outside, the dancing and drumming

restarted. Frank was saying to the camera, 'What a welcome! AMAAAZING!' Then he chuckled. 'And these are just a FEW of Benedict's wives!'

'No one but a few good Smaark men will disturb us here,' Jonny said.

I looked about at my surroundings, which were as they always were: a floor of loose limbum bark polished by bare feet; dusty crossbeams; rafters sticky from the tar laid over them by repeated applications of woodsmoke. A mouse bickering with another in the thatch. Three or four mosquito nets were curled out of the way like giant webs and in the corner sat a curved platter that acted as a fireplace – traded from Ambon village, because their clay was better than ours.

'Thank you, Jonny,' I said, meaning thanks for harbouring me even from my own people, which is to say the whiter-coloured ones.

He said nothing, but his eyes were warmer now that we were alone. Suddenly slightly bashful, he regarded me with affection.

'So much fussing about. The truth is, you do not like this much . . .'

'Not when I don't deserve it, no. A wonderful effort, though. And really, really appreciated. I'll never forget this day.'

Jonny studied me a moment. I remembered that this was something I'd been forced to grow used to, six weeks during the *banis* as he watched over me – those bold mahogany eyes reinforced by that unwavering brow.

Jonny went to the water butt and filled a plastic beaker. 'You have sweated too much. You must now drink.'

I took the water, thanked him. 'Jonny, you'll want me to explain why I've stayed away so long, I expect . . .'

But I didn't know where to begin and in the silence Jonny took my hand – feeling for my fingers as he searched about my face. 'I am glad you are not killed, that is all . . .'

And I still said nothing, and I saw that I didn't need to.

———

Over that next half-hour, I showed pictures of my young children – Natalya, Freddie and baby Beatrice. I then laid out my gifts for the key individuals of the village, so that Jonny might check all was in order. When that was done, he leaned over to where the cooking vessels were stacked, in the corner to the right of the door. 'You remember this?'

'My little pot!'

Jonny said, smiling at it fondly, 'You came along with this on your first day.'

You carried my bags to this very house, I thought. *Helped by Elijah – he was only small then. Rhonda lit the fire and I made you tea. 'Father George puts more sugar in,' you told me, emptying half my last packet before sharing the remainder around your relatives.*

I picked my pot up, ran my fingers over its smooth alloy body. The lid had gone, the handle been replaced by a length of wire, but here it was after so many years, as if – like everyone else – expecting me to turn up at any time.

'I thought I'd never see this again,' I said. 'Oh thank you, thank you!'

Jonny said, 'I keep nails in it now.' And abruptly took it back.

Awkwardly, clumsily, my adopted father and I re-established our relationship, stitching together what threads we could find.

VI

Some time later, when I emerged from Jonny's house, I found the shadows long and the crowds gone. Simon was crouched defeated on a log.

Steven was saying, 'Often the very best films start out like this . . .'

'Like what, a total cock-up? Benedict has *got* to start giving up control.'

Frank was scanning the lagoon with his binoculars. 'No, just a fish eagle,' he said.

Simon took another drag. 'I'm not even a smoker.'

We settled in. Os sorted his red medical bag, and Simon his batteries and memory cards. Steven huddled with his helpers – who, it was becoming obvious, adored him, just as he adored them. Wendy the cook heated up more spam. Mark was occasionally seen tiptoeing catlike between the raised houses with his boom mic; Frank, bird book on lap, also went off to explore the village. Children with dribbling noses crept behind, examining his tyre tracks.

When I passed through Kandengei, though, I was everywhere tailed not by mischievous boys but ghosts. Close at hand, the bachelor hut where I used to sleep – when not disturbed by the eligible young ladies who arrived on moonless nights. Further off, beyond the scarlet hibiscus, the house where, as a homesick twenty-five-year-old pursuing his lonely path, I had tried to save the girl whose smile had meant the world to me.

Over to the right was where my *wau* planted a coconut in my honour – the palm now swayed overhead, offering a friendly shade to passers-by. A little further, where Jonny had told me I might find it, the spot where Martin was laid to rest. Tucked between the roots, decorated with petals, was a cardboard sign – 'THiS IS MARTYNe R.I.p.' – pegged there this morning for my benefit, as a gardener might mark seedlings in a vegetable plot. My *wau* was also buried near, Jonny had said, and I eventually found his allocated space beside that of Sebastian – just another five-foot length of mud.

Here, then, the Kandengeis dwelt, just as before – the living and their dead. Even now they held together as best they could, fending off and welcoming ghosts like me, bonded by a swirling river, its many taboos and secrets. Through the ages they had united with their clan members – totemic eagles, bats, turtles, kingfishers and sago trees – against everyone else.

Should I have committed myself wholly to the Niowras, somehow tried to make their world mine? Looking around now, I thought I might have tried harder. But I could feel it already: the more rooted I was to this community, the less I was rooted to my own.

———

I spend the next few days in this unattached condition, thinking that I must do my best for Frank but also for Jonny. *Perhaps his people were right all along*, I think to myself. *The 'white man' is a spirit adrift. We've weakened the community ties that once bound us, become detached from the land on which we depend.*

And I proceed further through the village towards Maans's old house feeling the apparent truth of it – that I'm floating along exactly like one of the Niowra dead spirits in their unhappy limbo state, not sure which people or existence I am committed to any more.

I call out for Emma and down she comes, taking great care, these days having to pick out the stronger of the wooden steps, but her loving, half-buried twinkling eyes facing forward as if she's worried she'll lose sight of me. 'Wumbunavan! I do want to shake your hand. I do!'

She grabs onto me, holds me, regards me. Tears are left to run off down her cheeks as she brandishes a photo. A younger me must have given it to her, because there I am in Hampshire with my mum and dad, brother and sister. Together we are smiling to the camera in front of the drawing-room fireplace. I am freshly back from my travels and the photograph of our five beaming faces is a better record than any that I have of that time; for all these years, this sweet woman has safeguarded what was then dear to me, back in the land from which I'd come. Katie, Stewart, me, with our lives still ahead; our dad not yet frail, our mum not yet taken from us – cancer, one Christmas Day in the morning. 'I will keep it here for you,' she says, seeing me so profoundly moved. She squeezes the picture to her breast and without further explanation begins her arduous climb back up the steps.

A male figure, up ahead, looks slightly familiar. He wears a singlet and a reversed baseball cap.

'You remember me? It is Joel!'

'Joel?' I think back to the boy I once knew – the crocodile marks proud across his wide chest. That boy has gone, replaced by a middle-aged man whose face is angular and inflexible, like an old wood mask. It has grooves carved across it.

'*Wanbanis* . . . welcome back.' We hold hands and I look again, searching for the previous Joel. There is no lustre in this one; his shoulders barely show their scars. And they are very hairy.

'Of the Smaark boys, there is only Saun, Kennedy and Stens left,' he tells me, though I don't want to hear.

As he talks, I find I'm still picturing the other Joel, the one with faintly amused eyes who was the most musical of the Smaark fraternity. An image comes to mind: a boy with one foot forward, leaning back as he languidly beats the drum tucked under his arm. I cavort in circles, at Martin's suggestion singing 'Old MacDonald Had a Farm' – because this might raise morale, 'and also this is your national anthem'.

Joel is still speaking – and the passage of time seems to be measured in the interring of the dead. 'Kumbui, Pinga, Nau, Lamin, Warbee, Maans – they have all been planted in the ground. Lamin Wogu, though, he is still alive.' He munches a betel nut, spits, continues the list of deceased.

'Steven too is planted,' he says, finally turning his attention to our *wanbanis*. 'And Will and . . .'

I look over his face, its thick outer surface worked over by the sun and insects. The last time we were together we were young, looking forward; now we are together, looking back.

'I'll see you around,' he says. 'I'm glad you are here now.' He reaches out a hand and for a second or two holds tight my shoulder.

After dark, I rest out on the veranda with Jonny. The air that licks over us, percolating steadily from the lagoon, is sweet and warm; the waterside boughs are lit by the moon. A wicker chair, designed for Frank's transportation south through the interior, bides its time, stowed among the mosquitoes in the longer grass.

'They did the black magic,' Jonny murmurs, looking about at the moon shadows for whoever or whatever might be listening. 'Like *this*.' He shows me, making a spear head of his hand then jabbing it fiercely into his wrist. 'That,' he breathes. 'That is how they did it to Martin.'

'Sebastian, too?'

'The same. I told that white man with the big camera it was regrettably malaria. He was happy with that.'

Jonny and I do not mention Martin or Sebastian again. We look upon the glittering water, the occasional abrupt swirls caused by some creature of the deep. Sometimes this creature lifts to the surface, a large fish panics, flipping desperately to save itself.

The night passes by. A silent ripple approaches but slowly dies. The bats cross the stars, the palm leaves divide the sky.

We go to bed only much later. Jonny snores and Frank – installed in a mosquito net nearby – shifts about on his inflatable mattress. Occasionally, he lifts his legs with his hands, one at a time, to turn them.

'Frank?'

'Benedict, I'm fine. Just all the jostling over the last few days.'

In the morning, he looks terrible – utterly drained. 'A night of dry shouting,' he tells me. 'I just wanted to scream. It's like that sometimes . . .'

'So sorry, Frank. Last night I wasn't sure whether I should fetch Os.'

'No, I'm best left alone. One of the joys of being shot in the spine.

Feels like a hammer is being hit repeatedly inside my right leg. I don't go on about it – it's kind of boring for people. But I'm lucky. Some have it much worse.'

On my way to brush my teeth at the waterside I discreetly update our medic. 'His broken nerve-endings,' Os says. 'Doesn't bode well.'

However, Frank can rest up for a while because today there'll be the formal celebration of my return.

———

I make my way through Kandengei, to where the village backs against the forest. The fence which screened us as *bandees* has, of course, long gone, but there remains the spirit house that it once surrounded – the imposing saddle of thatch dropping precipitously towards the clay, the two wooden eagles that ascend to the skies from either end. The interior is the same, too: the hardwood slit gongs, the worm-ridden posts, the block of cold air held between. Only those on the benches that line both sides have changed – because the Senior Men, the *jinbungees*, sitting up on them are now us. The old men who once ruled here are gone. All except Lamin Wogu.

I remember him well, from the *banis* days. The keenest of the beaters, he had smooth skin, a quick energy and a short, precise gait. He preferred to thrash us before the heat of the day. He would seek out a betel nut to chew – that was how we knew the time had come.

Today, though, he is alone, rolling a cigarette from a piece of newspaper, and shrunken on a stool.

I greet him in Niowra – '*Apman andinya!*' – and he doesn't so much as look up. I try to make conversation. '*Tgurt*,' I say, pointing at his seat.

He nods, satisfied. I have remembered correctly.

And I find myself feeling relieved. I am fifty-six. I could lift this dry, reduced old man with one hand, but still I'm afraid of him.

At the far end, my peers are waiting, all dressed up in their head-dresses, leaves and shells. Again, they are indistinguishable from each other, plastered over in chalk and grease.

Lamin Wogu is brought out into the sunshine; he is provided with a collapsible aluminium chair, as might be a pensioner to watch the progress of a cricket match upon the village green. A little further off, just as near as they are permitted, the women and children are assembling on the grass with palm switches and fibrous skirts.

Simon hoists the camera, Mark raises his boom.

'*Wanbanis*, we begin?'

I nod my consent to Norbet and, still inside the spirit house, he smacks a palm bract down hard on the mud floor. This prompts the answering call of a crocodile, a gurgling whoop that emanates from behind a short fence outside. Thwack! And again a gurgle. Thwack! And again, five times. Five, it's always five.

I know my part. Though I'm wearing laced military boots and khaki – more like a wayward member of a 'special ops' jungle unit than a Niowra – I lead my *wanbanis* outside. A thousand eyes are on me – Wumbunavan, the tales of whom they've so long heard. And again I hear the rattle of the fence that imprisoned us, and smell the rich clay that adorned us, and taste the dried fish they forced us to eat till we were fat.

We stomp about, counting out the beats. Once more, the crocodile patrols its riverbank. And soon the women join us, wiggling their russet sago skirts and stroking the air with their leaf flags. We dance together till it's done – and at last I am back. And I am content to be back.

———

'Steven, let's head off,' says our director after quite a while. For three solid hours he has heroically endured, on top of sleep deprivation, a temperamental camera and blistering heat. But it's all over now. He has filmed from every imaginable angle the monotonous stomping, an interminable dirge composed of only a dozen words.

We troop back to our quarters for Simon to be rewarded with much-needed refreshment – only to find our progress interrupted by a forthright lady who's examining a fishing net. 'Afternoon,' she says, barring the way. 'Hey, what you doing, filmin' all that big men's stuff?'

She begins what rapidly turns into a full-blown speech. 'We womens did all the catching and cooking when boys like Wumbunavan here was in the *banis*,' she says, still inspecting the net for holes and plucking out snagged leaves. 'Not the old men.'

Simon sighs, lifts his camera once more to his shoulder. The woman speaks with gusto, hurling her wet hands around – which have sizable knuckles and surprisingly well-maintained fingernails.

And I remember, with a jolt. It all comes back to me – even to the puce varnish that once patterned those nails.

'Women's rights,' she goes on. 'We need to talk about that!' And she does talk about it, at length, not once looking up at me. Finally, she's come to a halt, scribbling her name illegibly on the 'release form' to signify her consent to use the interview.

'Quite glad we did her, actually,' says Simon, heading onward. 'Just what we've been missing. A female perspective.'

And I feel glad, too. For the Typist has, all these years after she was, as a girl, sent along to me, found her voice – and her audience. She has called out; she has been heard. Nor would this be the last of her kind.

Days pass. I renew acquaintances. I explain to Frank how it was. Sometimes, petitioners call by. They submit invoices in advance for boats, engines, a dredger, cement to reinforce Martin's grave ('Totall Estomated cost is $5,800') and reparations because, sure enough, the troublesome Korogos had one day brought a war party here, smashing up the gardens on the pretext that I'd revealed the secrets of the initiation.

In short, all is as it always was. I dig for wildfowl eggs, I fish. And when I go down with food poisoning the boy who leads me to the toilet throughout the night is Martin's young brother, Michael.

'He is following Wumbunavan like Martin used to,' observes an old lady from the darkness. 'So that he does not have to be alone.'

'But I want to be alone!' I say to myself.

That too, is always as it was.

And so, once more, I find myself taken back by the Kandengeis, and reintroduced to the life that I once lived. For a second time, the community has helped me disconnect from my world in order to connect with another.

VII

On the evening of our departure, we assemble around the fold-up dining table, clutching our stomachs and eyeing Wendy's prawns with suspicion. Steven outlines our proposed route inland. We'll cut west, back up the main Sepik, hoping to spot a lesser bird of paradise before turning inland to the Central Range. This way, Frank will at least have seen something, should he succumb to an infection and the whole expedition goes what he terms 'pear-shaped'.

Os gives his medical briefing. 'It's only going to get harder,' he begins. *But we've hardly gone anywhere yet*, I think.

Frank gives the wicker chair a go. Once off the beaten track, four men will carry him, bearing his weight on their shoulders with the help of the poles strung along the sides.

'Up!' says Felix to the carriers.

'Fine view,' says Frank, once he's airborne. He asks me clever questions about the clan boundaries marked by trees – apparently you can see them from up where he is.

The sedan chair is judged a success. The occupant's legs are secured with a bungee cord to stop them dangling, and we are ready.

Early the next morning, we load the canoes and say our farewells. Last aboard is Jonny, as we reverse from the shore; the women shriek and whoop, and we are away.

Soon we are back on the main river, then cutting south-west up the Wagu. The trees recede and the breeze peels away even the most resilient of our mosquito passengers. 'That's a pied cormorant,' Frank says to no one in particular, as he scans the indigo skies. Sometimes his binoculars pass left and right – 'Brahminy kite?' – and sometimes up and down – 'White-bellied sea eagle!'*

The water here runs clear. We can discern darting fish, a gravel bed and, swaying across it, long strands of weeds that flow free. To the left, inland, pied herons pick their way through a broken comb of reeds. Terns drop, water breaking in glassy sheets from them as they arise.

Jonny is quiet, now that he's away from home – his muds, his cloaking passageways of *pit-pit*, the obligations that secured him day and night; he wrenches another betel nut from his depleted branch and sinks further into his seat.

By contrast, today Simon is full of energy. 'Glad to be out of the fetid boglands!' he announces to the world – and we wonder if he's persuaded Os to part with one of his 'happy pills'.

'Benedict,' says Simon. 'You said your father wasn't around much when you were little. So, I take it you came here to PNG because you were looking for a home.'

'No, that's not at all the case, actually.'

'But what I don't get is why you didn't choose somewhere pleasant,' he continues. 'Like this.' He takes a moment to contemplate the loose wisps of cirrus, the whistling ducks, the bright waters. 'Nothing lurking in the shadows.'

'In all honesty, where I ended up wasn't a big deal to me. Or if it was, I thought it was a price worth paying. I was a fanatic really – thought I should do whatever it took. Perhaps we're all like that at twenty-four.'

'I wasn't,' says Simon, blissfully regarding the smoky, turquoise foot-hills of the interior, visible now.

Once ashore, Jonny picks up a stone – pink, micaceous, either igneous or metamorphic. It's only ordinary, but it's not the mud of home. He puts it in his pocket as a souvenir.

---

* When it comes to what birds Frank saw, or thought he saw, I've done my best, but can't be totally relied on to recall the species exactly.

We unload – the rucksacks, the hard boxes, Frank.

In among the trees we go, scrambling upslope, clearing the way for the sedan chair. And here, bathed in the seething fug that I haven't known for thirty years, I feel it again, what I felt when young: the thrill of being dwarfed by such a quantity of life.* Everywhere, other species are busy – hissing, chewing, sucking, panting. A moth flaps by – blunt white face like that of a miniature owl. Damsel flies hang before us like twigs of brass.

In this act – proceeding into tropical forest – all is made clear to the human being: the competitive matrix within which we all exist. Here, so much will be asked of you. Impelled by the forces of evolution, every species must seek advantage – till the day rises when each is cast down by the laws of entropy. The chief lesson is this: strive onward while you may, because all things fall apart.

Frank, too, is looking around in awe and – his face upturned and stippled green in the chlorophyll light – uses his binoculars in place of his legs to get a closer view. There aren't many creatures to see among so much foliage, but you can sense them, thousands upon thousands engaged in the struggle – thrips, stick insects, mantids and, for example, locked within the skins of these tree trunks, the larvae known as 'flat-headed borers'. Black fire ants run by. Banded hornets thunder through. And all the while the roots of these columnar trees – ascended and descended by termites, occasionally strung with vines – wrestle with those of their neighbours. They block them, they choke and poison them. A hundred, two hundred feet up, the neighbours join battle again, seeking advantage by thrusting up, bearing down, extending their sensitive tips to allies and enemies.

'So glad to be back in the forest,' I say to Jonny, as a Macleay's swallow-tail dances before us – a zigzagging flicker of hickory brown. I look about once more at the amassed greenery, breathing in the oxygen that the vegetation has just now breathed out.

Jonny says nothing. He plods on. Dutifully he sticks to his place ahead

---

* In Papua New Guinea, there are more than four and a half thousand species of vertebrate alone. See A. Allison, 'Introduction to the Fauna of Papua'.

of me, his bare feet treading the sparse leaf bed as his worn teeth squeeze down on another betel nut.

Already, I can hear the bird we've come for. The creature is issuing a liquid, throaty chortle. A large voice, too. He's called the 'lesser' bird of paradise but, when he spreads himself, he looks the size of a pheasant.

We round the hill. The chortles seem to follow. Frank calls for silence. He's placed on the ground. We peer right up to where a trunk spreads out, along with the plethora of staghorn ferns and orchids the tree has hoisted up there.

Again, we hear the birds; we see the leaves waver. 'Two or three of them,' says Frank. 'Very active.'

They are chasing each other. Flirting? Fighting? Nothing was very visible yet. I step forward and back through the undergrowth, seeking a better vantage point. Frank, meanwhile, must do his best, leaning back and forth between the trees.

A guide points. He's spotted something. '*Em nau, lukim!*'

There is a flash of amber – the bird flying off. Then another, in pursuit. 'Keep missing them,' says Frank, as he's carried hither and thither along the path. 'Felix, will someone PLEASE lower me down – slowly! – and move me to the wheelchair.'

The chair does little better. Everywhere, Frank is hindered by the emergent shrubs of the forest floor – the ensnaring briars, the bellicose roots.

And I see it truly for the first time – not the bird of paradise, but how remarkable my companion is, refusing to have his wings clipped but instead coming all the way here to the rainforest, regardless of obstacles. Whereas, here in the trees, I can go back or forward, take a side-step or duck down, Frank is constantly positioned at the behest of others, and his eyes always a metre from the ground.

'*Lukim!*'

'There! There!'

'You see him?'

'NO, I DO NOT EFFING SEE HIM!'

The bird flips, swings. The sun is behind him as he, a tight bowl of ochre plumage, spreads like a fan. He chuckles and burbles, seeming to glory in his halo of light, all the while accompanied by the cries of subordinate males courting from distant branches. I enjoy the glimpses – the blond and tawny wings, the flaring of the light as the bird effort-lessly sways and warbles or moves on again, burning like a comet as he endeavours to please his silent female.

'Frank,' I say. 'He's diagonally along from that slender branch. Follow it along to where it divides to the right.'

'This is worse than ever. Worse than not seeing them is being brought all this way – only for everyone else to see them.'

The lovely creature alights, closer at hand. It's directly overhead – as clear as day.

Frank misses the bird again. 'As if he's taunting me!'

We can only watch and hope. Its gorgeous rusty breast, its wings of leaden gold. Flopping, billowing. A sense of excess, as if nature here has permitted more than the usual leeway.

'Got him!' exclaims Frank. Quickly, he snaps the bird with his camera. That seems to matter: to capture the thing, hold the moment before it can again evade him.

'Melodic, mysterious, tantalising . . .' says Frank. He regards the space where the bird was, only a moment ago.

That night, again Frank doesn't sleep. Maybe it's his excitement, or maybe it's the pain of his shattered spine, or maybe it's the pain of having seen the rest of us weave through undergrowth as he once did.

Through the next day, as we veer south in two canoes across Chambri Lakes, Frank snoozes with an umbrella propped over his head, either to block out the sun or to block out us.

However, our spirits are high; we have one bird 'in the bag' and the film crew chatter light-heartedly as we cut another slice of spam. Occasionally, we slip through pearl-flowered water lilies, or we slow so as not to upset the small canoes of fishing ladies as they pick like spiders at their nets.

As the sun lowers, the waters to the west are a quivering silver on the flat, riparian fen. Ahead, yet further to the south, the hills steadily grow darker; they appear bolder.

'Hunstein Range,' I say.

'Tomorrow will be the hardest day yet,' Os says. But this time it really will be.

—

Beyond a floating grass island lies the village where we'll stay the night. Here, at the base of an isolated hill, is a spread of reeds and from among these a hundred little faces peep out.

As our canoes ply a corridor through the marsh, the faces abruptly vanish. An erect figure marches towards us, resolutely parting the morass of high grasses with long disciplined strides. He's a smart-looking fellow of about fifty, and stands rigid before us, his strong, uncompromising toes gripping the reed stems as we try to tie the canoes to something that won't drift off.

He begins addressing us, the children behind giving him plenty of space. 'So, my name is Joe, and I am the Official Reception. As a former respected member of the Australian military I would like to welcome you strongly to our village of Paliagwe . . .'

We find a patch where Frank won't sink and he speaks on our behalf. '*TANK YU TRU*. WE ARE VERY HAPPY – VERY *AMAMAS* – to be here.'

Joe indicates a way through the reed beds. 'About turn!' he yells, and the children, like us, fall in line behind.

'Sulphur cockatoo,' says Frank, wheeling himself along. 'Up on that branch – eleven o'clock.'

As we proceed, Joe says, 'When I heard you were in a wheelchair, I thought, "Oh shit! He's going to be fat. Too heavy to lift." But you are not at all like that.'

'Try my best to keep trim,' says Frank, as he stoically negotiates the soggy terrain. The wheels cause it to issue a continual stream of belches and burps. 'Much further to go?'

We squelch our way to firm ground, and there discover an airy, dappled environs of kempt huts, pruned shrubs and well-positioned starfruit trees. The grass underfoot is kept immaculate – as short as a tennis lawn. There are neatened up sago palms and behind them a sloping wood –

and this, like the semi-circle of villagers (both menfolk and ladies well turned out in white, laundered blouses), also looks well-drilled.

'You might tell these people here,' Joe says, pointing a finger at the population as they move in closer to inspect Frank, 'how you came to be this way.'

'You mean, how we came to be travelling through Chambri Lakes?'

'No. How you ended up a cripple.'

With that, Joe commands the youngsters to sit cross-legged in front of their eminent guest. Those who disobey are told they'll be boxed around the ears if they don't do so sharpish.

Frank is very obviously in need of sleep, but with immense generosity of spirit takes a steadying breath and begins. It is a biblical scene – beneath the palm trees, the multitudes gather around to listen as if to a parable. The story even starts like the tale of the Good Samaritan – though rapidly diverges.

Frank tells how the Arab strangers approached him in the road, offering a greeting – 'Peace be upon you!' Then the first bullet hit home – like the numb shock of being punched. Further bullets tore through organs and splintered vertebrae.

Then the altered life which followed. 'I look at it this way. Either you can feel sorry for yourself, or you can get on with it.' The children listen, mouths gaping, noses running. 'I'll tell you what, though, coming to a beautiful place like this for me makes this journey so worthwhile!'

And everyone looks about at their home of malarial parasites, obstructive reeds and death adders.

'You are a brave man,' says Joe. 'Like a true officer.'

'One thing I want to make clear: I haven't come away feeling more invincible, just because I've survived. If anything I feel more vulnerable.'

But Joe doesn't translate this. That a wheelchair user has made it here is proof of his miraculous abilities.

In the early morning, after Joe has demonstrated how he deals with the adders – you rub a special pebble ($29, plus post and packing, from New Delhi) three times on the bite – we punt a short distance through the shifting grasses to the forest that rims the south-west quarter of the lakes.

There, in shade provided by a stout acacia, the Paliagwe carriers get their lifting instructions from Felix and the rest of us a medical briefing from Os – for today we must hike eight hours over the Hunstein Range. 'If Frank is dropped, I'll command "Clear!" And everyone will stand back. Even if Frank looks fine, there's the risk of internal bleeding. Or his legs might shatter – osteoporosis. All clear on that? I will assess his condition and then we continue, or we don't.'

Off we go, the whole cavalcade. Caspar leads with his bush-knife and floppy hat; next, the four Paliagwe men bearing Frank aloft and then fifteen more, ready to take over. Felix, in his rugby shirt, tentatively murmurs encouragement and checks on his charge – 'Are you quite comfortable, Mr Frank?' – while Steven stays on the other side, tending to Frank as a courtier might his king. Os tramps studiously behind, emergency red medical bag on his back, then Jonny, the silent figure that precedes me. To our side, attached by electrical cable to Simon and his camera, is Mark, wearing his headphones. His microphone pivots this way and that, sampling the squishing of our feet, creak of the chair, the itching creatures of the understorey.

As we wend uphill, the procession makes a splendid spectacle – not so much a scene reminiscent of a more colonial era, Francis Rolleston Gardner borne along like John Hanning Speke half blind through the woodlands of Central Africa, but more like a charming interlude from *The Wind in the Willows*. We are doing our level best to pull together, as might Badger and Ratty.

The day hots up. Each step through this dense, watery air is now made with concerted effort. There is less chatter. And Jonny looks smaller and smaller as he walks with his heavy feet further and further from Kandengei. I take over the filming, running back and forward, capturing what I can. The many trials and onerous duties of this particular film shoot have finally caught up with Simon, who is flagging towards the rear.

We all do what we can, though, throwing our hearts into this endeavour for Frank's sake. The Paliagweans are especially impressive; without a fuss, they swap places as they tire. 'Don't be proud,' Os keeps saying. 'If any of you feel you might slip, let someone else take over.'

But no one slips. Each man is diligent, each man plays his part.

A sense of momentum possesses the journey. There are some thirty of us here, overshadowed by these sweating trees, willing on this idea that began six years ago in a gentleman's club with a chance remark. One of us had had a dream – not of money or self-advancement but of acquiring a moment of beauty at whatever the physical cost to himself. All those here understand that; they want his dream to live not die.

An hour passes, then two more. I monitor Frank's face. But although it's wet and gaunt, it's a face that's not as gaunt as that of Simon, our much-abused director.

We stop for a break and, once we have opened our snack boxes – more tuna and spam – I have time to inspect the fallen leaves. The scene enacted around my boots is frantic. Between the acquisitive root hairs, pale hyphae extend their miniature fingers over the thin substrate, prying apart cellulose, entering under-surfaces that microbes have already softened. The invertebrate marauders are also having a go – an ichneumon wasp is sawing off what it can, a millipede hurriedly chewing.

Simon lies down heavily beside me, flattening the lot. 'Not meant to be like this,' he murmurs, weakly. 'Dick's instructions were that I break you, Benedict. Better for the programme, you see? "Break that explorer!" he said. "Break Frank too!"' He dozes off, there on the path, as the first ants move in.

We've had half an hour's rest. It's time to be on our way – and this means disturbing Frank, who doesn't look at all broken. He too has been having what he calls 'a decent kip at last'.

One man ducks out, another slips in. Frank sways a bit but there never seems any likelihood of him being dropped. After six hours climbing we come to the territorial boundary – to us, just another enigmatic tree among ten thousand enigmatic others. Waiting ahead among a whirlwind of yellow birdwing butterflies are a score of youths from the village of Yembeyembe. They'll be taking Frank from here.

We are at the crest of the Hunstein uplands now and, peeking out through the leaves, I can see our destination further south, hidden in a garland of stationary cloud.

Somewhere just ahead, steeped in those clouds, would once have been the Yaifo. And as we continue in their direction I begin to remember the boy called Feefee flipping a pig's bladder about with Ashkai, his permanently disgruntled playmate. Then Sawi lifting my blue rucksack, and Korsai taking it without a word, before leading me over the Central Range to safety.

What I witnessed afterwards was only the beginning of the stampede for gold. Who knew what had befallen the Yaifo since?* Altogether too painful to think about.

But still I do, as we traipse down the other side of the Hunstein ridge. I think of Korsai – so slightly built and retiring. And at first I'm able to think of him as I wish to, on our climb over the Central Range: the squeak of moss as it twists beneath his slender feet. Then, before I know it, I'm thinking of him sieving the tailings in an illegal side pit, up to his thighs in the slurry. He leans on his shovel as before he used to lean on his bow. Feefee is slumped beside him – he lives two years longer but then there's an incident involving dynamite (they're not infrequent). Ashkai meanwhile is trying his luck over at Malumata. You wouldn't fancy his chances either.

———

We've more or less made it to Yembeyembe; there's only the matter of negotiating a reasonably narrow but very deep stream. With their usual proficiency the carriers somehow with their feet locate sure ground to assist them in transporting Frank over the turbid water. For the rest of us a successful crossing means tottering along a submerged pole, so the villagers come to watch us take it in turn, placing small bets on who'll fall in.

At last, we emerge into a clearing. Flowering lilies and trailing strands of purple and mauve bougainvillea frame a pretty enclave of thatched dwellings.

---

* The huge international concern known as Porgera Mine was opened three years after, in 1990. This became the largest open-cast gold and silver mining operation on the planet. It has created a pit five hundred metres deep and annually extracts thirty million tonnes of gold ore, according to the official figures of the Porgera Joint Venture (PJV), which is operated by Barrick Gold. The mine employs many hundreds of its own security guards and continues to be an important source of national income – and of social and environmental controversy.

Frank, our precious load, is laid safely down. We congratulate each other, shaking hands with the carriers and giving them a round of biscuits. Os breathes out, looks heavenward – 'No one wants to be known as the one that dropped Frank Gardner.' And together we look out over the swift waters of the Solomoi to what lies ahead: across the river, which downriver joins the Korosameri, are the lowermost slopes of the Central Range. It is here, just below the first smudges of mist, that we will reach our journey's end among the birds of paradise.

Not far away now, and things are looking good. We think things will work out.

They don't.

VIII

Early the next day, Frank stirs in his mosquito net. 'Morning all!' He's had an excellent night's sleep, he says. 'Tell you what, though, my bum is a tad sore from sitting so long.'

Frank already has a picture to show me. He's photographed his buttock in close-up, as he might an interesting mallard.

'Better get Os in to have a look.'

Os comes over, kneels on a single meaty leg by Frank. He doesn't like what he sees. 'Pressure sore. I'm going to get a second opinion.'

'Thing is, I'm not someone who gets them,' Frank says. 'Others do – but I'm really fortunate that way.'

'Probably we'll just rest up a day. Give it twenty-four hours, take a view then.'

But it all sounds a bit ominous. The fear is septicaemia, of course. The nurse – patched by Mark through to Frank's mosquito net from somewhere in New Zealand – talks of the remoteness of our location, of weather windows and of civil unrest. Civil unrest?

Frank says, 'Benedict, the decision is out of my hands.' He makes a joke of it. 'Os has been chatting up a Kiwi nurse. You know how he is!'

'I'm so sorry, Frank.'

'The curse of my injuries,' Frank says, briskly, 'is that they still come back to dog me, twelve years on.'

'I can't help but feel bad. You remember when you told me in the UK that you've done with pain? Well, I've put you through more pain – for what?'

'I've seen the lesser bird of paradise. I've seen the welcome the Kandengeis gave you, the welcome they gave me. So many things here that I'd never imagined I'd experience in my life!'

'Even so . . .' And I realise how fond I have become of Frank's little routines – the kitbag he likes to have on his knees, the shoulder bag he hangs at the back of the chair, hooking it on with two outward twists of the handles. I'll miss him.

'Every day is a bonus. That's how I look at it – and I've had a fantastic time. I really mean it.'

And that fantastic time is over. The dream we all shared – Frank and I, the crew, but also the Kandengeis, the Paliagweans – is suddenly dissolving around us. Felix, Caspar and Jonny look on appalled as we quickly pack Frank's things.

Simon seizes the camera and tries to grab a last word from him – only for the helicopter to arrive half an hour early.

Down it comes, causing the trees around to shudder. It settles among us, a raucous machine painted a garish orange and yellow. However, Frank notices that its flank is adorned with a resplendent bird of paradise. 'Raggiana,' he comments agreeably to the helmeted pilot. The pilot, though, is peering at the clumps of low sky; he tuts as he raises his clipboard and estimates the net weight of his cargo: one disabled adult and his wheelchair, one medic and one hefty red bag. 'Exquisite, those long tail streamers,' adds Frank.

Felix completes his final act of service, hoisting him aboard. 'I love you,' he breathes. As Os and then Frank are buckled up, he reaches into the helicopter as if to stop him leaving.

'Benedict, we'll continue this one day,' Frank then says – or perhaps he doesn't because I can't hear. The engine is screaming, the rotors turning. Felix and I step back, and Frank gives a victory sign as the chopper floats upwards, gradually ascending into the heavens.

Stunned and dispossessed, Simon, Mark and I mooch around the spot where Frank left us. The villagers watch with everyone else for what will happen next.

I jot a few thoughts in my diary. 'The pain, the mosquitoes, the thorns.

It's as if we need to pass further through Purgatory before we attain Paradise. We simply haven't suffered enough.'

I go to be with Jonny, who's found a dry tree trunk to perch on by the river. Despondently, he takes up another betel nut and looks out at the waters that flow into his Sepik and there mingle with the waters of home. He lifts his head, hopefully. 'We are finished?'

'Expect so. I think we'll both be going back where we belong now.'

Jonny nods, understanding well enough what I mean. 'For you, home is called England. It is a long way off.' So far off, it's somewhere hardly possible to imagine – cold instead of hot, night instead of day. I begin my goodbyes by slipping my own wristwatch onto the wrist of the man to whom I am a son.

After, I rejoin the crew. Felix is staring at his feet. So is everyone else, at theirs. To cheer us up, Caspar marshals a few boys to climb the palms and knock down some coconuts.

'Going to take a while to get us all out of here,' Steven says. 'This is an editorial decision, something for you not me to decide, Simon, but might I suggest we head up to Bisorio, see if we can cobble an ending out of this?'

'What's Bisorio?' says Simon, not exactly enthralled by the idea. 'And is there any more of that disgusting 3-in-1 coffee available?'

'Old mission station. Years ago, Benedict hiked from there up over the mountain.'

'Which mountain?'

'The one we can't see. Too much cloud.'

'Well, better than just kicking our heels, I suppose.'

The prospect of visiting the old mission station doesn't much appeal to me either. The forests will have been stripped of rosewood, kwila, black-bean, red cedar and whatever else was worth shipping to China.* Also, I've had quite enough of scraping through my past. But, as someone observes, 'there's sod all else to do', and so we slump into a canoe and motor down the Solomoi, then, after an hour – maybe it was more –

---

* PNG is China's single largest supplier of tropical logs, and whether sold off by *bikmen* at a village or national level the timber almost all goes there. China owns a third of PNG's national debt. See *A Major Liability*, published by the campaign group Global Witness.

meet the confluence with the Korosameri. We turn upriver to Bisorio, wondering if it's worth the effort.

After a while, I take a bit more notice. To the left is the river bank that Tsogomoi used to gaze so fixatedly at – although that was a lot further upriver – and I'm pleasantly surprised to see the forests as I remember them, thickly piled up on the slopes behind, murmuring as they always did, entirely indifferent to our failed expedition. The insects chirrup and click; a Blyth's hornbill clacks over the tight canopy – rising with each wing beat, dipping before the next – and just occasionally the foliage trembles as something larger shifts.

And now I'm beginning to remember Bisorio Mission – the clothes pegs on washing lines, the lawn mowers raising their sweet smells. I'm recalling George, over in his workshop, sharpening knives on the grinder. He's telling a Bible teacher that he must re-double his efforts, regarding the outreach programme. 'As I keep saying, it's no good the Yaifos staying in the bush. They must come down to the mission, learn about Our Saviour.'

By the time we're drawing near Bisorio the sun is low – right in our eyes – but that doesn't explain why I don't recognise the mission station. Where I expect there to be the Americans' neatly planked houses, and miners in them swigging beer at the end of a day's shift, there's only the odd local shack.

The gold rush has come – and gone. That much is readily apparent. And Bob, George, their hopeful congregation . . . they too are missing.

What leftovers there are now appear – and with a slight air of desperation I feel, they empty onto the beach with a clatter and rush, spilling like a bucket of shells. The children have pot bellies and rusty hair – malnutrition – and even in the dusk we can see their skin peeling away.

A bigger man than the rest steps forward. His shirt is so clean and his eyes so self-assured we know that he's not from here.

'Joseph,' he says and bids us a very good morning. He wants to express his thanks on behalf of the population of Bisorio.

Thanks for what? I'm thinking.

'They are gone now,' he says, noticing I'm still looking for the mission houses. He strokes his well-groomed moustache as he walks me over to the falling-apart huts.

'Who?'

'Them white people. They that helped them here talk to Him above.'

'All gone?'

'A long time back. They stopped these people buggering about with arrows, brought the Good News of God Almighty, and then they all pissed off back to America or somewhere.'

I'm still looking for signs of what I used to know – the trimmed lawns, the wooden steps up to well-hinged and netted doors. All I see are trees standing about, their only companions head-high grass and creepers – and the hollow-eyed children being mothered by what look like ancient women.

So I search instead for the airstrip. But again, not a trace; where I once jogged with George, there are only more vines grappling with the resurgent forest.

'No schools, no medicines, no services . . .' says Joseph. 'But these people are pleased that you are here at least,' he adds – as if any white man will do.

'The gold?'

'Came to nothing. The white men too – they came to nothing. There's gold down at Malumata, and bloody plenty of it up at Porgera, but not here.'

'I see. And why are you here?'

'Heard you were around the area, so dropped by. You have food and money for handing out?'

'Beni – you remember him? Bit of a dubious character, practised black magic, they used to say.'

'My father. He's been dead a long time. You got money?'

'And what about Tsogomoi?'

'Off somewhere. He doesn't like it here so much.'

'You remember him?'

'Sure, I remember him! You made the boy famous.'

'Oh, you know who I am?'

'Everyone knows who you are! You're the white man who was happy to eat the same shit that we ate! And then you walked up to the Yaifos.

You took Michael – he must have been fifteen, sixteen. Shit! Everyone remembers. But I was just a kid.'

——

We take possession of a ramshackle house and there Wendy begins her 'cooking', as best she is able. The atmosphere amongst us is grim. It's not just Jonny now pining for home. 'Always a thousand solutions,' Steven used to say, but there's no solving this one.

We wait for our spam, joining the scaly population of Bisorio Mission in their unhappy state. Sometimes I listen to the forest out there in the night – the swaying tree limbs, the lonely trills and screams – and once again that land across the water seems to be an expression of something forever unobtainable; once more the birds of paradise, up in the high branches with the orchids and fig-wasps, seem to speak of a state of grace, an exquisite freedom denied us. *Long ago, people came down from the mountain, having heard news of a Paradise,* I thought to myself. *And we were intending to go up. Either way, we're now all of us stuck down here, the wrong side of the River Styx.*

A day passes, while Steven arranges for us to be air-lifted out. Tracked by Simon and Mark, I walk about the old mission station, picking through my tangled memories, combing them out.

Gone, all gone – the workshop, the veranda with its money box, the missionaries you could watch through the net windows enjoying their nut roast while the sickly gathered, whispering like the insects around the porch light. Gone too are the coins you might earn by hacking back the forest, gone the shop to spend the money in. All these things have been swept away by the river in which the locals were baptised. It's as if the Korosameri had had enough. The red tractor you could still view, but it was on the riverbed so only at times of low water.

'Missionaries trump the indigenous and gold trumps the missionaries,' concludes Simon as we film what we can through the bushes.

And nature trumps all of us, I think to myself.

Steven buys two pigs to cook up for the Bisorios. Caspar takes charge, organising a *mumu*, a proper highland pig feast – lugging stones to the base of a fire, then burying them with the meat, taro and sweet potatoes, and sealing them with the banana leaves layered on top. The entire population of scrawny adults and children eye the strange heap as it smoulders like compost for two hours.

'Done!' announces Caspar and lays out the steaming vegetables and pig chunks. Felix, meanwhile, doles out portions from a massive tub of rice. The rice is too hot to hold in your hands, but the children hold it anyway, scalding their fingers then mouths.

Soon, the food, just like the mission station, is gone. We too will be gone, shortly. First thing in the morning, if Steven has sorted it properly – and he always does.

Except that, while milling with the crowds, I'm approached by a tired man who's just hurried in from the trees. He seems to want to sell me a Victoria crowned pigeon, which looks upon me regally from where it's confined to a string bag.

'You remember me?'

'I fear not,' I say, but I appreciate him bringing me the magnificent specimen, and take a moment to admire its ruby eyes, smooth maroon neck, blue-grey wings and dainty lace crest. I decide to buy the creature and release it. 'This poor thing might as well have a happy ending,' I mutter to myself, 'even if no one else does.'

'Michael,' the owner says in Tok Pisin. 'My name is Michael.' He looks up at me, blinking like the bird, waiting for me to remember.

'Michael?'

The figure before me is a far cry from the boy I knew. His hands are the worst – skin layers coming away, as do certain types of potatoes when overboiled. His cheeks look leathern and his eyes desolate even as he smiles, eagerly willing me to remember him.

I take Michael away from the hubbub. Alone with me at our portable table he consumes packet after packet of biscuits. I watch as he eats. The hinge of his jaw – once so plump – is a bone that's knotted with tendons. His face, just like the rest of him, has been put to hard work these thirty years. Seemingly all that remains is gristle and muscle, and as he scratches himself his skin makes the sound of nails over flock wallpaper.

'Such a hard walk up the mountain,' Michael says, munching away. 'And those people dancing about, wanting to kill us . . .'

'Michael, they were your relatives.'

'They were wild people!' Michael looks around for more biscuits. There are none.

'You've seen Tsogomoi lately?'

'He stays in Malumata or somewhere. Of course, he is an old-aged man like you now.' Michael's eyes come to rest on our tins of tuna.

'The Yaifo,' I say, handing over a box of twenty. 'What happened to them?'

'Most, they stayed up there.' He nods through the decrepit hut wall to the mountain.

'At one of the mining sites, you mean?' Michael might as well have the spam too. I begin rooting through Wendy's chaotic trove of supplies. 'Tragic. Not as if they were ever likely to become rich.'

'No, no. I mean that they stayed put.'

I come back to the table. 'What are you saying, Michael, that the Yaifo are still hiding away up there?'

'Still there – or thereabouts. But we don't go up. And no one from Bisorio has yet walked over the top as you did.'

'No one in all these years? Michael, surely they have. Why wouldn't they?'

Michael rubs his calves, remembering the climb to the Yaifo. He doesn't think it's so very strange that no one wanted to hike even further.

'What about George and Bob? They made no attempt to convert the Yaifos after I left?'

'Oh, they did, they did. Bob said he would not give up while the Lord gave him strength. And maybe the Yaifos guessed this because they sent a party down the mountain to tell him to stay right there.'

'So that was the end of that?'

'No, he walked up anyway. But only just. He arrived almost dead. Some Yaifos said that this would save them from killing him. But he then stood up and told them to accept Christ and turn away from their false god.'

'And did they?'

'Not so much,' says Michael, thinking about it.

At this key moment, Wendy, a lady of some size who is not to be messed with – she takes much pride in her quartermastering abilities, just as she does in the indifferent dishes she serves up – strides in. She regards me with disapproval and Michael with scorn, as she swoops up the discarded biscuit wrappers with a mighty fist, then with great ceremony counts the tins that I've piled before Michael. She restacks them out of his reach and, with a mix of menace and relish, marches to the door saying she's off to 'have words' with Steven.

I listen to Wendy's feet pounding down the steps as the incredible thought sinks in: Korsai might not be dead. He might not have collapsed beside a spoil heap.

'But talk to Tsogomoi's son, maybe he knows more. He's just arrived, you want to see him?' Michael picks up the tuna tins – they join the pigeon in the string bag – and outside asks around for a boy called Gibson.

It's twilight before he's found. Only aged sixteen or so, he has a crown tattooed on his brow and doesn't look much like his father. Whereas Tsogomoi had cheekbones that provided a strong frame for his pensive face, Gibson has lively eyes set prominently in rounded cheeks.

Unfortunately, dozens of Bisorio's listless converts gather around us when I produce photographs from my first visit and it's hard to get much from him.

'Really the best person to talk to is my father, not me,' he says in Tok Pisin. '*Mi man bilong bus, em tasol!*' I'm just a jungle man!

'But does he ever mention the walk we did?'

He stares at me, perplexed. 'Of course! All the time! He won't stop talking about it!'

'And the Yaifo. You think it's true that they really do still live up there?'

'Oh yes, they hang on up there, all right. No one can get them to come down.'

'And do you know who is alive and dead? You've heard of Korsai and Sawi? Or Feefee and Ashkai?'

'I do not know. Sawi is maybe dead.'

I picture the woven bag. *So, I'm too late for Sawi . . .* I think sadly to myself. But I suppose this is only to be expected. 'Korsai – he's alive, though?'

'Maybe yes. Maybe no. I don't know these names. The last of those people are up by the top of the Wilifa river, not the Yaifo now. Sometimes, you can hear them sing out – that's what my father says.'

Although after a while Gibson turns out to be quite a playful, forth-coming character, I learn little more from him – and nothing more from Michael. But even this information is a lot to absorb. The people I knew as the Yaifo have, against all odds, pulled through.

I go to the river to have a quiet think, as Tsogomoi used to. I watch a bird – a willie wagtail – dab and spin, free to cross the Korosameri as it seems we're not. Then I'm joined by Simon and Mark. The sun is lowering fast and Simon reminds me that we're here to make a film: this is our last chance to come up with an ending.

'What we need is for you to express a final, compelling sentiment,' he says. 'Try to wrap everything up in one sentence.'

We struggle with various takes as the light grows ever poorer.

'Sometimes life works out like this,' I say, mustering my only useful thought. 'There are no happy endings because Paradise is, by its very nature, unobtainable.'

However, Simon says, 'This is not the ending I'm paid to come up with.'

So, just before we lose the light completely, I try again, holding up Frank as an example to us all. At the risk of making him sound more like Jesus Christ than ever, I close the programme by quoting some of his parting words, enunciating them slowly and weightily, as a vicar in a pulpit might close his sermon by referring again to the scriptures. 'And so, we should try to follow His example, reminding ourselves that every day on this earth is a bonus . . .'

'Cut,' says Simon sadly. 'I'm off for a fag.'

———

In the morning, I go to wash in the river and it feels like yet another baptismal cleansing, only in my case I'm trying to wash away numerous memories of Papua New Guinea – so many outstanding, remarkably open-hearted people that should be locked in my past.

For the Yaifo at least, things have turned out all right – or better than was to be expected. The same could not be said for Frank, but he has made the most of this opportunity and that is important too. We have had our chance – Frank is safely out of here and the chopper is coming for me too, shortly. Time to resume our lives.

Only, I would have liked, just one more time, to hear the Yaifo yelling across the slopes as they used to. And as I wave to Jonny (relieved of his burden, he sits straight-backed, replete with more betel nuts in the homeward-bound canoe) and the helicopter banks sharply away from the Central Range, I allow myself to imagine the Yaifo tipping back their heads, then opening their lungs to address their world. No good being sentimental – their lives, beset by chest infections, intestinal worms and malign spirits, usually end before sixty. But the Yaifo's songs told of their presence on the mountain; they were asserting their right to exist, at this time, at this place. Even now – below me, the early mist unravelling along the Korosameri – Korsai might take a moment to pause on a well-loved trail. He stands tall, patient, as if to be counted among the trees. He listens for an answering call.

IX

Yet my dealings with New Guinea did not end that day. A few months on, our illustrious patient had recovered and was asking to go back. Just as surprising, the insurers who'd underwritten the TV production were willing to entertain the idea.

'Four filming days max, that's all we're allowed,' Simon informed me by phone. We'd fly directly to the highlands and seek the one bird of paradise that it transpired Frank had been wanting to see all along, the King of Saxony.

Our plane, a Dash 8, taxied unsteadily around the lopsided tarmac of Tari airport and came to a halt. 'I'm really gunning for this!' said Frank, then peered out of the window. A brick-coloured piglet trotted beside its owner like a dog and through the perimeter fence – constructed of clumsily hewn stakes – several men were goggling at us, looking like a delegation of keen horticulturalists with their bush knives and earth-stained, askew hats.

We climbed aboard the vehicles provided and found ourselves passing through the Huli villages – each burnt to a crisp. This was a punishment from the police for recurrent bouts of communal violence. However, the highlands were pleasantly cool and, though this was the rainy season and many birds of paradise surely 'in moult', Frank was determined to finish the job.

Thankfully, Simon on this attempt would be properly supported – not only by Steven and Os, but by a wildlife cameraman, Ralph. Our sound man would be Nick, who wore a flat cap and cut a suave figure with his boom mic – like a member of the aristocracy, out for a stroll with his Labrador and shotgun. Furthermore, our base camp would be Ambua Lodge, a luxurious-sounding tourist retreat; we'd have the use of their bird spotter.

Little wonder Simon was in such good form. His eczema had cleared up and that afternoon as we drove through the rolling uplands – basking just now in glorious sunshine – he could at last afford to smile.

The rain set in half an hour later. It bucketed down. Through the torrent we looked with foreboding at the moss thriving everywhere – on the wild bamboos as they dripped, the wooden gate of Ambua Lodge as that too dripped. There were well-worn runnels in the thatch, and this was colonised by what botanists call 'cushion bog flora' and those epiphytic orchids that favour only the wettest of habitats.

However, there was exciting news. Felix, chief of the carriers, was here to greet Frank, and although he was finding it chilly away from the swelter of his home down at Chambri – 'Mr Frank, it is like the air-con is stuck on' – he was pleased to report that the local helpers had already been familiarised with the sedan chair. He directed his Huli team like a conductor of an orchestra. 'Up!' he called, raising both hands. 'And now, Mr Frank, the setting down.' He laid his hands to rest.

What with the rain, there'd be no lifting today. Notwithstanding, Frank was soon manfully carving across the saturated lawn in his wheelchair. Despite the garden being hemmed by vicious stakes – the same as the Huli deployed around their villages as a first defence – he managed to spot a blue bird of paradise ('dull female, she looks miserable') before sinking.

The afternoon went by, washed in a dreary, otherworldly light. Children peered at us like bedraggled meerkats from a hillock at the entrance gate and all sound was dampened by the damp.

———

The next day begins exactly like the rest. With no duties to speak of, I wake before everyone else, examine the insect dead and wounded – they lie about, wings snapped off or in tatters, damaged by a night of battering the security lights – and wonder if today will be the day Frank sees his bird of paradise.

I'm kept company by Jonathan, the night watchman. 'I have just the one wife, not the two,' he complains bitterly. 'How can I even afford another unless my first wife does her housekeeping properly?'

He keeps an eye on the nearby highway as it looms below us in the first light. Lazily he waves his rifle to indicate the direction of the Porgera Mine, further off. 'Trouble reaches us easier now. They can just catch a lift. Or idle up here on their feet.'

I tell Jonathan about the Yaifo, who are not so far from the mine.

'They had better hide themselves well, then,' he says.

The spritelier members of a group of elderly American bird spotters now appear. I chat with them at the water urn, as they queue for their herbal tea. 'Darn shame about the fog. We've had a good time, though. Hey, I'm Mary, by the way. Mary Roberts. And this is Don. He sort of tags along.'

Don regards me through his round lenses that are placed low on his thin nose and alarmingly expand his genial eyes. 'When we married, I promised I'd follow her to the ends of the earth. So that's what I'm doing here!' Cheerily, he waves Mary's bird book; he has gaffer-taped the PNG section together and cut off the rest.

The film crew begin to pitch up, and then Joseph, our bird spotter, who has skin like worn basalt; it lies in a long fold down either expressionless cheek. Already we've learned that he tends to stand too close to us, and is immovable, like a heavy statue. This morning at the breakfast table he has on his wet waterproofs.

When Frank rolls into place, I notice that he has what looks like fruticose lichen sprouting from his chin. 'I haven't seen a mirror in days! Given up shaving because they're all out of my reach.'

'The butter tastes of bananas,' Nick informs him, and Frank is just about to test it when a Ribbon-tailed Astrapia is sighted in the hotel car park. The female bobs about, plucking berries from a low bush, and then an eager male. Swarthy, no larger than a blackbird, he has a turquoise sheen when his breast catches the light. Twin feathers stream like white satin from him as he doggedly flies after his disinterested mate.

Frank hurtles off with his camera and we eat our scrambled eggs, watching through the window as he edges nearer. Vehicles reverse noisily around him – it's the Americans heading out.

Afterwards, we too patrol the road for birds. Benson, at the wheel of the minibus, wears frayed woollen mitts and likes very much the complicated manoeuvre which involves avoiding the ditch while we turn to go back the other way; this we do a lot.

The light fades. Day One is gone and we've yet to film anything of note. We have a stiff drink to calm our nerves.

The second day slips by and we elect to spend the end of it further up the mountain, where the forest yields to sub-alpine grasslands and shrubby heath. Frank and I will try our luck sleeping outdoors.

With Benson at the wheel, and Joseph the bird spotter with his flat, lacklustre cheeks staring grimly out, we drive up through the smothering cloud until we reach the spot where the road is being widened – this to ameliorate access to a new liquified natural gas facility. The workers clustering at the battered red cedar look like highway robbers.

'STOP!' yells one of them, not bothering to swivel his 'GO' sign around. We are held here while he chatters to Benson.

Up and up, until we find ourselves through the cloud and bathed instead in sun. There's razor grass, a hint of a tarn, and grey skeletal trees. Here it is that we'll sleep – off to the right in a delightful valley bowl, known locally as Lai-iba, banked with myrtles, *Nothofagus* and laurel.

With the help of two carriers, Howard and Henry, I find a meadow of cushion herbs, and among the buttercups and potentilla weave a reed thatch for our simple shelter. That night, Frank and I gnaw the sweet potatoes I've left too long in our campfire and listen for birds as the water vapours move around and about us, wiping the valley sides.

But not a peep – just snoring from Frank. Though Frank claims it's snoring from me.

'Didn't sleep a wink,' comes a croaky voice from a bivvi bag. It's still only four thirty in the morning. 'But wouldn't have missed that for the world!'

We peek out from our leafy den. The valley is enveloped in blue haze, laid over us like a net.

Frank props himself up. 'You hear that?'.

We listen.

'King of Saxony! Sure of it.'

Maybe Frank's still half asleep, because I hear nothing.

We speed off downhill for breakfast. 'Still no ending in the can,' says Simon, who's starting to look like a wreck again.

There is only this afternoon and tomorrow left and, for want of anything else to do, we go to film a bunch of Hulis dressed up in their traditional finery.

Behind a wooden gateway which has received a lot of axe blows, half a dozen characters, joined by our Howard, line up on an apron of grass that looks like one of those display areas which the *Parotia*, among other more ground-dwelling birds of paradise, devotedly tend.

'Well, here at last is what we've been looking for,' says Simon sardonically. The Huli men are adorned with magnificent birds – or chunks of them. Hornbill beaks dangle from necks, cassowary thigh bones have been shoved in belts as daggers. However, most of the body parts and feathers are reserved for their wig headdresses – the King of Saxony enamel-blue brow plumes, the apricot quiffs of the Lesser and Greater, the electric turquoise sprays of the Superb, and entire squashed specimens of the Blue.

'Tremendous!' Frank exclaims warmly to the Hulis. And quieter, 'Let's hope one or two died naturally.'

Now for the performance. The seven men, faces coated with toxic-looking acrylic, line up and slap their diminutive drums, unhurriedly synchronising till they indeed do slap at the same time – and then hop, hop, they are off. The display of hopping, well-greased youths is impressive indeed: the bobbing of their leaf kilts (technical term, 'arse grass') and plumage startling. Between each dance bout, the men rescue precious fallen feathers, and this we much enjoy too. But it's not what Frank is seeking.

'Let's go back to HQ,' he says, making the best of it. 'Get some scoff.'

On the Sunday, the sun as usual rises only faintly. Jonathan, the night watchman, talks of the second young lady he's pursuing – 'she doesn't understand that she needs a man who's seriously hard core' – as finally, the cloud lifts. Then sinks back down again. At our feet are heaped the night's invertebrate toll. Occasionally, more moths fall from the walls like chips of loose paint.

However, it gives me comfort to think of the Yaifo wrapped in the same cloud. I've known many resilient communities through the years, but the survival of the Yaifo in the face of the twenty-first century spoke of something even more extraordinary.

———

The American bird spotters are back from an early outing. Mary says she has news, and she imparts it hurriedly as we queue for the hot water urn, mugs in hand. 'Right by the roadside! Up at that Bailey Bridge! Just the one male. Oh my, Benedict, he was quite something.'

When I inform Simon, he greets this exciting intelligence with a bitter sigh. He'd hoped it was all over.

However, he agrees that we should make a last effort.

First though, he wishes to clinch some heartfelt words from Frank, who's insisting on not faking anything.

And while Simon and everyone else is willing Frank to agree that his quest is concluded, I find that I've begun pacing back and forward, thinking of the Yaifo not so far away. 'Really, I should go back,' I keep muttering to myself. 'Find out if Korsai's alive.'

Just before four in the afternoon, the time the King of Saxony favours for its afternoon display, Os checks our drinking bottles. 'Are we all watered up?' he says. 'Right lads, the final push!'

Frank is upbeat. 'I was just going to do a final stint in the car park! I'd settled for that!'

Simon, though, is not upbeat, as Benson takes the wheel and we accelerate up the road. The strain has been all too much. He is prostrate on the back seat, clutching an empty bag of sweets. 'Just need forty winks,' he says.

Today, as it happens, marks the beginning of the end for the birds of paradise hereabouts. The road has been successfully enlarged, opened up for all and sundry, and now the bitumen is to be laid down. The entire section reeks and steams; it has the odour of Hades as it despoils the Paradise we're meant to have reached at long last.

There is much reversing, and much of Benson executing his five-point turns in frayed woollen mittens. Ahead is Frank in the Toyota; he cranes out of the window, still able to believe that he will, in the last half-hour of the last filming day, see a King of Saxony.

Then, by two yellow construction vehicles sprawled by the roadside where they've been gnawing like beasts, we stop. The road workers are singing raucously in their grass hut, the 'GO' sign laid against it, and Frank, up ahead, appears to be fascinated by something in the treetops.

We park up behind his vehicle and get out: Nick the soundman, Ralph with his camouflaged big lens, Simon with the tripod, Joseph with his long flat cheeks.

'See it?' says Joseph. 'Here, look.' He hands me his binoculars. 'A hundred metres up, and a hundred and thirty off.'

The bird dips and flips. Frank is perfectly still. It matters not that the diminutive bird today looks like a sparrow, that against the cloud it is a uniform dark grey, that the streamers that bizarrely extend from its head are hardly visible to the naked eye. Frank is caught up in the wonder of what's been newly revealed to him.

The King of Saxony is alone, swinging on his bare twig.

'As if it defies gravity, the laws of science,' Frank says, and the crew edges a little closer.

After a long while, during which Frank says nothing, he mops away a tear. Then he speaks. He explains that he's remembering a time from his childhood. His dad was at the piano playing 'Carnaval', while Frank was playing cards. And on those cards was depicted a bird of paradise. 'We'll go there together some day,' his father had said.

Frank falls quiet.

Simon gestures to me to stay clear. 'Let him have his moment.'

'We have such short lives,' Frank resumes after a while. 'I'm beyond thinking we'll see our parents once they've died, but my dad would have been so proud to have known I got here to see this . . .'

It's a wrap. After what feels like a respectable interval, the crew lower their gear and we go over to congratulate Frank, each in turn – me,

Simon, Steven, Nick, Os, Ralph, Caspar and last of all Felix. 'Mr Frank, I will miss you.'

There are cheers, there are sighs of relief, there are slaps on the back.

Then the moment's gone. A sickle bill flies over, startling us with its call – 'ratter-tat-tat'.

'Like a machine gun,' says Frank, eyes darting left and right. He is no longer a small boy with a deck of cards, the Schumann washing over him. 'An M16,' he says, looking for where it's coming from. He's not in the highlands of PNG, either, he's reporting from a war-zone. 'No.' He corrects himself. 'Heavier calibre. More like an M60.'

It's like his shooting, all over again.

There remains the filming of the 'end credits' – the Land Cruiser steadily heading homeward, its red rear lights aglow as the mist closes in once more.

Then we climb aboard for real. 'Fathers and sons!' exclaims Simon, as we speed off. 'That's the programme's underlying theme. The viewer begins to understand that for Benedict and Frank it's all about fathers and sons.'

The film has its ending. Dick, the executive producer, passes on his congratulations to all concerned and reveals that, though he personally is retiring from television – 'I've always fancied the Italian Alps' – there is already talk of *Birds of Paradise: The Ultimate Quest* picking up a BAFTA.*

I, for one, wish the film well – but know that I'll never be induced to watch it.† What matters is that for Frank the quest is over, and we can move on. And to that end, I look out over the highlands in the direction of where Korsai might possibly be, lost to time and the fog like the rest of the Yaifo and just about everything else around here.

---

* It didn't.

† I was induced to see the second half, which I thoroughly enjoyed. Frank gave me a call and, with Os, we viewed it at his flat with a bowl of his own version of spaghetti – better than mine – on our knees.

PART THREE

WHAT LIES ON THE FAR SHORE

I

Somewhere in the process of helping Frank achieve his journey, I had begun to feel compelled to complete my own.

Already, out there between those dripping trees, I had begun to entertain the idea of a serious lone expedition – the sort I used to do. I would, just one last time, revisit the past – journey back to the Yaifo to see how they were faring – but also the restlessness of my earlier years. This felt unfinished. Frank had found his bird while I had not.

All I asked was that I undertake this final journey as I had the others. I would take little with me and if things got tricky, as they had many times in my youth, then I would come up with a solution with those whose home this was.

However, even as I began dusting down my boots, there was something very different about this expedition – a sense of disquiet, even from those who felt they knew me. 'Suddenly got a chill that I'd never see you again,' a cousin wrote. 'Why is that?'

I did my best to remind everyone that I used to spend month upon month travelling in the rainforest with no possibility of help; on two occasions, I had trudged on for weeks alone.

It was no use. Not only had everyone forgotten that this was what I'd dedicated my adult life to doing, they had forgotten that this was once what we all did, at one level or other. Off we went – bicycling to India, hitching down South America or catching the Magic Bus to Marrakech. Our loved ones heard nothing of us for months, while we occasionally picked up an airmail envelope – chalky blue, marked 'POSTE RESTANTE' – from the back of a dusty post office somewhere in Madrid or Rio.*

The indigenous people, not us, were the experts of the rainforest, I went on. To be blunt about it, they could get someone out quicker than any rescue party could get in. Besides, though somewhat older than was ideal, I was still fit. (The boring reality was that, to stand even the vaguest chance of entering sympathetically into anywhere remote I always had to prepare myself with the rigour of a track athlete. The same applied now.) And I detailed various predicaments from which I'd extracted myself. For example, once, in Sumatra, I'd even sewn up my chest with a boot-mending kit, without the use of an anaesthetic. No one was much reassured. The bald fact remained that I believed in doing it on my own terms (which were as close as possible to 'native' terms) or risk death.

From my diary:

Wednesday, 27th September
And now goodbye to my little family.

Lenka [my wife], proud of me, I think. She trusts in me and the faith I have in what she calls 'The Jungle Occupants' – even if no one else does.

At bedtime, Freddie in his red pyjamas talking incessantly about his Lego and his special invention – a cardboard box which he fits himself in, a slot for his eyes, to suck CO_2. 'It's called The Machine For Saving The Planet'.

The children, like animals before an earthquake, sense something is about to happen. Natalya wanted me to read on and on from Anne of Green Gables, *as far as possible delaying the moment I switch off the light. Later, Freddie climbed into my bed, then was constantly seeking*

---

* Gone were the days, lamented the Irish writer Dervla Murphy, when the young severed their apron strings. 'Now the familiar is not left behind,' she wrote, 'and the unknown has become familiar even before one leaves home.' The veteran traveller went on: 'Unpredictability – to my generation the salt that gave travelling its savour – seems unnecessary if not downright irritating to many of the young.'

*in his sleep to be near me. Occasionally there were grunts and snuffles
from little Beatrice, who'd clambered in on the other side.*

In order to get this expedition right, I needed time away from the
concerns of those who cared for me. The next few days I spent in West
London at my friend Susanna's empty house.

It was a tried and tested procedure: all alone now, I laid everything
out on her floor, and there on a rug worked through different scenarios,
second guessing what might go wrong.

My health in particular might go wrong. Malaria, I could treat –
there'd be pills in my survival kit and duplicates in my main pack – but
not dengue fever, a virus delivered by a day-flying mosquito, the symp-
toms of which include a fever and haemorrhaging. Crucially, this element
of my expedition I'd have no power to control. There was no cure, and
no realistic prevention – and the disease was considerably more prevalent
than in my youth. I should hurry through the lowlands it favoured and
avoid spending time either side of the Central Range.

To clarify my thoughts, I studied my original 1:500,000 aeronautical
map. For the first time in an age, I traced the contours, and the valleys
and peaks laid out in the warm hues of honey and pollen. Next, I shuffled through my old photos, reminding myself of what I'd faced three
decades ago.

These years on, how fragile that first expedition looked, as we were about
to head off: a bright morning at Bisorio Mission, the sun not yet high. Me,
fresh-faced and in shorts, like an overgrown schoolboy – socks pulled up,
just as my mum would have wanted; Tsogomoi, only aged seventeen,
sporting his mining hat to mark the occasion; Michael, even younger, a fat
child cautiously looking out from under his special yellow cap. To the rear,
overshadowed, told to face forward but still confused as to why we were
standing here like this, the two Yaifo youths on whom our lives would
depend. And there in the foreground, our five deficient piles of baggage.

'Can do the trek in fourteen days but give yourself eighteen,' I decided.
'Get in as fast as possible to avoid dengue, then get out. That means a
helicopter to Bisorio – not just extremely costly, but goes against my
entire ethos.'

I placed the map in a plastic sleeve and wondered again if I might avoid the expense and intrusion of a chopper. No, I could not.

At the last moment I also found space for the string pouch, the one Sawi swapped for my plastic sponge bag. This would serve to remind me that my journey was a strictly personal trip; I was checking up on old friends, nothing more.

That said, I was going somewhere unusually remote and I should see if someone might lend me a video camera to record anything of interest. October Films, a TV production company in North London, very generously offered, so I went along with my big green rucksack to see what they'd let me have.

'You can also take along a sat phone, if you like,' said Martin, the tech man, sorting through the cables. 'I've got a spare from Lev,' he said, naming a prominent, well-loved adventurer. We eyed the lovely phone as it sat on a shelf amid lithium batteries and adapter plugs. But no, I would not be tempted.

It only remained to have a final quick chat with Matt and Jos, who'd be the producers looking at any material I had time to film.

'Probably the Yaifo are these days more tech savvy than you, Benedict,' Matt said. He was an intelligent, good-natured bloke in black-rimmed glasses who tended to look down at his empty notepad when I talked but took everything in.

I reassured Matt that I was not, despite what was generally thought, someone stuck in the past.

'Just a little bit?' offered Jos. He had a bottle of wine and a birthday card on his desk, wore a chequered shirt and had a cheery face, with eyes that were boyish but at times very exacting.

'With every aspect of our lives so interconnected,' I said, suddenly forced to justify this short trip and my life's work on a more intellectual footing, 'perhaps we should disconnect ourselves more than ever. Few people these days ever stand back.'

'I get it,' said Matt, and thoughtfully twiddled with his biro. 'An interesting take: we live in an echo chamber, just passing around the same information. We are not owners of phones but owned *by* phones . . .'

'Also,' I said, 'we've forgotten the importance of learning to take risks.'

Matt nodded. Twisted that biro. 'Children not allowed to play conkers, et cetera . . .'

'Wait,' Jos said, suddenly sitting up. 'This expedition is risky? Just how risky?'

'I'm just saying that letting go, accepting the need to take risks, is more important now than ever.'

'Hold your horses . . .'

But Matt's mobile rang. Jos checked his phone too, and said he had to dash to a meeting – and so onward with my green rucksack, together with a letter absolving the TV company of all responsibility.

On the eve of my departure, I went for supper with Frank in Wandsworth. We talked of the film shoot, two years ago now, and the time we'd spent in our homemade shelter – a rough few hours endured prostrate on wet tree ferns, shivering as the cold set in. Strange that for both of us such a perishing night was the best night of all.

We raised a glass, ate our pizza and Frank said, 'On a more serious note, please tell me you're breaking the habit of a lifetime and taking a phone with you.'

'No,' I said. *Why would I do a thing like that?*

'Just tuck it into the bottom of your rucksack. No one need know.'

But I will know, I thought.

This led to a conversation about Charles Blackmore's army friend Henry Worsley, an exact contemporary who had died aged fifty-five not so long before, having almost completed a lone trek across the breadth of Antarctica. With nine hundred miles behind him, and only a hundred and twenty-six to go, utterly exhausted, he at last called in assistance – 'I've shot my bolt.' He was flown to Punta Arenas in southern Chile, and in hospital was diagnosed with peritonitis.* I pointed out that Worsley did take a sat phone – but sadly died anyway.

Aside from the issue of whether I should chuck in my conviction – that it was right to place my entire objective and well-being in the hands

---

* Later, after what transpired in PNG, Blackmore wondered if – like himself at times, and conceivably like Worsley in the Antarctic – I entered what he termed 'the death zone', a state when it begins to seem heroic and fitting to die rather than 'surrender' and get yourself home.

of my hosts – at this late stage in my career, or whether an adventurer was much of an adventurer if they felt they had to call home when in trouble, the problem was that many forms of danger – a burst ulcer, a flash flood, an attack by a bear – came quickly. 'Taking a phone might even be dangerous!' I said to Frank. 'Phones give people a false sense of security.'

We agreed to change the subject; we shouldn't end on this note. We shared a crème caramel, had a final glass of pinot grigio and then Frank wished me luck. 'See you on the other side!'

That was the last of my goodbyes, and now I was walking across Brook Green with a thirty-kilo rucksack, feeling better because I was at last free from the weight of everyone else's anxieties. 'Don't try to rescue me, please,' I wrote on the way to the airport to those who were good enough to read my occasional posts on Twitter. 'Where I'm going in PNG you won't ever find me.' And I took comfort as I boarded a plane from a few supportive words sent by a complete stranger. 'Once you are out there,' she wrote, 'you'll be safe.'

———

On 25 October 2017, I was once more back in Wewak, where a couple of years before I'd launched out with the film crew, and long before that had hung around with my *wantoks*.

My cut-price room at the surprisingly expansive 'Boutique Hotel' was as stuffy and damp as the rainforest – which was the way I needed it to be. The helicopter flight had been confirmed for early the next morning and around me were stacked rations to feed six men for twenty days.

I did my daily press-ups and I paced the room. And I began to have grave doubts about the wisdom of what I was doing. Soon, I was thinking of like-minded souls who had lost their lives through the years: Rod Coatman, who'd drowned with Tilman, but also the mountaineers whose crevasse fields, arêtes and pitches I'd grown up reading about – Peter Boardman, Joe Tasker, Mick Burke. Later, Alison Hargreaves, but also, in the Bornean forests, Bruno Manser, the Swiss shepherd who devoted himself to the beleaguered Penan nomads. He had handed me his simple name card and not long after vanished into the interior forever.*

Why had I never experienced such trepidation when younger?

'It's because I'm a dad,' I told myself. I tried to weed them out – fears of others and fears of mine. Which were truer fears?

Adding to my sense of foreboding was the afternoon sky – clouds first racing through, striated and mauve, then solidly wedged together over the hills like a jagged block of slate. The oncoming storm was unwilling or unable to break.

I gave a last recharge to my camera batteries – there were wires snaking everywhere – then reviewed my supplies, purchased the previous day from the Chinese stores with the assistance of a suitably well-built taxi driver.

The storm did then break. The wind ripped through and the water spilled down. Droplets exploded on the Boutique Hotel's many roofs and adjoining fixtures; they ricocheted from expansive verandas. Lovely pipes spouted, fancy gutters spewed. Such was the deluge, and such my state of mind, I in all seriousness began contemplating whether God had sought fit to intervene: he wanted me spared. Or the opposite: he wanted the helicopter flight delayed so that I'd have fewer days to complete the trek and thus suffer more.

Onward into the night the rain drummed. Later, I woke to an image of Freddie looking up into my eyes.

'Why am I doing this?' I said to myself.

Then later, 'No, that's the wrong question. I should ask, what are the rest of us doing, that this act is seen as strange?'

---

* Manser travelled to Malaysia in 1984 and lived for the next six years with the Penan, organising blockades of the logging roads to protect the ecosystem being devastated with the active encouragement of the authorities. Reputedly a bounty was put on Manser's head and he disappeared in 2000. 'He thinks he is their saviour,' an official told me in Kuching at the time. 'Like a man born to be king. But these simple people wear no clothes! Like they are monkeys! They wander about eating nuts and rats!'

II

Thursday, 26 October. Due to re-emerge in eighteen days

From my diary:

> *Dawn at last. Overhead, the sky passive, drifting in whale-blue
> lumps. The air still wet. My excitement, my dread. My heightened
> awareness – a heightened sense of living. As if I'm already in danger.*
>
> *I went over to the drenched gate keeper – his cardboard hat is
> ruined. I asked his opinion. He thinks the clouds will lift.*
>
> *I must assume, then, that we are 'on'.*
>
> *Is this, then, the difference between a project going according to
> plan or not – someone feeling so alive and someone ending up dead? Is
> this what we want, those of us who seek something beyond home –
> unpredictability, the thrill of the roll of the dice? NB: 'To die will be
> an awfully big adventure.'**
>
> *I went to my room, made myself look at the pictures of my children.*

Whatever my eventual fate, this particular venture would begin incon-
gruously, with departure at the civilised time of seven fifteen and in a
complimentary hotel bus. The cook, hearing of my intentions, felt moved
to dish up extra portions of bacon and eggs.

---

* From *Peter Pan*. J.M. Barrie was a friend of 'Scott of the Antarctic' and the play first performed
in 1904, the year Robert Scott returned from his Discovery Expedition.

Despite the deep pools of water in the rutted track to the far side of the airport, the minivan driver too thought the helicopter would fly. 'Them pilots stick low, try to squeeze between the trees and the clouds.' Slowly, we made it to the back entrance. With each successfully negotiated pool, there was less and less to stop me.

At the gate, the security guard struggled with the chains that secured it. This obstacle, too, seemed like another chance for me to reconsider. But no, the guard invited us forward.

The pilot was in the hangar, circling his aircraft. He had close-cropped hair, and moved quietly and economically as he went about his job. Clean and efficient, I thought, trying to assess him. Like Tsogomoi, he's reserved but conscientious.

'Angus,' he said. 'It's my pleasure to be flying you from here today.'

'A Kiwi, am I right in saying?'

'Got it in one.'

I showed him my old yellow map, spreading it on a table beside the oil barrels and hand tools. 'When I was here, years ago, this is what pilots relied on.'

'Well,' he muttered wryly, 'I won't be using this.'

Angus placed a finger on the Central Range, portrayed in crinkled folds. 'I envy you that you had that time. I mean, a time when there was so much that was unknown. What map do you use nowadays?'

'Same one. Very small scale but the essentials are all there.'

'Right,' said Angus, smiling – then he stopped. He tipped back his baseball cap, revealing some more of his diffident face as he sought to assess me more carefully now.

'Don't worry. I'll be travelling with the Papuans – much more reliable than any map or GPS.'

'Not if you're flying a chopper, they're not.'

Angus weighed my eight white sacks, which were labelled in fluorescent tape with unambiguous instructions such as 'FOR THE MARCH: DAY-SNACKS ONLY' and 'FOR BISORIO: LEAVE BEHIND'.

The chopper was wheeled outside, its rotor blades neatly folded like a bird at rest.

I was found to be within my weight allowance, so Angus suggested one of his 'boys' filled my water containers. 'Better than anything they drink at Bisorio, I bet. Anyone expecting you there?'

'Nope. My first job is to track down someone called Michael. He's not one of life's little rays of sunshine when it comes to walking up mountains, to be honest – at least judging by the last time – but if he does agree to come along, he'll act as my GPS, as it were.'

'Let's hope he doesn't malfunction, then,' murmured Angus, and proceeded to the safety briefing.

Before long I was strapping myself in, and suddenly we were away – the helicopter's eerie vertical lift, then the shift forward – and now Angus's voice was in my headphones as he notified traffic control. Out along the runway, over the perimeter fence, and next we were thumping over the woods where lived the contingent of Niowra who had jobs, and where once I had been Wumbunavan.

'How are your nivs?'

'My what? Oh, my nerves. Well, I feel better now that we're on our way.'

There was not much more to say during the journey. I had my job to do, he had his.

I pored over the scenery that was visible through the windshield below, familiarising myself with what, from up here, looked abstract, no more than a rumpled carpet beneath our feet. I was painfully aware that soon I'd be deposited in the pile of that carpet – and needed to be ready for whatever lay within it.

That sago thatch is dark because everything's totally soaked down there, I reminded myself. *Those people looking up, walking on, scurrying about? They're just the sort of strangers you'll be depending on.*

Rough grasslands to the south gave way to trees, which gave way to the Sepik flood plains. Further south yet, the main channel wound on through, lazily slicing off corners – pitiless as it isolated whole communities with a twist here, immersed others with a tuck there. Beyond, the trees again accumulated, riding the lower undulating hills – and then up the Hunstein Range, then down. And here the cloud thickened to create a firm ceiling; we seemed to bump along its underside.

Below now, the village of Yembeyembe, where Frank was evacuated.

Not far to go. But even on higher ground there was water sparkling back up to us from between the palms, and when we did come upon the Korosameri it was twice the size of the river I remembered. A turbulent swathe of water drove onward over what were once tree crowded banks and expansive beaches; some houses appeared to be floating. Was this even Bisorio? We circled – once, twice. There was nowhere obvious to land. Angus pushed back his baseball cap; he craned forward. We angled to the left, then the right. Below us, men scattered one way, then back, as we looked for where we might set down. They ran about, they waved their arms, their hands, their shirts.

'Think they're directing us to that bit of muddy grass,' Angus said. 'Right by the waterside.'

We descended. Lower and lower, until we were hovering just over a surface that must have been submerged till an hour ago – every leaf blade was smeared with the river's sticky, putty-like grey trail.

'Not sure it'll bear our weight,' said Angus.

The people of Bisorio were gaping not at the helicopter skids as they tested the mud but through the windows, trying to work out who had come to be with them. They were clutching themselves as the downwash pressed what ramained of their American hand-me-downs. Some of the men gave a thumbs up. This might mean we were welcome, or mean we'd chosen a firm spot.

We settled to the ground, waited to see if we sank. When the chopper blades were hardly turning and the grass once again stood straight, I opened my door – and now felt the heat, heard the whistle of insects and the lapping of quick water. Scores of questioning eyes were on me and the humidity weighed heavily.

My arrival seemed too quick. *Matt and Jos were right*, I thought. *I'm not cut out for the modern era of explorers.* Two hours ago I was having a slap-up breakfast. Now I was with people who looked in shock, wondering if, despite everything, some unexpected good had come their way.

I stepped out. The crowd stepped back.

I waved, and they did not.

'*Nem bilong mi em* Benedict,' I explained to the only welcoming face. '*Mi save*,' the man said. I know.

Though he had big, friendly eyes his eyebrows steadily fell as I failed to recognise him. '*Nem bilong mi em* MICHAEL,' he sighed, with a tragic air.

He didn't look like Michael. In the last two years he had aged another ten.

I grabbed his hand anyway, Michael warmly grabbed mine, and then I stepped aside to assess things. I had to keep a clear head – decide right now if I needed to go back with Angus. Be brave enough to do that, if necessary. Close by, the river that I must cross: the current was fast, and where I had to disembark on the far side there was no bank: the water swirled chest height among the trees. However, the Korosameri was also fast receding – everywhere on the foreshore were pebbles painted with silt where they'd been recently discarded by the flow.

'Not impossible,' I decided. 'Might lose a day but if Michael does feel able to help, together we'll find a way.'

Behind me, Angus was already unloading stuff. The Bisorio men stood stock still, eyeing up my sacks while the women did the work, hoisting them into a pile.

'Best of luck, mate,' said Angus. Then we shook hands – and he suddenly adjusted his cap and murmured, half looking away, 'Wish I had the guts to do what you're doing . . .'

This was a generous thing to say – and, from someone who seemed by nature to be reserved, came a little unexpectedly. But before I could thank him, I found myself with the Bisorios being battered by flying vegetation and wind. And now the chopper was gone too – hacking north, startling a couple of ornate fruit-doves.

I turned to greet Michael properly, with a big hug. But he, like everyone here, was still watching where the helicopter was last seen, disturbing the palm fronds.

'So . . .' Michael said, finally. He raised his expansive eyebrows, letting them do the asking.

I was forced to explain, in front of the whole population as they wondered about my promising bags, what I hoped to accomplish here. The women giggled and looked away bashfully, and the infants scrambled up their legs to be safe.

'*Mi laik go long hap.*' I pointed tentatively up into the cloud seething on the other side of the river. '*Long ol pipel bilong Yaifo.*'

Michael nodded. 'And I'll of course gladly accompany you,' he said without hesitation – though he didn't look entirely glad as he stared in disbelief to where I'd pointed.

Frowning grimly at the prospect of what lay ahead – all over again, the dreadful slog into oblivion – he told the children to lend a hand carrying my things to his house. Along the squelching bank we went, everywhere evidence of the river that last night swept through: branches had impaled huts, leaves were enmeshed around the stilts that supported them. The Korosameri again had exerted itself – an unimaginably large and unrepentant snake, forcing on through whatever it pleased.

As we walked along, me thinking about the serpent river, how it had so easily wiped out all hope of anyone finally having their Paradise here, Michael alternately laughed and sighed. He was thinking back to when he was fifteen. The pride we had once shared in our achievement but also the ache of his thighs, the wear on his shoulders from the baggage. '*Long wai tru,*' he said. A very long way.

We reached a hut more elaborate than the rest. The sawn planks were suspiciously similar to those that once floored the houses of Bob and George. I dipped my big boots in a pail, to clean off the mud – just as everyone else dipped their feet. Up the delicate steps I went, breaking two on the way.

And anyone else from Bisorio who was not already in the hut now piled in behind me. I was surrounded by the whole lost flock; they could still believe that I might have brought something more than news of an imminent departure.

'They are hoping you are sent from God,' said Michael.

No, I said. Not from God.

To give myself time to adjust to my surroundings, I asked if someone might boil my pot of water in the living space beneath the house. I opened the sack labelled 'KITCHEN GEAR' and all eyes were on my hands as I untied the string. Even after Michael asked everyone to leave, there were thirty or forty Bisorios left. Two hundred others waited with their dogs around the fireside below us, yakking and coughing and spitting.

I indicated the thirty-kilo sack of rice and two bags that I'd brought along for the community – 'BISORIO ONLY', the label stated: 'MOS. NETS, BUSH KNIVES, FISH.' We went downstairs to dish them out.

I loathed this, my act of benevolence that told the congregation that Paradise did exist, just as the missionaries promised, but far away from here.

The contents were divided fairly. Seventeen bowls, seventeen families. Same with the tuna. Ten tins per family, a hundred and seventy tins in total. Once again, thanks to the white man, Bisorio had become a distribution centre, a repository for the less fortunate.

'It is from his church,' Michael explained, stretching the truth somewhat.* 'We receive this,' he told the crowd, 'in the name of Jesus.'

'Amen!' an old chap said enthusiastically, but the rest sat about with their swollen bellies and, without smiling, took whatever they were given.

Back upstairs, Michael and I passed around plastic mugs of tea and, to the accompaniment of the men laboriously expectorating and dogs snarling and copulating, we got to know each other again.

'So, is Tsogomoi somewhere nearby, by any chance?'

'*Nogat.*' Michael shook his head, then he lifted his eyes and pointed with them towards Malumata, downriver. 'With one new wife of his.'

To get some peace from onlookers, we pottered through the settlement; all those people who'd been milling below Michael's house now milled close behind us.

Among the trees I found a fragment of lino. No longer a floral luxuriant orange, it lay there drab, sodden and buckled, like every piece of leaf litter subjected to the flood. 'From George's kitchen floor,' said Michael. 'You remember? I used to clean this every morning with a bucket and cloth.'

We identified the spot where Michael used to do his kitchen duties; it was mid river.

'I did tell Bob that his houses were in the wrong place.'

'He wouldn't listen, even though you are a white man, like him?'

---

* The donation, in fact, owed itself to the generosity of an anonymous viewer of *Birds of Paradise: The Ultimate Quest* who was moved by the Bisorios' plight.

'Bob just smiled. I said I had a degree in environmental science, but he said he had the best adviser possible: the Lord God above.'

Parting the bushes, we came across George's bathtub, and next, held high in a tree up with the bird nests, a plastic cone to mark the runway.

And at last I told him. 'Michael, I'm afraid I'd like to head out as early as tomorrow, if I can.'

Michael issued an involuntary groan.

'And I'll need to recruit a few people . . .'

Even after all we'd long ago been through together, or because of it, Michael was expressionless for a moment. 'It's all right,' he then said, offering a slightly forlorn smile – but not yet quite resigned I felt, to a repeat of the long grind upward. 'If this is what you want, then we'll do what we can.'

The rest of the day we spent fruitlessly asking around for anyone who knew a way to the Wilifa river, also known as the Saromé, where the Yaifo were said to be. 'There are bush men like Gibson who might help,' said Michael, 'but without him, what can we do?'

I went to sleep at nightfall to save torch batteries – and to save my body, lest we did leave tomorrow. And in the dark the children sniffed and men coughed and the dogs copulated some more.

Friday, 27 October. Due to re-emerge in seventeen days

From my diary:

> *Before the sun was up, I went to check the state of the river. I found that the waters had continued to drop, exposing a coarse black sand. A stroke of good fortune – as if I'm being given permission to cross.*

I explored the newly exposed beach, looking for landing points on the far shore. The early light was pale, the air smelt good; all was quiet. The mist was burning off the trees – a mass of wet foliage simmering noisily, like a pot of liquid on the stove.

Not a sign of human presence over there, I thought. I watched the unmoving trees. Masterful, standing tall. Heap upon heap of boisterous vegetation, extending up, spilling down.

Michael was also up early. He sought me out, padding over the beach stones and through the loose pockets of ooze. Did I detect a limp?

Clutched in his hands was a book entitled *Satan*. I wondered if Michael saw my re-arrival into his life as a test of his faith.

'I can't find anyone to come with us,' he said. 'We wait two days, what do you think?'

What I thought was that the ill-starred community – or just Michael – was hoping something would happen in those two days to deflect me from my goal – and who could blame them?

'Everyone has gardening duties,' he explained. Michael was trying his utmost just for me, I could see that. If we ever did accomplish the journey I would, apart from any payment, owe him a massive debt of gratitude. Even so – for who in their right mind would actually relish the prospect of such a trek – he was hoping I'd change my mind, his eyes loitering now, trying to catch mine. 'Those who might come with us say they first need to stock up on food for their wives and children.'

'You've checked absolutely everyone?' I asked, feeling disappointed with myself. This was always the way: the inevitable tension between someone who arrives vulnerable and alone because they believe it is wrong to impose, but who has – notwithstanding their good intent, and notwithstanding their desire to collaborate on all matters – a hope like all explorers to pursue a cause that is their own, a dream that has its origins elsewhere.

'So,' Michael said, hoping to conclude the matter, 'everyone is busy.' He shrugged. '*Ol man I gat plenti wok tu mas*,' he repeated for further emphasis.

A large fly was circling. Noisily, aggressively, it spun about us. It simply wouldn't go away. *Utterly fixated*, I thought. *Like you, Benedict*.

'Michael, let's ask around together.'

Michael examined his legs. He seemed to be contemplating what they might, despite his best efforts, still have to undergo. 'Even if you find men, the floods may have washed away the rope bridge.'

Bridge? This was the first mention of any bridge.

I looked about for the obsessive fly; it seemed to have given up. *And I should give up too*, I thought. *I'm too old for this*. Then I located the fly – sparse bristles on its back, wings like a twist of cellophane. It was crouched possessively on the toe of my left boot, rubbing together its forelimbs as if planning what next.

'Benedik,' Michael said, a little sorrowful for me, 'you do not have some women and children who worry about you?'

He had a certain point, of course, and the last thing I should do was persuade anyone here to come with me against their will or better judgement but suddenly I loathed Bisorio Mission Station – this broken dream, this shattered promise. Everything and everyone here expressed hopelessness. The ground was grey, the skin was grey.

Michael and I walked back, slowly, across the beach. At his house, sharing out biscuits with a few onlookers around the fireside downstairs, I wondered what to do. 'Too hard,' Michael repeatedly tutted, pressing his victory home. '*Em i hat tu mas.*'

Someone called Teo then spoke up. He had a trim beard, a quiet, attentive manner, and, though so softly spoken, now proceeded to ruin everything for Michael.

'What's he been saying to you?' he said, addressing me directly in Tok Pisin. '*Mi laik go wantem yu!*' I want to go with you!

Another man joined in. He was called Thomas and wore a decorative line of circular tattoos along his brow. A third, Barnabus, said he wasn't even interested in how much I might want to pay him. '*Sapos yu baim mi liklik o bikpela, em orait tasol.*' All three insisted on coming – they wouldn't hear otherwise.

By now, Michael was stroking his calves as if to reassure them.

'We all want to go!' they exclaimed and then looked at Michael. 'You must tell him!'

Michael said nothing; for my sake too he had done what he could to dissuade me.

I said, 'Does anyone here even know the route? Let's sit and talk it through.'

'We do not know but we can try our best,' said Teo, speaking for everyone.

'This is the land of our fathers,' Thomas said. 'We want to see what they gave up.' With a single thin forefinger he described through the air a notional route we might take, crossing the river and then ascending through the ancestral lands.

Michael was not looking – but he saw that he must succumb to the inevitable. 'We go!' he exclaimed. He bounded forward and began ordering everyone about. '*Yumi skelim cargo na go hariap!*' We weigh the loads and leave immediately!

This was such a sudden turnaround, I wasn't sure I was quite ready. I took Michael aside and explained that I needed to look these men in the eye and let them know that I wanted them not as guides but friends. He too must not feel coerced by me or anyone else. If events turned out badly, and they might do, then we must sort things out ourselves. There wouldn't be another helicopter. 'And here's the main point, Michael: my life is no more valuable than yours.'

'*Em tru,*' Michael said, not believing for a second that his life was worth the same as mine.

Soon he was engaged in a conversation with two others wanting to come along. Michael was doing all the talking – and only after a while did I realise that the men were deaf or mute, or both.

I added their names to my list. 'Bee-o,' I wrote in my notebook, 'is thin-boned and I'm afraid won't manage if called to carry a double load in a crisis. Kwa-an stands more erect, but even so . . .' But then I thought of another who had what was conventionally termed a disability. I thought of the things Frank had felt able to achieve – and gone on to achieve. And I thought of how much harder it must be for each and anyone here in Bisorio. Yet these two latest volunteers had found a way to get by – or perhaps much more than that. Even just standing here, keen to depart, they showed pluck, they showed resolve.

'They are knowledgeable men,' Michael said, allocating them only fifteen kilos each to carry. '*Em save long plenti samting.*'

I invited the six men to sit with me and talk about what we were about to do. *It doesn't matter that they're a rag-tag bunch*, I said to myself. *Perhaps it's better that they are.* They weren't motivated by money; their hearts were in the right place.

We agreed that we'd take the circuitous route downriver to Michael's garden, see if we might come across Gibson, who was seen near there only two days ago.

We talked some more, my new acquaintances slurping copious amounts of tea – before passing the mugs on to everyone in Bisorio who wanted some too. And thus it was we used up a full day's ration of sugar – but this was all right, because it was their way, and we were in this together.

'*Yumi go nau*,' I said. Ready now.

———

The loads were lifted. Children stood back. We trooped along the waterfront to the mooring point. Wives walked behind, some lent a hand. It was nine thirty in the morning. The sun was already fierce.

Quickly, we loaded ourselves and bags into a dugout, and two boys pushed us off into the Korosameri, punting a short distance upriver, then deftly swinging the craft into the main current. The prow turned with the flow, finally nudging the shallows of the far side.

We were across. We had done nothing more than slip to the other bank of a local river, but this was the side of the river I'd thought I'd never visit again, and the simple act of stepping ashore seemed loaded with significance. This forest, with its gleaming leaves, I already knew was not always going to be pleasant. I wouldn't find Paradise here – not Eden, not the Elysian Fields where 'the happy souls reside'. This trek might even finish me off, deliver me to Hamlet's 'undiscovered country', the one from which no visitor returns. But I'd taken my fate back into my hands, and, just for now, to be once more on a testing journey, this felt like the most exhilarating thing in the world. I had not been daunted. I had not been denied. I was across the river and in a land that I'd once felt was beyond my reach, somehow forbidden me.

My companions too were excited as they cut lengths of bark for their head straps. As they fixed them to their loads, they peeked through the bottle-green light: the cicadas hissed, the tiger parrots cried out and a lone regent whistler watched.

We set off due east through trees that were, until this morning, half submerged. Stray leaves were stuck fast to tree trunks, elsewhere skewered by thorns. Mosses trailed from where they'd been wrenched and these hung heavily, water seeping from each as it might from a face flannel after someone had just pulled the plug out. Everywhere creatures were already restoring their fortunes. Anthills were being refashioned, nests and paths relaid. Frogs once more threatened and entreated each other, branches shed their loads. Order was again established, life resurgent, and we too felt part of the general endeavour.

Thus far, all was proceeding well. We tight-roped along roots through the sumps of creamy mud; we deviated around dams of washed-up trees, the palms with bracelets of spines.

But all this could end, and at any moment – and most likely for me, at the bottom of the innumerable creeks. 'Maybe this will be the one that kills me,' I'd say to myself as I teetered along another greasy trunk. My boots were already weighted by a kilo each of dough-like clay.

Two hours on, and we were experiencing the various practical aspects of having two deaf people with us; we couldn't call out for them as we threaded between the bushes and gullies, and only one of the men, Kwa-an, being able to speak but not hear, had the ability to call out to us when he fell behind.

Furthermore, when we regrouped, stopping for a smoke in the heat of the day, both men were several sentences behind as we discussed our options from here. Bee-o had to flap his hands to get attention. Kwa-an was always interrupting.

However, I could see that both men were well liked, and not just because they only ever showed good will. They were valued for their contribution, having learned to make themselves useful, as we all must do in life, but it seemed also for their unique perspective: Bee-o favoured a position on the edge of our group, where he could take an overview of things. He darted in, tapped a shoulder, pointed out a fat pigeon, an advancing leech.

As we contemplated what lay ahead, I wrote in my diary:

These men in whom I'm entrusting my life remain an unknown quantity. To be brutally frank – as I have to be – two of them are not physically the strongest men I've known, and Michael our 'leader' is

perhaps secretly nursing a foot injury. In short, I'd do well to shore up
this expedition; I'd feel a lot happier with Gibson alongside.

Before we moved on, I jotted my navigational notes, sketching our
position near the confluence of the river called the Yogapass. 'All water,
for now, drains north to the Korosameri, and thence east to the Sepik.
If I'm injured, this, for now, remains my way out.'

We ascended the west bank of the Yogapass, traversing pebbled side-
brooks, slipping between high, sleek trees and explosive sprays of
bamboo. Then a wade across to the far side, still tracking by my compass
south-south-east.

This left bank was composed of wide beaches laid with stones the size
of street cobbles and scattered with tree trunks dragged from upriver.
They lay about like monstrous ribs, stripped clean and bleached white.

Out in the open it was easier to watch Michael, who was still, it
seemed to me, favouring his left leg. Finally, I stopped him, and he owned
up to his injury: he'd put an axe through his foot about a month ago.

'Michael, you should have said!' And for his sake, I should have
properly checked before we left, I thought, angry with myself for letting
him come out of the goodness of his heart.

He nodded guiltily, and I reassured him that I'd take a proper look
later. For now, he tied the big toe with the electrical tape he'd been
carrying for the purpose and onward he soldiered.

By late afternoon we had reached his garden house, a location known
as Sintao-pa, and here, while everyone else was puffing away on their
cigarettes, I began the laborious process of removing what felt like my
armour: the unstrapping of my survival kit from my waist, the unlacing
of my boots, the unwinding of the crepe bandages – these to safeguard
my ankles – next the socks . . .

Leeches had to be picked off, all items wrung out – the socks ran red
with blood. Sometimes, Michael called out for young Gibson.

I wrote in my diary:

Michael sounds like a lonely dog howling. As the sun went down and
we ate up our rice and tinned fish, there was further discussion. The

bridge, Michael felt, was a couple of days away. Others chipped in with
their view and, now that everyone had had a moment to think on it,
they too agreed that the bridge is unlikely to have survived any storm.

So, we're retiring to sleep with the prospect of the journey ending in
a matter of days, not so far from this river with its dragonflies. (They
skate on its cold draught; the globe-eyes that hunt the crinkled fields of
water are a cerulean blue.)

'We do not know for sure the bridge is ruined,' said Michael just
now, consoling me as I hung my mosquito net. But for the first time on
our hike he looks quite chipper.

Saturday, 28 October. Due to re-emerge in sixteen days

Before the sun was on us, the first sweat bees were busily crawling over
my shirt. I drove them away and then recovered my still-damp footwear.
Ants were colonising my socks – placing guards, forming supply lines.

I treated Michael's toe while he looked with trepidation at the mountain base which we could now glimpse through the lower wreathes of
cloud. Once we were on the move, he again called out for Gibson, yelping
only half-heartedly now – the dog that's lost hope.

We crossed the river to the right, west bank, where we broached the
forest, and at a brook known as the Yei-pa prepared ourselves for
the climb. It was a pleasant spot, an enchanting loop of clear water
accompanied by a dappled shingle beach. Skinks warmed in the sunshine
and then a beautiful oriole appeared, its head and body a black and
burnished yellow. This was joined by smaller songbirds as we refreshed
ourselves and sorted our loads.

'They don't know humans,' Michael said, as the birds settled down as
if to enjoy our company, oblivious to the stones being catapulted at
them.

Then, a crash in the undergrowth. It might be a pig. But from out of
the shrubbery stepped someone whose face was radiant. He had a crown-
like design tattooed over the bridge of his nose, in his hand a shiny
object – it looked like a kitchen tap – and he was about to change
everything.

III

Seeing me, Gibson stopped to make himself presentable. He scrubbed his mouth with his forefinger, working away at the betel nut stains, then wiped both hands on his shorts. At our last encounter, in Bisorio, he had been sixteen years old and a little overwhelmed. Not any more.

He took a seat on the pebbles beside me, chattering to everyone, half in English, half in Tok Pisin. 'You are going to the Yaifo? Haha! My father used to tell me the story of his journey with you when I was a little boy – but only to scare me. Haha!' With his every movement, Gibson was disturbing the glade; a squad of lorikeets sailed off and, from further away, several Papuan king parrots, cackling fussily in pairs.

He handed the tap to Michael – 'From George's bath,' Michael observed, buffing the chrome with his grubby shirt.

I gave Gibson various pictures of his father, from the original trek – 'Nice!' he said. '*Papa bilong me!*' – then I produced the wristwatch I'd brought along for Tsogomoi as a present.

'Oh, for me?'

'No, for your dad.'

'But Tsogomoi is a bushman more than me, haha! He won't need this!' He strapped the watch on. 'It lights in the dark like the moon, or it does not?' He tucked it into his shirt, testing whether the dial was luminous.

'Your dad must have been even younger than you,' I said, and was about to express my appreciation for what he had done when Gibson turned his attention to the tap.

'Gen-u-in-e,' he said, struggling to read what was embossed on it. 'Del-ta Pro-duct, Indian-a-polis.' Gibson got to his feet and passed it around. Soon, everyone wanted a go, opening and closing it as the men of God had done. 'Hot' the enamel label proclaimed, but nothing it promised any more came out.

I had begun to see that Gibson was always on the move – and possibly always at play. Before he could slip away, back among the birds and geckos, I asked him whether he'd come along.

'You want me to walk up to the Yaifo like my mad dad?' He laughed some more – 'Haha!' – and delivered an affectionate slap to Michael, who grimaced, caught off balance.

It was clear, though, that he was proud of his father. He looked again at the pictures, caressing the image of his dad as he'd never seen him: quick and vigorous, still with the lustre of youth.

'I've told Benedik that the bridge has probably been swept clean away,' Michael said. 'And that really there isn't much point trying.'

'And I've told Michael that I still want to try,' I said.

Gibson sat down. Then stood up. He weighed each bag in turn. 'You must take more food! Last time you bought only little tinned fishes and rices and my father said he thought he was dying from starvation! Haha!'

He prodded my rucksack, inspected a bush knife blade. All the while I was waiting for him to tell me he'd come. I needed this maverick – possibly a liability – to save the day, as his father had done. All seven of us watched Gibson as he huffed and tutted around us, governed by his considerable life force.

'We go!' he said. '*Yu mas redim olgeta samting!*' Get everything together!

'The bridge . . .' began Michael.

'Benedik, you must wait here for me to catch some big fishes. And Michael, he must find some big sweet potatoes from his gardens.' Gibson again whacked him. 'Haha!'

With this, he was off. He gave Bee-o a friendly kick, mimed a spearing motion, and the two were gone. Then they were back again, carrying eight fish – the sort known as 'rubber mouth'. These he ordered us to shove onto sticks – 'Hey, you stupids! No more talk-talk, now you cook-cook!' – to roast over a fire.

By this time, however, our minds were elsewhere. A second storm was approaching – already the canopy leaves were stirring.

Quickly, it was agreed: Thomas, Teo and I should stay put, guarding the provisions against pigs, and everyone else go back to the garden house. All being well, the storm would quickly pass, and they'd return at first light with the extra sweet potatoes.

The first drops fell before we had rigged our shelter. Soon, the rain was whipping through the trees, initially tearing off dead leaves, next the live ones. We plaited palm fronds for walls, strung my tarpaulin as a roof, then dug troughs to divert the surfacewater as it quietly gathered itself and began to run towards us.

We had no option for now but watch the rain hammer everything around. The night came; water rebounded on us from the dark. We huddled together as the walls and roof sagged. Soon we couldn't gauge whether we were being drenched by water from the sky or rising from the creek.

'*Yu go silip,*' Thomas said. You sleep. The lightning snapped and flared. '*Mi bai singaut sapos tait wara I kam.*' I'll call out if the flood waters come.

Cross-legged, he began his vigil, listening as best he could for any surge of the main river. I didn't sleep either; I wanted to be ready to hang on as best I could to the trees. Through the whole night the three of us steered the water here and there, filling pots, emptying them a bit further off. Hour upon hour we waited for the Yogapass, wondering whether the river would take us away.

Sunday, 29 October: Due to re-emerge in fifteen days

Only at six in the morning did the rain stop. Shivering and soaked, as if from a long swim, we investigated our surroundings. The brook had become a deep, milky pond. The trees that yesterday had seemed ebullient, as if making a collective effort to beautify the dell, were this morning still dispensing huge showers of left-over raindrops, along with enraged black ants that bit us if they could. Near at hand we could hear the Yogapass – and that too sounded angry.

We waited by our battered shelter to see if the others in our party could cross over – and this they eventually did succeed in doing. But meanwhile every creature around us was quieted, every tree weighed down. And when the yellow oriole again took up its pretty whistling the bird no longer seemed such good company. 'His black head and clever raven eyes this morning have a sinister aspect,' I wrote gloomily in my diary as we slumped in our former haven – now a muddy sink. 'He's a hooded pitohui. His flesh is poisonous.' And so was washed away any remaining illusion that an Arcadia was to be found for any of us this side of the river.

There was a certain tragicomedy about our motley crew, as we headed out – from time to time Gibson whooping for no obvious reason, our former leader Michael padding along in disconsolate silence, and Barnabus, Teo or Thomas trying to get the attention of a deaf man behind and another one ahead, and me stopping to remove the empty packets of SNAX biscuits with which everyone else thought to signpost our trail.

But we were on the move again. I looked this way and that through the twilight understorey – daubed by the sopping leaves, licked at by day-flying moths and butterflies. On every side, untampered life: 'jewel beetle, elongate, its carapace glossy, even its superb antennae metallic', I jotted as we walked, 'a spider with four prominent, disquieting eyes, blue hairless legs', trying to be a reliable witness. Up the steep slope we zigzagged through the montane forest in the direction of Hanamata, Gibson's home, and saw not one sign of any path or the humans that had once frequented these parts. The trees here were able to spread as best they could, easing out their rivals, laying down their acids, fostering new insect alliances. They tolerated their weight of mosses, stretched out their limbs. For the taller members of the plant kingdom remained all-powerful here, and we did not. These trees competed, but they were also a community – social creatures which bickered but also supported each other, nurturing those of their ilk. They bequeathed shelter, genes, practices and useful networks to the next generation and together, through diversity, brought resilience, just as among human beings where we ruled.

Gibson traced the streams, keeping this one to the left, another to the right, as they gradually shrank to a trickle. Reaching each watershed, we would look out as best we could, judge where we were relative to the next valley in the drifting mist. I would take a couple of compass readings, scribble a few observations and then press on.

Clay turned to stone. We ducked under fallen trees, sliced through lianas. Stretching up, diving down. I was perspiring so much the leeches were abandoning me. Unable to tolerate the salt in my sweat, they retreated to where the mud was more thickly caked. The flies, on the other hand, seemed to smell the possibility of flesh wounds. Of the eight in our party, it was me they picked to follow.

This effort may be for nothing if the bridge is broken, I reminded myself, and redoubled my efforts to enjoy the red bark of a pencil cedar, the flight of a glider lizard. We, the living, were bottled here together, inhabiting the same mottled world, sharing and disputing it. A large sow marshalled her stripped piglets, or a cassowary sauntered through. And hanging everywhere the solitary and the more social wasps, with their dangling yellow legs.

Already, halfway through the day, I was finding it hard to be the vigilant person that I must be to keep safe. My scarf loosened – and, as if spotting the error, coral-red ants poured down my neck like links in an intricate chain. I slumped against a hollow stump, only for bees to burst out – swoosh, like an explosion from a barrel – and we hurled ourselves flat. This was the way of things out here: death came with a single slack act – you angered the bees and received their stings (renal failure). You loosened a dead branch and it snapped your ribs.

We crossed rivers – extended poles over, fashioned pontoons, or tied rattans round our waists to steady us. All along the way my companions reached into the trees, extracting solutions from them. 'The lack of what we would call common sense is a lack of connection with our world,' I said to myself, so tired now I wasn't sure if I was quoting myself or someone else.

In the afternoon, we came to the remnants of a garden – which looked much like the rest of the forest, but for the odd banana palm dwarfed by a wealth of biomass keener than ever to make headway towards the sky. Whatever man-made system had once been imposed here, it had long since succumbed to the natural order. The clearing had closed, what light had once been shed by humanity was gone, and other species in turn now sought to make their mark.

'Things were better in those days?' I asked Michael, as we poked around for any sign of houses.

'*Nogat,*' Michael said firmly. '*Olgeta manmeri kisim sik. Na ol poret. Ol nogat kaikai.*' Everyone at that time got sick. They were frightened of their enemies. They didn't have food.

Teo, Thomas and Barnabus were still looking here and there in vain, hacking at the thicket where once grass and their kin had lived. They shared Michael's dismal view of the past. 'That was a time of fighting,' said Teo. 'Up until the days of George and Bob, our people hid away from each other. And they grew hungry because they couldn't maintain large gardens. They were always being attacked. No one even slept.'

Even so, the three men mooched about, disappointed at not having found even one post or blackened fireplace rock. The forest had taken back all they once had.

'No one knows how it really was,' Gibson said, joining us. '*Yumi no save long trupla tok.*' We don't know for sure.

'Perhaps the Yaifo know,' I said.

Up, up, then down, down. And now the flies chasing after my body seemed to have become more acquisitive; they charged at each other, demarcating territory – as if the prize was within their grasp.

Sometimes I tried to reassure myself. 'It's not because you're old, Benedict! It was just as hard-going when you were young!' To look at him, Michael felt the same – just as thirty years ago when he had lumbered along in his wellingtons, plaintive eyebrows forever asking for another biscuit.

'We keep walking,' called Gibson from up ahead. 'Michael, though you have only short and stumpy legs you do not slow down.'

Only reaching the next ridge could we afford to think about the bridge that may or may not be ahead. We could hear the river two thousand feet below, the booming of tumultuous waves as they lifted to us through the competing calls of crickets and birds.

———

Nearer and nearer to that incessant sound of fast water. Soon, it was echoing off the tree trunks. Closer still, we caught sight of what must be a gorge – we could see a ribbon of bald rock and spray. However, we now came upon a newly erected shack. We smelt pig urine, spotted fresh footprints.

'Who are these people?' said Gibson to himself, as he examined the shelter. 'I do not know.'

In a stupor after the eight-hour march, I watched steam uncurl in loose tongues from the thatch.

Michael arrived. 'I think there is no bridge,' he said, sounding encouraged. Then he frowned, seeing the hut. 'But what is this doing here?'

We worked our way down through a glade of tree ferns, and here at last was a clear view: the river thumped violently through two black walls, pulsating and bellowing as it twisted, occasionally turning back on itself, transforming from white to olive green as it slowed.

'Oh!' said Gibson, ahead, having to speak up as the water seethed. 'I think that is Mawiva, my daddy's brother!'

Above the chasm was suspended a small figure. He wore a formal black jacket, as if he might later be going out for dinner, but was presently edging out along two cables of vine that had been laid side by side to where they were secured at the far bank. Over there, four or five helpers waved to acknowledge us, but only briefly; they were almost oblivious to everything but the task: passing materials among themselves without a word, as an advance party of safari ants might seek to rig a bivouac. Before us, above the cascading water, were being placed the first elements of a brand new bridge.

Mawiva too was working quickly. His face was a little more severe than his brother's, I felt, but at this distance it might have been Tsogomoi himself once again helping me. He looked in extreme danger, hanging in the wet updraught, paring a length of rattan with his teeth, then chewing it to be as malleable as rope. Unable to bend down without toppling, he was using his feet to string a series of loops from the two main strands. A couple of men on our side of the river slid out a bundle of poles, and these Mawiva strung from the loops, engaging them as one might spread curtain hooks along a rail.

Steadily, he knitted with his hands and feet, establishing a thoroughfare through the air, where an hour or two ago there had been none.

I retreated from the river, pondering on this extraordinary stroke of luck. *Michael weakens*, I thought to myself, *only for Gibson to step from the undergrowth. We come to an impassable gully, only to be presented with a bridge.* It would have been foolish to allow myself to think this journey was 'meant to be' – but even so, I could hardly believe my continuing good fortune.

We commandeered the new shack, which had yet to be discovered by cockroaches or any of the usual pests. I examined Michael's foot – bearing up very well, all considered – then began the laborious procedure of unfastening myself from my various bindings.

The bridge-builders joined us; they were chilled to the bone and sopping wet, and said little until we had fed them with our tinned fish and rice. Then I got out my photos, and Mawiva released brief flashes of a dazzling smile at the sight of his brother Tsogomoi from long ago.

However, suddenly there was also an urgent matter to address: Thomas, Barnabus and Teo – our three strongest men – wished to go home. 'We have seen our ancestral lands,' said Teo. 'And it is enough.'

This is a serious problem, was my first thought. *We might not be able to continue.*

'Samwell will come along in his place,' said Gibson, indicating the largest of the bridge-builders, who lay flat on his back stuffed with our rice. 'A loyal boy. He's a good one.'

'We'll need more than just him . . .'

'And also Alex.'

But Gibson didn't attempt to describe the qualities of Alex.

I noted in my diary:

A gentle soul, he listens to our conversation with head tilted. I see that he wears blue flipflops and carries a bag of knitting.

But – we have a way forward.

The force of the march will take its toll mainly on me. While Gibson leaps deftly along, I thump from rock to rock in my boots, or have to search out whatever is obscured in the mud that will bear my weight. Already there are aches in my joints. I must last another two weeks of brutal percussion; this will be a question of preserving myself as best I can through each hour.

Though the forest is wearing down everyone, already I'm shown to be the weakest – weaker than the deaf and dumb among us.

Monday, 30 October. Due to re-emerge in fourteen days

My diary reads:

We woke early, to assess the bridge. This glowed when played on by the early sun and was just slightly quivering. It looked like the trap of a giant predator.

The structure is not designed for someone of my height and weight – nor is it quite finished. Before I was a third of the way, it uttered a dire cracking sound. Then the whole thing began to swing. I had to endure the agonised face of Mawiva as he watched me edge along his precious creation. Reaching the far bank was only the first stage; from there I had to descend a makeshift pole that for now served to help our expedition down onto the far bank. Bee-o – because he is the lightest member of our group – lugged over our bags one at a time. Unable to hear us, or to communicate any of his doubts, he looked extremely uneasy. Behind, a dog howled, too scared to attempt the journey itself but for some reason nonetheless longing to tag along with us. Eventually, it was carried over, although rather ignominiously.

Then we were away, walking up through the tree ferns. Gibson's

pace was quickening as he sensed home, the isolated hilltop settlement
of Hanamata.

Behind Gibson came Samwell, who's someone of slow, methodical
movements. Then Alex: a shorter, lighter stride. His voice is high; he
carries his flipflops for the march, parts the leaves with delicacy, and
protects his red embroidered bag from the continuous threat of thorns.
If you walk too close behind him, all you ever smell of your
surroundings is his soap. Yet everyone accepts Alex, just as they do
Bee-o and Kwa-an. He is not married – but nor were there howls of
laughter when I asked.

Behind tramp Bee-o and Kwa-an in their world of silence and
finally, like Christian in The Pilgrim's Progress, *Michael trudges his*
way as if through the Slough of Despond, not the slightest interested
any more each time Gibson halts our progress to indicate another of
his relatives' plots of sweet potatoes. We are entering mist-forest now.
Beneath my boots, the hollow crunch of the pitcher plants –
Nepenthes spp., *each jug speckled like the breast of a song thrush.*

Then suddenly, up there in the clouds, the trees fell back to reveal
Hanamata – a scattering of huts straddling a grass-capped ridge.
Huddled figures, all female, gawped as we wheezed up the final rise.
They said nothing, just backed away, still shredding rods of sugarcane
with their teeth. Gibson laid his bag triumphantly on the ground. 'We
are home!'

Before I could do the same to mine, however, he dragged over a young
girl that he wanted me to meet. 'Surprise! This is Tsogomoi's daughter.'

Clad in a washed-out yellow shirt and skirt, which spread down her
small ribcage to her knees, the girl waited obediently to be inspected.

She was about ten years old, and though quite slender and with
remarkably placid eyes considering the present trying circumstances,
overall she looked fit and healthy. Only, her skin everywhere was coming
away, beset by worse than the usual fungus.

I shook her hand warmly, wanting her to know that it meant a lot to
meet any relative of her father. She smiled timorously, then we both
wondered what to do next.

The return to Kandengei. The *wanbanis*, or fellow initiates, ready to escort one of their number home after thirty years. Copyright © David Osborne

Preparing for impact: helped back into another time and place by Jonny Gowi. Copyright © David Osborne

Emma: three decades on, together with the picture she was safeguarding of me in my other existence, in a Hampshire 'drawing room' alongside the loved ones who had first launched me out.

The welcome home party – the austere and often dreaded *geigo*, or spirit house, behind.
Copyright © David Osborne

Doing whatever it takes. Renowned journalist Frank Gardner with film crew in the Lai-iba valley, while searching for the male King of Saxony bird of paradise (from left to right: Os, Steven, Ralph, Nick, Simon, Frank and Joseph our bird spotter).

The quest continues. In scenes at times strangely reminiscent of a by-gone age, Frank Gardner is carried onward through the upland grasses, the lowlander Felix at his side wearing a great many layers while Os, our trauma specialist, speeds along at the rear.

Return to Bisorio Mission – view of the Korosameri in flood as pilot Angus and I circle in the chopper, looking for a landing place.

On the far shore. Michael begins the ascent.

Gibson, son of Tsogomoi, displaying the watch meant for his father. Michael, less amused, visible behind.

Crossing Mawiva's hastily erected vine bridge. Bee-o was the lightest of us, so given the task of taking our baggage over, one piece at a time.

Gibson lowering our provisions down a temporary pole from the incomplete bridge.

Our three latest recruits resting on arrival at Bisocode – the higher slopes of the Central Range and an uncertain reception by the Yaifo still ahead.

Images from the original journey taken along to try to establish the fate of Korsai (photographed wearing decoration indoors) and the boy called Feefee (shown in all three pictures) – both likely to be dead.

Self-portrait with an old friend.

Lost and found: Korsai dancing one last time.

Nearing the ridge on the way out (Raimond with red cap in the shadows, Koi-ak-kei nearest, Ashkai with yellow necklace, Alex to the right).

'The creature inclined its head to observe our approach with interest . . .' Even today there were parts of the Papua New Guinea's Central Range rarely frequented by humans.

Safely delivered – so we thought. Samwell (furthest right) and the rest of our party resting on arrival at Fiyawena Mission airstrip, Jokei addressing them (third from left, windsock behind) while other converts look on.

Any suggestions? At the abandoned mission house, Fiyawena – Samwell (left) in his floppy hat, Alex reclining, Soli in the foreground, Latinai adjacent to the decorated alcove and stove. 'Jesus had compassion on them.'

'You can heal this lizard condition,' Gibson suggested. 'That will be very pleasant for her.'

I looked again at the child – her flaking sheets, her arms to her sides. Standing so speechless, pale and isolated before me in the mist, she appeared, to me in my depleted state, like something unearthly that had come down to be among us from the heavens.

'There's not much I can do for her,' I said, and then felt like someone denying his heritage as a European.

'Oh,' Gibson said, perplexed.

'So sorry.'

'Dear me,' Gibson said.

'We could try Canesten, I suppose? It's an anti-fungal.' But frankly not up to this job.

The girl was still awaiting her treatment. Pallid, silent and perfectly expressionless, she hovered, as I say, like something supernatural before me among her clouds.

There was no hiding it: Gibson was very disappointed in me. He said, looking hard into my eyes, 'But my daddy even gave her your name!'

'Named after me?'

The girl held her palms outstretched, ready to receive her cure.

'Yes, she is the new Benedik.'

IV

From my diary:

I extracted my tube of Canesten. Handed it to Gibson and he packed this new Benedik off, telling her to rub it all over. We retreated indoors, which meant being in the dark, because in the highlands there are no windows.

Harriet, Gibson's young wife, built up the central fire, saying not a word. The sapwood crackled and sparkled but mainly smoked. For a while, the six of us were too tired to do anything other than cough in the tar-laden air.

It's been a struggle even to get out my notebook.

I wonder about 'the ox-boned Samwell', as Gibson calls him. Much the largest and strongest of my companions, he's said to be a son of none other than Sawi, the Yaifo who gave me his woven pouch. However, Samwell shows not the slightest interest. Reading between the lines, his father's relationship with his mother lasted only the one brief encounter.

But what then DOES excite Samwell's interest? Can I trust him if it comes down to it? At first I took his quietly-amused smile for mockery; he's as wilful as me, and as obstinate too. Though I also like that about him.

And Alex. How resilient is that body that he handles so tenderly?

However, I must look to my feet – more important for getting out of here than my hands – and the rest of my falling-apart body.

On the trek I will only weaken. It's a question of the degree. I've checked my leech bites – circular, like the wounds made by a drill; my skin is torn here and there like my trousers.

LATER:
Have had my tea. Feel a bit restored.

Along with Gibson I've looked back downslope, traced our progress over ten or eleven watersheds, establishing where we deviated to avoid landslips, treefalls and so on.

As I write, the forest lies below me in blue sweeps, filaments of mist parting and closing. 'Unspoilt,' it's tempting to write.

Odd how this notion of the pristine fascinates. We seem to need to seek out those left in an 'original' condition, or anyway, earlier condition.*

Like Paradise, the perfect condition is a state we are condemned to search for but which we are destined never to regain. Not on earth, anyway.

I remember in Venice, speaking at the Arsenale at a conference boldly entitled 'Understanding Risk': my main contribution seemed to be my statement – not entirely accurate – that 'I'm not a risk-taker. I'm a challenge-taker.'

Risk, mortality. What we gain, as human beings, in return for surrendering the Garden of Eden. But the knowledge we were meant to receive by digesting the forbidden fruit – which was probably a pomegranate, not an apple – was INCOMPLETE. We'll always need to learn more.

---

* I had in mind, perhaps, the peculiar allure of those TV shows in which the companionable presenter is deposited as if alone in a remote community – though our welcoming hosts were always given the more picturesque designation 'tribe' – whose hunting prowess, animalistic rites, apparently weird foodstuffs and scanty garments or voluminous furs speak compellingly of exoticism and 'Otherness', a society that keeps company with the wild. In an era in which we have brought about so much environmental destruction, here is a chance for us to be among beautiful relics, a people sold to us as being in a more 'natural' state. It's a televisual take on the Noble Savage – the epithet often attributed to Rousseau, though he never used it.

Also speaking at the conference was Marcus du Sautoy, Prof. of Public Understanding of Science. Before all was lost in a fog of grappa, Marcus was erudite on the 'know-able', the 'unknown', and the perfect state. He likened the edge of my drinking glass to the seemingly perfect. Under a microscope, the rim was pitted and rutted. 'So, we face the possibility of knowing the form, but not necessarily of obtaining it.'

The rest was lost to me – so I had to buy his book, a dozen of which always seem to accompany him, like Os's red paramedic's kit, for people seeking assistance.

'Paradise,' he scrawled for me in the frontispiece. 'Benedict, I hope you find it.'

I've gone to bed early. It's seven p.m. – scarcely dark. Each night, I'm retiring earlier and earlier, I thought to myself as I rolled out the sleeping bag. As if I am no longer out here to explore our planet but in retreat from it.

As I lie here, occasionally an orange flame reveals the women as they extract another tobacco leaf, lay it onto the ashes with care – as one might a damp banknote till it's crisp – then roll it between thumb and forefinger to smoke. All the while they listen to the men, smiling knowingly at their idle chatter.

Alex also listens to the men as they natter on. (He has eased into the role of our washer-upper – and thankfully is economical with our bar of expedition soap.) 'On our first walk up the mountain Benedik used to do all the cooking,' Michael says, releasing another little moan. 'In those days he did all the washing up, too.'

Tuesday, 31 October. Due to re-emerge in thirteen days

So far, so good. Of the eighteen days I'd allowed for this journey, plenty, in theory, remained. We had an extra two in hand, and I could thank my lucky stars that, whatever the eventual cost, I had seen views that no one of my kind – aside from a younger version of me – had been permitted to see.

We were meant to depart at 'sun up' – we were always attempting this – but the two men who yesterday were happy to replace Bee-o and Kwa-an this morning thought better of it. Three young ladies having a quiet smoke outside were, to their exasperation, recruited by Gibson instead.

Having received the bad news, Namee and Nessie – also Seleena, aged eleven or twelve – remained in a conspiratorial huddle, cigarettes the size of Havana cigars clamped in their lips, arms crossed, determinedly looking away from us, as they blew out smoke and sneakily eyed the hideous loads.

'Anyway, it's better we arrive with some womens,' said Gibson. 'The Yaifo will be then less worrisome.'

Michael proceeded to tell me something he'd neglected to mention before: that there were rumours of fighting on the other side of the Central Range – and precisely where I was due to reappear in Hewa country, towards the mine at Porgera. The Yaifo might misunderstand our intentions.

'You do not worry!' Gibson said, weighing our bags with his usual enthusiasm. 'We will sing out to them or somethings.'

The women's blue tobacco clouds rose through the dank air and I asked if I might say goodbye to the girl called Benedik. It was as if I was leaving a fragment of myself behind.

But, like the early mist, she had vanished – and so I gave her gift, a kitchen knife, instead to Bee-o. I pressed it into his hands, so he understood this was for him alone. He examined the quality of the edge, then grinned as he slipped it into his bag.

As the others looked on, they showed no surprise or jealousy but nodded, satisfied. It was true, then, the meek did sometimes inherit the earth.

The ladies placed our sacks in their *bilum* bags, along with their sweet potatoes for the road.

'Jeeeeezus!' the first gasped as she lifted it.

The next tried. 'Shiiit!'

And the next. 'Fugging!'

In turn, they tried each other's loads, yelped and thumped them down.

To raise their morale, I offered each new carrier a packet of SNAX biscuits – and at this sudden upturn of events they each released a hiss of pleasure as they took theirs in turn – then, also in turn, kicked the dog as it moved in for its share.

The women led off promptly, heads bowed and issuing a trail of gasps, dirty sniggers and smoke.

Before following on, I took a deep breath. 'One slip,' as Os would have said, 'and it's game over.'

Bathed in streaming cloud, every surface now slippery, we traced the course of the higher streams upwards through increasingly twisted branches. The trees were cold to the touch. There were steep descents, then steep ascents. Then all over again – easing through blackwater mires, scurrying over algal screes. This was as much a mental task as a physical one. And never an indication from Gibson as to what might be required of us next – a four-hour climb, a ten-minute plummet, or just flopping over another crumpled, defeated-looking tree.

Finally, around three in the afternoon, we came to a slender rise that Gibson called Bisocode. We would stop here, staying overnight in the solitary shack that he and his father had once built.

At last the forest canopy was below us – the bulk of it – and we might again look out. The swiftlets burbled, a 'two leaf' tree glistened, each fresh shoot and twin blade weighed by the clinging mist. Samwell laid himself out on the grass, Alex reached for his knitting, and I flicked off my leeches. A fat bee lurched by, assisted by an uplifting breeze, and my friends and I had reason to feel pleased. At long last we were free of the noisy trees and all they housed.

Or so I thought. Then a big ant approached. Solitary, his abdomen hairy, he was sizing me up; he dabbed me with his soft mouth parts, sampling my damp skin. He seemed to take courage; like a lone alpinist, he made his way steadily towards the summit.

Wednesday, 1 November. Due to re-emerge in twelve days

At six thirty in the morning we were ready. Below us, the clouds puckered, responding to the earliest sun beams of the day. The mountain issued the sweet, melodic phrase of a ground robin, and a cascade of notes from what I liked to think was the sooty, tit-like bird that is known as the 'friendly fantail'.

My diary reads:

Michael was standing beside me as I was listening to the knots of birds chorusing. He was more interested in what else lay to the north – the moss-clad treetops dropping down and down to the Korosameri.

'Benedik, we have come a long, long way,' he said, with heavy meaning. 'The Yaifo are not so far off now . . .' He gestured despairingly towards yet higher slopes and next his expressive eyebrows rose to their most pitiful. Michael was asking permission to leave.

And, of course, he must. What an extraordinary act, to accompany me all this distance up here. I will never forget this.

I loaded Michael up with painkillers. He embraced me with his dry hands and, looking at Gibson, said he hoped we'd take care when approaching the Yaifo.

Gibson took this uncalled-for advice in good heart. He agreed that Sawi's son Samwell should go ahead, call out to the Yaifo and smooth over any fears they might have.

'No good they think we have come to fight!' he said, and this only made me worry more.

We turned to Samwell to ask his view. But he was in his customary pose – as if on a slab in the mortuary, although legs crossed at his hairy ankles. He lowered his hat further over his nose and grunted.

Michael and I hugged once more – and, as he looked on me a final time with his tragic eyes he gave the first suggestion of a genuinely warm and open smile. And this smile broadened as he turned to go. He knew he had done all he could for me. Off he went back down to Bisorio, reduced in weight but also height, like a bent old man as he pottered stiffly homeward. I'll be the same by the expedition's end.

The ladies led off, bent under their bags, but not before Gibson had added a cooking pot to each. They tottered up the first slope, issuing their blue smoke and curses, and I walked close behind.

Soon, the first flies joined me. By eight in the morning they were my constant companions. Sometimes I had to stop and close my eyes, as rivals moved in and squabbled.

Up and up. The trees about us were quieter now; the clouds worked through their branches, teased apart by twigs. Everything else was still – even the flies that had been fighting over me laid low. We walked on in silence, listening to the clanging pots and otherwise only our feet as they squelched, releasing squirts of tannin.

At last, a ridge. Far, far below us, we could hear another substantial watercourse, this one punching through the forest like something embroiled in a fight.

'The Yaifo are there,' Gibson said, pointing with his chin at the unbroken spread of a hundred million trees. 'Somewhere down on that Wilifa river.'

We studied the descent we must make through the loosely stacked mist, Gibson beside me on a tree stump, bouncing first on one foot, then the other. While we deliberated, looking out over the land of the Yaifo's, the three ladies faced inward in a circle, puffing away madly on their cigars.

'We must sing out, in case some of those Yaifo people are near. Like our daddies used to do.' Gibson turned expectantly to Samwell, who was gazing out alongside us, strapped tightly into my big green rucksack.

'Gibson,' came a measured voice from under the brim of Samwell's hat, 'you are a man who is very good at making a noise. YOU sing out.'

'Well, I will sing out,' said Gibson, huffily. 'But Samwell, you are too big like your hat, and also a son of Sawi, not me!'

Satisfied with his rebuke, Gibson opened his lungs. And the sound he made vibrated eerily all around us. I hadn't heard the like for thirty years and it felt not like a call to a settlement that was somewhere up ahead but a summoning of the past. 'Waak, wup, waak, wup!'

We waited as Gibson's voice carried over the valley to the far slope. Further and further his voice journeyed, dropping down and then down, then soaring up and up. But no answer.

'Actually, there is no point,' Samwell said with evident pleasure. 'The river is too loud for anyone to hear us.'

That river was a mile or two below here, I supposed. For a couple of hours, I slammed into trees, skated on roots, skidded down mud shoots. I seemed to be teetering on the brink; any moment I expected a bad decision to end everything.

By mid-afternoon, we had picked up an old trail. We decided to stick to it, and Gibson had just grandly announced that it was now time for Samwell to call out to the Yaifo when the heavens opened. We could hardly hear ourselves speak. Puddles formed; these then joined to create pools, and these united to cover the whole of the forest floor. We sloshed on, examining blazed trees, repeatedly losing the path. In our faces the wet leaves flapped, around our feet the groundwater spat.

The river itself we found to be concealed by tall trees that pitched over a rocky channel. Across this was strung a bridge that, from this distance, looked composed of old twine. For a while, pelted by the rain, we threaded the rickety structure with fresh strands of creeper.

Cautiously, one by one, we made it across. The sky cleared as we again followed the trail, and then all was quiet but for the thudding of the river below and the trees overhead draining.

Gibson had always been a joker – not any longer. Sometimes he looked to Samwell, but neither of them called out.

'We should announce our presence,' I said. 'Didn't we agree?'

'They will know we are coming,' Samwell murmured – and I remembered how it was before: the Yaifos ready for us with their bows and paint.

Gibson said, 'If they dance and sing about, you must stay very calm-some, Benedik. You do not talk to them either.'

'They will not understand Tok Pisin anyway, Gibson,' muttered Samwell under his breath.

The girls were placed at the back, Samwell at the front. We walked on, sticking closer together now. Loosened bark slammed to the floor. A pair of hornbills clattered through; there was the steam engine whoosh of their flight feathers, then silence again, only the soft padding of twelve feet as they picked out roots, and the dead thump of two boots.

All these years I had imagined it – the calling out, the answer back. But instead there was only the sound of the forest ridding itself of rain.

The ends of branches ran like taps; the larger, furled leaves filled like beakers, then, unbalancing, spilled.

We were near. There were footprints in the mud – dozens of them, showing as goblets of rainwater. Then, not much further along the path, the daylight broke through. We stood perfectly still.

Across the way lay a pig fence, erected like a stockade, and directly ahead was a crossing point, beneath a simple wooden arch.

We listened. Exchanged glances. There were none of the usual village sounds – the gentle cluck of foraging hens, toddlers singing dreamily as they scratched patterns in the clay.

We took the few steps nearer and from here we could see, silhouetted against the fusillade of light, one or two wooden shacks.

Gibson nodded to Samwell and gave his instructions clearly. '*Yu mas singaut nau.*'

Samwell did now sing out. He put both hands around his mouth, stretched out his throat. 'Ooo-wwhup! Whup! Whup!'

But no reply – not from the Yaifo, not from anyone.

Samwell led. One at a time we stepped through the archway and onto a rough sward. There we remained together in a cluster, the women at the rear, clinging as if to the forest.

'We wait,' said Gibson sharply. He was motionless now, and his eyes ahead, searching for clues: two substantial houses to the right, three or four now visible further up. But still not a child singing or wailing, not a hen pecking the dirt. And I'd never seen either this stillness or this tension in Gibson before.

First the silence. Next, the breaking of the silence.

From somewhere up ahead came an echo of another time. That echo was coming nearer – and quickly. Whoop, waap, whoop! Urgent, intense – it was just as I remembered it. Undiluted by the years, undissipated by anything or anyone that had come along since. At last, here it was, the voice that I'd hoped to hear again.

Whoop, wup, whoop! The assertive cries, the smash and disorderly clatter of arrows, the whack of bowstrings against palmwood. All this to the beat of feet on clay, hands brought to bear on drums.

'I think it's all right,' said Gibson, though he kept his eyes glued to the approaching mob – still a hundred paces away. 'The womens are coming out first. This way they show us they are not going to fight.'

A dissenting voice said, 'Unless they are tricking us, Gibson.'

The women were armed too. On their shoulders they wore mantles of ferns, but even at this distance the fronds barely concealed the knives each held upright before them in both hands. These vivacious characters – about ten of them – bounded towards us with their backs held erect, eyes front, jogging along with their armaments. The male contingent was fast coming up behind.

Thirty years ago, the Yaifo men had chosen to hide the women away: they might be about to lose their lands, their lives. Today, all this time on, though the outside world was still poised to do away with the community, it was surer of itself. What in the past had been a ritual of power, a display to signal strength, was today a celebration.

Forward they came – bows, arrows and knives to hand, limbs smeared in pig fat and soot. Across foreheads were strapped cowrie headbands, from noses curled pig bones. The canes around the men's waists rose and fell, and below these flapped clumps of leaves or trouser scraps. *If this is all I ever see of the Yaifo, then so be it*, I thought. *I can go home content.*

Not all the outfits of the greeting party were traditional. From one boy's head projected a large metal spring – it looked like a spare car part. Another wore a spiral of tin cans slung across his chest like a bandolier. Together the last survivors encircled us – jubilant, vindicated. I'd once thought these people had no future; I'd thought of them dead in a ditch. But they were not. The Yaifo danced on, giving expression to their triumph.

There was one old man among them, I saw. Every now and then he was having to have a little sit-down on the grass bank. Wheezing, his cheeks colourless, he wore the wire-like quills that had once projected from the nose of every male Yaifo.

He joined in the dance again, though already he was short of breath. And to think, this same man must have been one of those youths who, all those years ago, stared in fear or just stupefaction at me – their implausible boy visitor. Undoubtedly, back in 1987 I'd have shaken hands with him. But now he was getting on in years and he must know he would never again take part in this dance – the dance of his people which seemed to be the dance of life. I watched; it was almost unbearably poignant to see him make such a last effort.

Panting, he made his way again to the side. And only as I came up to him did I recognise his face. Though his body was weary, his slender hands looking heavy, laid down beside him with his arrows, he had the same timid eyes as ever, the same open-mouthed look of wonder. He reached for me with a thin hand.

'Benedik,' he said. He wouldn't let go. 'Benedik!' And again and again: 'Benedik! Beneediiiik! BENEEEEDIK!'

'This old fellow seems to know you,' Gibson commented, wryly.

'This is Korsai,' I said.

As yet, it was too much to take in fully. This small, bony man, partly encased in a spiral of rattan, had survived for three decades on a mountain wrapped in cloud, staying put on a diet of sweet potatoes, while while I – essentially just a bigger bony man – had used up my own years failing to find a meaningful solution while scampering among boulders, shales and snows around the whole globe.

'Korsai . . .' was all I could say. I kept on repeating his name, and Korsai kept repeating mine. These were the only words of each other's that we really understood – and they seemed to be enough. Once, we had shared an extraordinary moment in time; now, despite the different courses of our lives, we'd been permitted to meet again, and this was beyond expression in words.

Korsai hugged me tight and I hugged him back – trying not to squash the red quills protruding a foot's length from his face.

'Beeeenedik Beneeeedik!'

'Korsaai Koorsaaai!'

V

The dancing was done, and I went to acknowledge everyone in turn with a handshake. And each man, woman and child responded in the same way, loosely gripping my fingertips as a gentle indication of friendship. I understood that my name was known to every person here.

But of course I was anxious to know who else had lasted through the years. I scrutinised the faces around me. 'Could you ask if Feefee is alive, Gibson? He'd be about forty-five, now.'

'*Eba, eba!*' Yes, yes, came back the reply, amid lots of jumping up and down. 'He is alive! He is alive!'

Though not present, unfortunately. Feefee was at a second settlement, called Alibowan, which was a long day's walk away. But he too had made it through, and I smiled to myself, looking again at the healthy, smiling, decorated faces. Who would have thought?

The crowd was pressing in on Gibson, everyone talking at once. 'They are very overexcited! They wish to know who else you remember from that time.'

I searched out the photos from my first visit. There they were, the Yaifo of the old days, captured going about their lives in different moods – preoccupied, dumbfounded, nonchalant, gleeful – on deteriorating Kodak film, mostly at one-sixtieth of a second.

Those present today handed the images around, pressing them with their black fingernails. Tutting and sighing, they stroked the past, bringing it to life again – addressing these ghosts, calling them in.

Someone's uncle, someone's younger wife. The relatives were named, then handed back and forth, greeted again after so many years. Eeee! Oooh! Yeeee! Once more, the Yaifo might examine the faces of those who had been with them. Once more, they could be reunited with those lost to them.

I established who was living yet. Fenala, pictured as she was escorted from her hiding place, hands on her submissive head, tummy rounded with child, was also over at Alibowan. Keya-kei, shown patting the pig bladder with Feefee as a boy, was brought forward. These days middle-aged, and at present slightly breathless, he angled his head at his younger self. 'Is this me? The other is Feefee, but the second boy I do not know. Do I have the face of this child you show me?'

We turned to the photos again. 'Gibson, what about Feefee's other playmate, Ashkai. Just sometimes, perhaps a little sour-faced?' The camera had caught him well, hunched on a log, aged eight or nine, pointedly scowling.

'I think he is that strong fellow beside you.'

The Ashkai of today had an immensely powerful build and wore neatly tailored grass, front and back. A quill from a spiny anteater had been shoved through his beard, and a referee's whistle slung from his neck. A useful plastic cord, as well as two cane rings, was wound tight around his waist. He was scowling just as he always scowled.

We were escorted through a string of eight houses to a larger building at the end. Inside, Alex found a length of bark string and hung a saucepan over the central fireplace, but before I'd taken my boots off for our customary tea the entire community had joined us – so many people, hardly any daylight could squeeze through the doorway. Even the infants sat cross-legged, waiting to hear how it was when I first came among them.

I handed the first mug of tea to Korsai, who was seated beside Gibson in a prominent position by the hearth. 'You remember drinking this the last time?' I asked. 'You liked it, you said.'

Korsai took a brief, noisy sip and told Gibson that he remembered the drink, but this time it wasn't as sweet; there was something wrong with it.

The audience was patiently waiting. Korsai leant back; he slurped at the tea. He began.

'At that time, when I was strong and my eyes could look well, we hadn't seen white-skinned men. But we had heard about them! And our neighbours were leaving to be with them – we secretly watched as they left their gardens and their homes and they walked quietly down the mountain. Many of them were scared to go, especially the women and children. But we did not mind them going, because they were our enemies! Maybe now they wouldn't kill us any more – and maybe we wouldn't have to go and kill them!'

The story was being told with care as, back in the fourteenth century, a Viking might by the fireside repeat the words of a handed-down saga. As Gibson translated, Korsai checked that I was writing everything down. I did my best, slumped against a post, my feet crinkled from a day sealed in waterlogged bandages and socks. Stray leeches wandered off as the mud on my trousers dried.

'The day came when many machines were flying high over our heads. We told each other they were bees. "Bssssssss!"'

Korsai chuckled at himself. The other old-timers – every one of them younger than him – smiled, remembering and smoking, and occasionally adjusting the feathers and bones sticking out from them. But the children did not laugh at how things used to be; they remained deathly quiet. They hadn't seen a plane at close quarters either.

Korsai took up his story once more.

'We thought we had made a mistake not leaving the mountain and all would end badly for us. We were alone and many said that the world was coming to an end. More and more machines were buzzing through the air, sometimes quite near, and we thought strange people would come for us – maybe eat us.'

Even at the mention of cannibals, there wasn't a gasp or titter.

'And then one of them did come! On that day some men of ours shouted up to us from the lower gardens that we had then at the Yaifo river. They shouted a warning: far below there was a giant white-coloured man coming up. He was being led by Kaibayoo, who is also called Kai-pass.

'Hearing this, we were happy, because Kaibayoo was coming back to us from further along the valley and we hadn't known if he was still alive. But then we thought about the white man coming, and we were scared and confused. Maybe Kaibayoo was a prisoner of this giant.

'Yet Kaibayoo was bringing him nearer and nearer – quite slowly, and with another of our young men whose name I do not remember now.* We did not know what to do – finish the white man and have more problems on our head, or let him live and have more problems too. Also, we were not agreed. Sawi said the machines in the air were not bees but birds; we must prepare nests for them or they would be angry.

'Finally, it was decided that we should jump out on the giant white-skinned man – who is the same as this Benedik that you see here – and that is what we did. But I should say that there were two others with him, black-skinned, just like us, and later they spoke to us for him and told us not to be afraid. This is how it was in those days.'

The boys and girls gazed on me as I slouched against the post, trying hard to imagine me as any sort of threat.

Korsai had come to a stop. He was never a man of many words and these days he sometimes had that glassy-eyed look of those who have retired from the exertions of everyday life. 'But I am tired. Ask Benedik how it was at that time.'

I said, speaking through Gibson, 'That terrifying dance of yours seemed to go on forever! I told Tsogomoi to drop his bush knife, in case that's why you hadn't stopped trying to frighten us.'

Korsai said, 'But Tsogomoi didn't drop his knife! Yes. *Eba.* I remember this. So we grabbed it from him.'

'And still you didn't stop!'

'*Eba, eba!* Yes, yes! The dancing was going so well that we thought we'd dance a little more! And then we ended, because we saw you meant no harm and we felt sorry for you.'

'Korsai, we were so scared of you that day!'

Now the audience did laugh – first a snort from the adults, as Gibson translated, and then the youngsters, seeing that it was all right to do so.

---

* He was Akai, also known as Loweenō.

196

Here I was, a white man, one of those who were, for argument's sake, in control of everything beyond this tree-laden incline, and I'd been discovered to be a weakling. I felt the children's eyes on my feet – the skin on them soft and wet, every wrinkled surface like that of a snail – or watching as I searched for a new pencil. They examined the ungainly movements of a creature hampered in this house at every turn – the low-slung rafters, the bark floor that might break through at any moment.

'Well, we made friends,' Korsai said. 'Benedik, you learned our names, and how long we hope to live out our lives, and what we like to eat. And we learned from you what boots were and that your soap was not food. And then we worried about you, because you were alone and far from your own people, and Sawi said I must walk with you to a place where you would be safe. This was a difficult journey for me and Yado, especially because he was barely a man yet and also we had no path, and it was cold, so you, Benedik, lit many fires as we went along to warm our feet, because they were so suffering in the cold we thought they were dying. And that is how we came to cross the mountain for the first time, for our ancestors were from the river lands, far down below.'

Korsai again fell silent. The gaze of the audience moved from him to me, and back again. 'So. We have talked and it has been good,' Korsai said, looking at the door. He was concluding proceedings.

The Yaifo got to their feet and filed out – everyone except Korsai. When all was quiet, I dug around for the string pouch that Sawi had exchanged for my plastic washbag. Gently I extracted it from the water-proof sleeve in which it had been safeguarded every step of the way here, preserved from the humidity in silica gel.

'Oh!' Korsai said. He needed only the one glance. 'You have *that* still?' He examined the wing bone of the flying fox, the pin that served to secure its white, fibrous trim. 'Sawi said it was ancient and he would gladly give it to you. But then you offered him a new bag in exchange!'

———

Korsai led me to where I might bathe. Diligently trailing behind was his son, Noah, a boy of about eight years old who, like everyone of his age group, had gone to inordinate lengths to blacken his face for the greeting dance. He wore pieces of red and yellow cotton, the last remains of a shirt.

Father and son observed me from not far off as I washed, then escorted me back to where I might sit by the fire to warm. All the while Noah interrogated my face with his eyes, not saying a word as he pondered on all that had happened today – as well he might.

I wrote in my notebook:

Korsai is alone with me. 'Benedik! Benedik!' he keeps repeating, fondly looking in my direction. 'Korsai, Korsai!' I say back, and still these are the only words we can exchange and still that seems enough.

Just now, I presented Korsai with my extremely expensive bush knife – the one with hardened steel. He took it as if it was his anyway, nonchalantly slipping the blade inside the ring of cane that surrounds his midriff.

I got out my video camera to film us together – but he's only interested in seeing his own reflection in the lens. He's fascinated to look upon his glazed eyes, and also the two stripped plumes that extend from his aged face. The feathers of course remind me of the two that extend from the head of Frank's prize bird, his long-sought King of Saxony.

Thursday, 2 November. Due to re-emerge in eleven days

'Release', I found myself writing in my diary the next morning. Just that word: release. But from what – from not knowing? Release from my obligation to the Yaifo – or to my younger self?

A relief, certainly. By the close of that year, more rainforest than ever before had been felled within a twelve-month period.* But not here. Two-thirds of the way up a certain range on a certain island, a forest had endured.

---

* 'One football pitch of forest lost every second in 2017, data reveals' by Damian Carrington et al.

Left alone, mislaid, through the intervening years the Yaifo had become something mythical to me. I had held them steady in my mind's eye and now I needed to establish the truth of who they were.

I wrote in my diary:

The women are wary. Usually when Gibson asks them to talk, they scurry off to hack firewood or cook up a bowl of pandanus fruit. The older men, though, are keen to tell their stories. Se-ven comes along with his huge digging stick and dour face, and makes Gibson write the names of 'everyone here who is alive today because this has never been done, and perhaps will never be done'.

The girls listen in; they spit expertly into the fireside, with wooden tongs deftly flicking ash over whatever they've ejected. Sometimes a piglet, seeking out warmth, snuggles into the cooler ashes.

I discovered what I could.

'They are very decided, Benedik,' said Gibson, as he translated for a gathering of older men. 'They say that they are happier now than in the old days.'

I asked Gibson if they were unanimously agreed on this.

They nodded, they exclaimed, they spat into the fireplace with vigour. They gave all sorts of reasons, including their accommodation. Before, everyone used to crowd together in a single house, draw up the log ladder at night and prepare for the enemy.

'When you came up to see us, so long ago,' said Kalima, who was the nearest to Korsai in age, and wore a headband of small white glass beads, 'we were afraid not just of strangers but our friends!'

Se-ven concurred. 'We didn't eat well. We didn't even sleep well!'

'He speaks the truth,' said Korsai. 'We were awake all night, worrying about being killed. And then we didn't sleep because we went to kill others. This was tiring for us.'

'And then our neighbours left us . . .' said Kalima.

'And here we stayed,' said Korsai. 'And our gardens grew larger and yet larger, and our women and men were safe, and we were never again hungry. So, we were thankful to the white men who lived down there in Bisorio – because they took everyone else away!'

Gradually, over the course of that afternoon, my feet so bruised that I could only hobble now between their houses, the Yaifo filled me in. They were by no measure ignorant of the wider world; I'd seen as much on arrival – the foreign bits and pieces they wore, and also how they wore them. The meeting party had not been dressed as a cohesive team; they had no collective understanding of what it was to present themselves as a 'Yaifo'.

Were the Yaifo truly content? Thus far into my visit it would seem so – though they must have known that their population, although doubled to 150 individuals, more including Alibowan, could not be sustainable in the longer term.*

Friday, 3 November. Due to re-emerge in ten days

Another precious day passed, while we recovered ourselves and I learned what I could.

Of the eighteen days I had given myself to complete this journey safely, eight had already gone; I could spare only a couple more with the Yaifo.

I began to draw up a plan to trek to Alibowan, the second settlement – only for Gibson to caution me against going anywhere. There was still a major trek ahead of me – and among the Yaifo too there was talk of fighting on the other side of the Range.

'But has anyone actually died?'

'Oh, many!' said Ashkai.

However, no one knew for sure. And now something happened that distracted the entire community. A sudden fog descended and the talk everywhere was of three children from Alibowan who had not yet made their way home.

---

* Jakob Walters, the missionary at Niksek on the April river, estimated infant mortality at 60–70 per cent in the early to mid 1980s, when the mission was being established. 'Now they can even afford to laugh,' he told me – or a similar phrase. Up in the highlands, the infant mortality rate was considerably better. On my first visit I estimated it as more like one in ten or twelve. Nowadays, it would seem to be more like one in sixty or so.

The cloud settled over us, a disorientating cold nothingness that percolated through the village and above and below. All day, men were calling out into the whiteness – as if pleading with it. They called and called – and for so long that this became a terrible dirge, something of much deeper and darker significance, a haunting song not for the lost children but all lost souls.

VI

The mood of the settlement has further deteriorated. Everyone is sombre – thinking of the children or else dwelling on times gone.

My sudden appearance from out of the past seems to have conjured simply too many ghosts. Korsai too is staring into the void with his young son Noah; he's not calling for the mislaid years or mislaid children but seems to be considering the long passage of the future – which, sooner or later, lies for his son out somewhere in a world he's never seen. That future, too, seems to be lost in the fog.

And I am left alone with my thoughts.

When a sailor is 'lost at sea', that means they are drowned somewhere, like Rod Coatman and Tilman in the South Atlantic. When, on my first Amazon expedition, I was thought 'lost in the jungle', that simply meant that everyone else had lost all sense of where I was – although I knew my location precisely.

We are drawn to these tales of the lost. Our imaginations, set to – seeking to make out a pattern and thereby make sense of the void.

Our desire to reprise the tales of the missing was given exquisite free rein in the case of Percy Fawcett – a Lost Explorer searching for a Lost Kingdom. His central geographical achievement – adequate survey work on the Bolivian border – was of no interest to the public; but when he, a gentleman with mystical inclinations, disappeared for good, this was a different matter entirely. Fawcett had made repeated attempts to find

whatever it was he was looking for – and was known to have pored over
Manuscript 512 [in the National Library, Rio]. *I've seen it myself – a*
faded document dated 1753, describing purported discoveries by
Portuguese adventurers of an abandoned city. [Beyond a range of
crystalline peaks, somewhere thought to be in the Mato Grosso
towards Brazil's north-east, the remains lay half swallowed by jungle:
there were obelisks, there were gold coins, there were beardless youths
depicted crowned with laurels. At the very centre of a ruined town
square, the account went on, was a black column 'of extraordinary
height and size, and upon it was a statue of an average-sized man,
with one hand held upon his left haunch, and the right arm
extended, pointing with his forefinger to the North Pole.'*]

When Fawcett vanished looking for this wondrous place – or looking for
something, anyway – along with his son Jack and another inexperienced
younger man, Jack's friend Raleigh Rimell, here were all the ingredients of
the perfect mystery. 'You need have no fear of any failure.' But failure of
what? There was nothing much to go on. (Not even those memorable 'last
words' – from Exploration Fawcett, *the colourful rendition by surviving*
son Brian that not only served to glamorise further a not-very-important
escapade by a not-very-important explorer.) Failure that he might not find
the lost gold, the lost civilisation, the lost oil deposits? Fear that he would
die known only for doing a reasonable stint of surveying?

There were investigative expeditions – nineteen, when I last heard†
– and, from memory, reported sightings of a 'salt-and-pepper-bearded'
man by the roadside. We remain none the wiser. I've met a Brazilian
mystic who claims that Fawcett is to this day worshipped deep in the

---

* See *Explorations of the Highlands of Brazil* by Richard Francis Burton, 1869, the translations
by his ever-forbearing wife, Isabel.

† Including mine, though my aim was only to give voice to the Kalapalo, a people accused of
murdering him in the Upper Xingu. My one noteworthy discovery was that the bones proffered
by them were not those of 'their victim', Fawcett – as claimed by the distinguished pioneer and
advocate of indigenous peoples Orlando Villas Bôas – but shockingly belonged to an uncle of
Vajuvi, one of my Kalapalo informants. Villas Bôas had been trying to put an end to the never-
ending and intrusive speculation – see *The Bones of Colonel Fawcett*, my BBC 2 TV series. The
next expedition along employed my Brazilian guide and translator; the result was the highly
successful 2009 book *The Lost City of Z* by American David Grann, then a Hollywood film.

interior as a god. (I've been there and he isn't.) In summary: if Fawcett
wished for immortality, he need have no fear of any failure of that.

Lost Tribes, Lost Cities, Lost Explorers . . . While there is a blank
in our map of the cosmos, our hold on it is incomplete – and the odds
of our survival lessened. We are physically weak but brainy creatures
and things mysterious in space or time are an existential threat: we
must send out an explorer to make sense of them.

I contemplated these matters as the hours of my short stay ticked by.
And then I was given a quite different matter to think on.

I recorded the following in my notebook:

Gibson came over and sat with me. I knew him well enough to
understand he wanted to say something of importance – and he did just
that. 'I can't help you further,' he announced, eventually. He explained
that he must think of his baby son and what he called 'the Other
Benedik' – he means his niece, the young girl now completely smeared
with Canesten – and guide our three women carriers safely back too.

And this is absolutely fair enough. Only, it leaves me with only
Alex and Samwell. And though these days Alex is up and about,
scrubbing our clothes, seeing to my ripped black trousers with
vermillion cotton – Samwell looks done in. He is yellow-eyed, and
sleeps by day and night in a sheet, like a chrysalis.

Slowly, I have begun to accept that I won't see Feefee again – and
perhaps this is how it should be; something of the Yaifo ought to
remain beyond reach. In their elusiveness lies their strength.

Talk in the community has turned to my passage out of here. The
Yaifo are worried for me – just like the last time – and they heap
donations of sweet potatoes by the door. But no one wishes to help us
find a route over the Range.

'What about Ashkai?' Se-ven suggested. 'Benedict remembers him
as the play friend of Feefee, so he can go in his place. This is fair.'

'This is not fair at all,' said Kalima. 'The walk would mean the
death of him in place of Feefee!'

The Yaifo are afraid for three reasons, Gibson says. Afraid of the possible fighting, afraid of the cold up there, and afraid of getting lost like the children in the cloud. 'I would have taken you myself,' Korsai told me miserably. 'But like you I am an old man.'

I looked down at the legs that I have grown to know through the years – appendages that have got me out of (and into) so much trouble. I notice how slowly they are healing up. Even after four days' recuperation flies run up and down, exhilarated as they trace the cuts.

4 p.m. At last, after much further deliberation, Ashkai growled that he'd come along and bring a couple of youngsters too. More importantly, we will have Raimond, who is renowned for his trail-making.

I get the feeling the whole community is behind his decision: they're banking on Raimond getting me safely off their hands. Well, I think we'll be fine with him. He appears very solid in mind and body. Though he tends to mumble.

Sunday, 5 November. Due to re-emerge in eight days

Today being our final day, and needing to limber up for the rigours ahead, I climbed through the deciduous forest towards the white cliffs behind. Korsai tagged along with old Kalumbee, the two old-timers delicately picking their way through the saturated clay like long-legged birds.

At the top, my companions renewed their 'arse grass', deftly trimming it with a bush knife. Then Korsai plucked a yellow flower – a particularly lurid Compositae – and rammed this into his bed of twisted hair, which he wore gathered by a bark string. He tried the same with me but, my hair being straight, the two flowers slipped off. He examined them with surprise, as if it was their fault.

For quite a while, we rested side by side, surveying the view. A pretty bird – a spotted jewel-babbler, I thought – chimed its single note and bobbed its chestnut-capped head. Making himself more comfortable, Korsai extended one thin leg, then the other – the limbs that long ago with mine walked over the Central Range.

Below, the Yaifo settlement was visible just at present through the fog astride its ridge, positioned like a ground-nest. Otherwise, there was nothing but tree and low cloud for as far as the eye could see. Yet strangely the Yaifo that I remembered from long ago hadn't ever thought of themselves as remote. Rather, they had spoken as if they were the centre of the universe; in their mind, expanding to the distance were rings of lessening significance. There had been their hillside neighbours – hostile – and down in the lowlands the Sepik crocodile nations – even worse – and further off those who venerated not a thick-skinned reptile but the yam. Beyond the yam people there was to be encountered a limitless extent of water, and there dwelled the insipid people who were the dead.

But much was hearsay; news of the wider world had come with the cowrie shells gleaned from somewhere that lay in the outlying bounds of their knowledge.

The Yaifo, then, had had a pre-Copernican view of the cosmos: around them were arranged, like planets, forces of varying character and influence.

And in this they were exactly the same as us – for we all tend to view our lives as if we are at the centre of things. But how were those planets of their universe doing today? Judging by the evidence from Bisorio Mission Station (a flown-in god, his flown-off disciples) and Porgera Mine (theft, violence, ruination), all was not well out there. Despite the vast knowledge and power they had acquired, the white people hadn't changed in all these years. Still they promised, still they threatened. Today, as before, much in the outer galaxy would appear amiss.

Such, it is fair to say, represented the views of the weary old Yaifo men of my return visit, as conveyed through Gibson. But how had it come to this? It wasn't as if the Yaifo's origins were so very different from ours; the missionaries had painstakingly explained this.

'See, Korsai,' Bob had said – or words to this effect – 'we are all Sons of Adam. Forevermore we are made to till the soil, if you will, and you folks are on the self-same path of learning as us white men, but you got kinda . . . left behind.' Waylaid by your false god, this meant.

It was all very perplexing, Korsai had felt – and I could see why it just might be. Because at times, observed from my position out here, admittedly today through copious mist, it almost looked as if they, the Yaifo, who had maintained their dignity and their gardens and their right to chose, had fared better than everyone else.

—

Korsai and I descended the hill as silently as we had walked up. We were immensely sad, knowing that we'd never in our lives see each other again.

Kalumbee went ahead to pick a long grass stem for a new arrow, as he had done since childhood, and in the distance men could be heard still calling out over the valleys for the lost.

That last day, Loomakee insisted on cooking up a small pig on behalf of Feefee. 'This is what he would like best,' he said, bringing along Gibson to explain, 'had he known that you remembered him from when he was a boy. This meat will give you strength for the hard days ahead, because he cannot walk with you himself.'

And now came news that the missing children had arrived safely at Alibowan; there was a general sense of relief. All would work out for me too, it was felt.

The community assembled a final time, gathering beneath a shelter constructed in the middle of the settlement. We shared the pig and talked about the world at large.

'The young people want to know,' said Gibson, 'if they should stay or leave.'

I said this wasn't something I could decide for them.

'Yes, but they want to know. Should they go?'

'Go where?'

'They do not know.'

I considered the two options presented to them, Bisorio to the north, Porgera to the south. Neither were likely to work out well. I said, 'It's really not for me to decide.'

There was quiet. The audience thought it *was* for me to decide.

I asked Gibson to gently suggest they look to their leaders; I was just a guest.

There was a heated discussion. I caught the odd word. '*Wau*', meaning no. Or '*Biame*', I don't understand.

'So, would a road be good?'

'Really, I cannot decide for you.'

'What about a doctor and teacher? They sound good, but *are* they good?'

'Well . . .'

I wanted to help but couldn't. I hadn't come here to offer salvation or to transform lives. Nor was I in a position to do so.

'So, what is your final answer?' said Gibson.

After a mercilessly long and awkward pause, Korsai came to my rescue. He clambered slowly down the steps of his veranda and then softly issued the following announcement: 'Enough has been said. Benedik came a long way only to shake my hand. And this he has now done.'

Monday, 6 November. Due to re-emerge in seven days

'Benedik, I will worry about you on the road,' said Gibson, as I divided and calculated our remaining supplies. 'The girls, they are crying already.'

The three ladies did look miserable, but this might be the prospect of the walk back. I buckled on my survival kit and our small party headed into the cloud – accompanied by the usual doughty females on their way to outlying gardens. Reaching the top of a slimy clay hill, I called goodbye to Gibson; he called back. The wet forest beckoned, the crowds of well-wishers thinned, and Ashkai escorted me upslope as he had as a boy. Korsai, walking alongside with his son Noah, came as far as the beginning of the trees. He stopped and waved both hands at me – wiping the air rapidly, palms to me, as if cleaning a window. Gingerly he stalked his way back down the path, taking his son with him, and I watched as he disappeared – this time forever.

And thus the story of my visit to the Yaifo moved swiftly to its end – or so I believed. An expedition to trace a people, a friend, a lost piece of history, had proved an unlikely success. The fears shared by many had proved ungrounded. All would be fine.

True, I was by no means safe, but the task ahead was relatively straight-forward. Undertaking such a trek with the aid of indigenous people was, after all, meant to be my skill set. I was seasoned at this sort of thing. I must remain vigilant, that was all – and trust to myself and the people with me, as I'd always done.

VII

Throughout the day we made our way upwards. The mists came and went, the stooping trees creaked. Their leaves rubbed together; lichens flapped like sopping rags.

That evening I wrote:

We are on the move again and with this movement comes a greater sense that all will be well. Indeed, to survive we MUST now keep moving. There are few places to shelter before we descend to the Hewa [who are the Sepik-language people] *three or four days away. From there, it's several days further to the first road.*

Our group consists of Raimond, who's always somewhere ahead, chopping branches.

There is Alex, who stops to gesture prettily at the sky – he says it makes the rain go away. There is Samwell, whose face is now sallow; he's on my spare malaria tablets. There is Soli, a tireless lad of about sixteen with reddened hair that he encourages to spiral upwards. There is Ashkai, whacking irritably at any vegetation that comes near. His perennial discontentment – with existence in general, thankfully, not me – shows even in the way he attacks his own food, a sweet potato, which he keeps to hand, wrenching at it with his front teeth whenever we take a breather.

We also have Wag-ee, an endearing old codger who ornaments his hair with the fern tips he gathers; they hang as if growing from his short, greying locks, and as we walk he sings out of tune – in fact, SO OUT OF TUNE I wonder if he's lost his faculties; however, he's with us because he knows the Hewa, the people we need beyond the ridge.

Altogether stronger is Koi-ak-kei, a youth who wears only a bunch of leaves stuck in an army belt; finally, a boy called Kor-ma-be, who is only about seven, wears pieces of blue shorts and is trusted to carry our vital axe, which all day balances by itself on his narrow little shoulder.

LATER:

We have come to a hunting shack and will spend the night here. From now on, there'll be no path to speak of. But six days to go: we are on schedule.

It's very cold tonight – but that cold has drawn us together; we each hug the air that rises around the embers. We have cut firewood for when the worst of the chill sets in, placing it on a rack over the flames to dry. Down trickles its sap, sticky like blood.

Ashkai and Koi-ak-kei have begun a tune that I haven't heard in all these decades – stirring such powerful memories it's painful to listen. The song has the air of a plaintive hymn or lament. The words tell of the white cockatoo, the conifer, the waterfall, the betel nut palm, the bamboo; the men evoke the friendly elements of the forest, one by one, to be with us in the night.

But I feel better for the song; soon, all will be restful except for the snapping fire. Things might work out for the Yaifo, as well as for me. They may well hand over to a child called Noah, who like his namesake might save his family from the Great Flood that is surely coming.

Tuesday, 7 November. Due to re-emerge in six days

With the first hazy daylight, the first movement among us: arms were extended from blankets to stir the fire and raise some heat. As my companions each added their sweet potatoes to the embers I prepared my feet – dusting them, strapping them, booting them.

Then Raimond was away: he picked a line through the trees and raised his knife to the vines. Last in our party was Ashkai, who snatched a dozen leaves from the prize tobacco plant that someone once tended here, and rammed them inside his waistband before taking up his bag with a grunt.

I had to remind myself: few human eyes, if any, have looked on these particular tree stands we were now entering, each occupied by mini groves of liverworts and hornworts. I wanted to stop to sketch or photograph all I was seeing – the bryophytes, the leaf-hoppers, the cicadas like chips of bark, the hawkmoths, the crooked stone gullies and the giant striped leeches that stopped to smell the air – but I did not. Papua New Guinea is host to three thousand fern species, so it's thought, and almost that number of orchids – 2,800, though no one knows for sure.* But we were dangerously exposed out here – and felt it. I kept placing one foot in front of another, trying to savour what I could – the arena of a courting bird (fallen leaves cleared aside, a stack of select twigs readied like a bride price), the snake that was able to outpace us even in the cold.

I stumbled on, feeling the strength of my legs drain. After a few hours, I would lean against a tree just for the relief of its chilly moss pelt. Was it the river called Alibaiye where we strung a short bridge? I was hardly keeping up with my navigational notes either.

And onward, and higher. Up above me now, Ashkai chewed a ginger stem and hacked with his stunted knife, carving with his left hand a way through the silence – alongside Raimond, to his right. Half a day went by; Raimond checked a dry hole in a trunk – just the sort of snug retreat a cuscus might make home. As each man passed, they noted it for their return.

In the late afternoon, we were nearing the main crest. There was a hint of it, high up through the branches; it hung like a thicker curtain of mist.

'Potomuka,' Raimond announced proudly, and stepped aside to allow me to view the shelter that he had assembled from sheets of bark on a previous venture up here – judging by its crumpled state, quite a few years before. The rain began to fall – or perhaps it was just a wetter mist – and around us the dusk frogs clacked and the trees crouched.

---

* For latest research figures on this and other species, see for example the New Guinea Binatang Research Centre.

Once we had cut seven or eight fresh staves and re-erected what remained of the roof, then began the grim half-hour of building a fire among the sopping clouds. We extracted what standing deadwood we could, then split the branches to get at their dry insides. Raimond harboured the splinters, shaving off tinder with our axeblade. To block the wind we crouched in a circle, eyes smarting as we willed the first reluctant flames not to die.

When the fire did take – offering us no discernible heat for quite a long while – a five- or six-inch orange centipede rattled in and out of our bags, showing its venomous pincers.

Finally, we were warm enough to feel like talking to each other. The centipede had been discovered again and dispatched, the fire was crackling and Ashkai, undoing his bundle of tobacco leaves, positioned them on the hearth stones so that they could dry out with our feet. All that night he seemed to be turning the leaves as if baking cakes. And away from our fire the darkness spread around us and seemed interminable, floating in with the damp whenever the flames died down. We shivered together, clutching ourselves as we waited it out, longing for daylight.

Wednesday, 8 November. Due to re-emerge in five days

There was no dawn chorus. The sun barely showed itself. We stoked the fire some more, tried again to warm up our fingers and feet.

'It's not only me who is feeling more fragile,' I wrote. 'The Yaifo say their backs have stiffened up and yesterday their toes were so numb they kept stumbling.'

Time to be going – the binding of my ankles, the strapping on of sodden boots.

The trees became shorter and shorter. Bracket fungi swelled from decaying logs; mosses bulged from gaunt trunks. At last, after three hours' swimming through the heavens, we were on the ridge itself. We didn't celebrate our arrival up at the very top, or even linger – a driving wind swept over us and the view was only of more soaked trees. There were batches of toadstools poking into the dense grey air – these were otherworldly individuals which had delicate, glossy ball heads – but they too were shivering.

The descent was more dangerous. We must not slip – and yet, as ever, we must not grab any branch for support – the concealed biters and stingers, the spine-backed beetles that impale your hand. Down and down. Until the wet air was, we noticed, tepid in our lungs. Soon, our skin was beginning to dry out a little. The trees were taller, birds were nesting among them, insects ate through them. The sun once again shone; as we went by, creatures again looked upon us with large, enquiring eyes.

That evening, I wrote:

5 p.m. We are back down in the tropics – and again in dengue fever country. However, not far to go. A plunging brook that we've been chasing is now a formidable torrent called the Lai-fa. This too is reassuring – the river steadily making its way down, like us.

We'll sleep here, in the underhang a crumpled grey-brown cliff – like a huge ear as it listens to the fizzing trees.

We are on schedule – and the worst, in theory, behind us. We have picked up no injuries to speak of and we feel resurgent, like the yipping frogs in their nooks and crannies.

Ashkai – who is more ravenous even than the rest of us – despite all my protestations insisted we went to catch a tree kangaroo to augment our rations. This didn't take long. The creature inclined its head to observe our approach with interest – as if wishing to know what form of strange beings were about to consume him. Even at the very end, he hardly fought back.

That was an hour ago. Now, we are resting and the tree kangaroo is cooking in its juice. 'Tomorrow we will be with the Hewa,' Samwell said as we watched the tail begin to sizzle. 'They will know more.'

We all know he's referring to the rumours of fighting – and suddenly the prospect of being back among our own species is less comforting.

Also, I've caught my reflection in the camera lens, and – just as I always feared – at this stage I look VERY old. Will I ever again look the age I was when I started walking, only two or three weeks ago? I now see that I am being made to pay a price for this journey. It's only a question of how much.

VIII

Thursday, 9 November. Due to re-emerge in four days

Even before we came upon the first humans, there was something a little odd about the day. As we pursued the Lag-a river, negotiating the boulders, leaping through the spray, the ground began to shake. The stones under our feet shifted wildly and the cicadas went quiet as their trees juddered.

'What is it?' asked Wag-ee, the older chap who was accompanying us.

'Porgera Mine,' said Samwell, darkly. 'They are blowing things up!'

I said, 'Still too far away, I would think. More likely an earth tremor.'* We waited among the rocks for further shocks, wondering, like the disconcerted lifeforms around us, whether to move or stay put. Out there among the silenced trees, the whole mountain seemed to be expressing its unease.

But now we were approaching habitation. Thankful, exhausted, we made what we believed was our final ascent. We had reached Minini, which appeared to be composed of only five houses constructed from thick planks, the whole hamlet contained within

---

* Indeed it was an earth tremor. This heralded one much more substantial, which took place a few months later, on 26 February the following year. The epicentre of the second, 7.5-magnitude quake was 90 km south of Porgera and it was reportedly the biggest earthquake in a hundred years. See 'Papua New Guinea Earthquake: Tens of Thousands Need Urgent Aid', BBC, 4 March 2018.

an intimidating boundary fence – to keep out pigs or people, or both. Each door was shut firmly, and kept that way with the help of several padlocks.

Wag-ee went forward. He called out, sounding not relieved that we had made it to the margins of the outside world but worried. At this, a dog barked like a maniac, peeling back its lips and showing its teeth – before joyfully running forward and frolicking with him.

However, there seemed to be no actual humans here.

'Gold,' Samwell said, lumbering up behind me. The one word was enough of an explanation.

We were contemplating what to do next when an ancient fellow wearing a girl's pink watch, a blouse and a wide-brimmed cricketer's hat rushed from his gardens. He told Wag-ee that more or less everyone had left a while ago. 'A while' seemed to mean a year or two.

Much chattering ensued, as the antique gent – who, like Wag-ee, didn't seem to be quite 'with it' – sought to establish who we were exactly. While the two talked on together, the Hewa man fed a pet cockatoo sweet potato and gawped at me, puzzled by my hair, my skin, my height. Everything I did he found humorous – the way I undid my survival kit, how I threw myself exhausted to the ground.

'He cannot believe we have come over the mountain,' explained Samwell, wearily. He leaned his pack against the hut and slowly slid himself down. 'Especially you.'

It was only early afternoon, and we might yet be on our way, but on and on the two old men nattered while the cockatoo walked about on its clumsy black toes, inspecting us.

Eventually, we learned only that the gentleman had never seen the mine at Porgera, just the river of a strange colour that gushed from it. Sometimes a helicopter came. It dipped in the water, as might a swallow taking a drink. No one knew what for. Perhaps it served no purpose at all.

They're hydrologists testing for mineral contaminants, I decided. They're assessing the sediment load.

A woman appeared in what looked like a nightie. She was fortyish and smallish. More noticeable, her eyes were stern, bordering on violent.

She marched over with her mind made up: someone must cut through the old idiots' jabber.

She addressed only me, telling me in broken Tok Pisin and English what the man wouldn't.

'You not go any more towards Porgera! The road is blocked at Kolombi. Too much fighting. The Hewas against the Paielas. The Paielas against everyone. Machine guns, homemade guns, too many killing! White mans, they want to kill him too!'

'I see,' I said. I tried to read her – this impressive woman with her forthright eyes. She talked on and on, listing robberies and mass rapes of girls. She called them 'line-ups'.

'My name is Benedict, by the way. And you are?'

'It doesn't matter what I am.'

But it did matter. This information might even save my life. A school-teacher, was she? She was supremely confident and articulate, well-versed in male ways and not particularly impressed by them.

'Your friends will be chopped up, like you. The gold is making the men into mad dogs.'

'And there's no way around?'

'You can try to walk a long way. Six, seven days and nights, if you got strong legs. You got strong legs? To Mount Kare direction, but stay on the right – the back-side of Porgera. There you can get the road and a truck or something.'

Having imparted her devasting news she marched back to her own hut.

When Samwell lugged himself over to her, hoping to glean more, she sank further down on her haunches and began aggressively muttering and pouting – warning him off with her blazing cigar.

I wrote the following in my field notebook:

We've decided to spend a night here – rest before going on for four hours to the bigger settlement, Owaiee. That will expend a further half day but I need to make an informed decision.

Another matter to note: according to the fellow who's wearing girls' clothes and an Australian cricketer's hat, there's a small goldmining camp at Owaiee, down by the river – with a radio transmitter and a cook who feeds the labourers. Sounds organised.

If true, this is important. The man told us – at inordinate length – how the rocks have to be readied for the helicopter, placed in the sacks provided. The helicopter comes every Saturday for these sacks – if there are any, because the children nab them. (Apparently, the sacks are excellent for carrying garden produce.) Down the helicopter comes, loads up the rocks and whisks them off.

Anyway, there's a phone number we can ring from there. 'This number begins with a six,' the man said. 'Definitely six. Or is it a nine?' And dialling this number we can talk to the Bossman direct. 'He's all white-coloured, like you! Just ask him to take you quickly away from here.'

So, we rest – all except Ashkai, who has to fend off the resentful cockatoo because he stole the remainder of its sweet potato.

Somehow, watching Ashkai, I know that he won't take a step further. Nor Koi-ak-kei, nor the boy. The three squat together, awaiting their meal. Just like Michael and Gibson before them, they have done their bit. So, supper will become a farewell feast. However, there's much on my mind: including the (small but increased) risk of contracting dengue fever, should I indeed be delayed down here in the mosquito's habitat.

6 p.m. I've retired early, taking comfort in the routine – hitching my mosquito net, folding my damp scarf in quarters for my pillow. There is no real cause for alarm. Such setbacks are to be expected – and indeed have been accounted for. Importantly, the most physically demanding elements of the journey are over with. I know my body of old – how it stresses and how it strains. How quickly or slowly it recovers. I should last out – and at Owaiee can phone home to explain I'll be delayed. As for the threat of dengue, even if I do go down with it, the outside world is near at hand. Having said that, as usual it's not remote people I need worry about, it's problems brought by my own kind.

Raimond, Soli, Alex and Samwell will stay with me, I'm certain. All along they were to be my friends, not 'guides' – and so they are.

The alleged weekly helicopter – that too offers possibilities . . .
   But now I see that I'm not so different from the Yaifo as I first knew
them. Tomorrow I'll be much like Korsai was, many years ago, looking to
the skies, wondering if the goldmining presents a threat or my salvation.

Friday, 10 November. Due to re-emerge in three days

By daybreak, Ashkai had already gone with the two younger Yaifo and I was pleased. They weren't going to be embroiled in whatever awaited the rest of us. Not far off now was Porgera, and already we had seen the early signs – the silence of the houses, the locks on doors.

Raimond, Soli, Samwell, Alex and I walked on. We kept up a fast pace through hot, forested hills and finally reached the outer gardens of Owaiee. There in the rolling distance we saw a river unlike any I've ever known. The waters of the Laigap ran across our view from the direction of Porgera and were a startling kidney red.

We descended further, from time to time hoping to glimpse the mine – or whatever wound in the planet was bleeding in this disconcerting way. But no sign, only more undulating slopes, the withering heat and, ever nearer, that river spurting like a corrupted vein.

There were some forty houses at Owaiee – but this didn't make it any less of a ghost town. Through the untended gardens we walked, passing by more and more padlocks. By now the sun was high and bleaching the colour out of every object we looked upon, adding to a sense of calamity.

At long last, an elderly man craned out of a doorway and beckoned us into the shade for a drink of water.

Indoors, he passed around a grubby cup and first Raimond then the rest of us considered whether we should risk it. While the old gentleman's granddaughter – or perhaps new wife – baked some peanuts for us, we cooled down. I asked if he knew the phone number – the vital one, beginning with a six or a nine.

'Ahh, the number,' the man replied, reassuring me with a smile. 'The number of the Bossman. Yes, either a nine. Or maybe a six. Peter will know. Peter will dial it for you. Maybe you'll get out today and your friends can go home!'

On this promising note we waited for the mysterious 'Peter'. Outside, a line of youths padded by, each with a shovel, pan and sieve. Then they padded back again, having heard the news that the settlement had visitors.

The five of them crowded into the hut and waited for something to happen. Their feet were still wet from the river, their necks red, radiating heat from the sun. Alex played with his flipflops; Raimond studied his axe; Samwell swallowed some more of my malaria tablets with a handful of nuts. I stared at my mug of water, willing my chlorine tablets to do their work. Soli, the youngster among us, was the only one of our group who looked capable of going much further.

Finally, along hurried a man in his fifties with a happy, shiny face. He was wearing pin-striped trousers – the lower half of a suit – and an office shirt that was crumpled and musky. It seemed to have been dug out especially for this occasion.

'I am Peter of the Seventh-day Adventists,' he said, proffering a set of brilliantly white teeth as he smiled. 'Are you too?'

Sadly not, I said.

For someone used to all those geologists from Porgera regularly dropping by, Peter – just like the five goldminers – seemed remarkably excited to set eyes on a foreigner. He wanted to know how I came to be here.

After having told our tale as best we could, and Raimond and Samwell having reassured them it was true, I cut to the chase. 'This chopper, Peter, the weekly one . . .'

Peter lost his cheery demeanour. 'Brother, you must listen to me.'

I noticed that the five goldminers were already listening to him. Indeed, all conversation stopped whenever Peter or I breathed a word.

There was no helicopter, Peter began. Not any regular one, anyway. There was no miners' camp, nor radio contact with the Bossman – because he didn't exist. And nor was there any outside contact with anyone. There was no phone signal because the aerial had been taken to pieces by children. They'd sold the lot for one hundred and forty-seven kina.

I was brought up to speed on the situation – a central feature of which was violence. A long-running dispute between the Hewa and the Paiela had been exacerbated over the years by social unrest associated with the operation at Porgera, but also more sporadic and localised gold finds. Weapons had become more sophisticated, and surges of anger – normally restricted to communal tit-for-tat disputes – had become more far-ranging and unpredictable. Much of this I had known long since, from my own research, but it would now seem that I had arrived at the time of one such flare-up. 'There was a killing again yesterday. Just the other side of the river.'

'But one man only this time,' said one of the miners.

'And a few women and two pigs,' said another.

I discussed various possible routes out of here: these entailed me heading not south across the Laigap as intended, but along the Range, west or east, to an airstrip. I'd request a flight, as I had done many times before.*

'But I have good news for you, Mr Benedik!' said Peter, a plan suddenly formulating in his head. 'Set off right away to Fiyawena Mission Station. Tomorrow the pastor is coming to baptise those who refused last time. You see? The Lord is watching over you too!'

'Are you sure the plane is coming?'

'The plane is for sure coming tomorrow morning. Or – if cloudy – he comes on Tuesday. But my associate has been praying for tomorrow. So, let's say tomorrow.'

Let's say Tuesday, I thought.

'So, you do not need to worry,' said Peter. 'Ask and the Lord will provide!'

'We can't be certain he has provided it yet,' I said, a bit uncharitably. I tipped a sachet of salt and sugar into my water to begin rehydrating myself and, as I did so, rolling up the emptied sachet to create a stirrer, noticed my hand was shaking. Perhaps just a touch of flu.

'Mr Benedik, you must have faith!'

'Yes,' I said, not entirely satisfied. 'Yes, I suppose I must.'

'Do not try to walk to Mount Kare with your tired men, just catch God's plane!'

---

* Usually with MAF, the Mission Aviation Fellowship, a Christian organisation of highly skilled pilots that serves mission outposts, 'because we're passionate about sharing Christ's love beyond where the road ends'. Such was their expertise, and willingness to serve regions that were not commercially viable, in remoter PNG obtaining transport this way was still standard practice.

'Hmm . . .' I double-checked that Fiyawena had a radio transmitter, so I might explain my delay to the outside world, if necessary.

'Oh, of course! This is only a small matter.'

Not to me, it isn't, I thought.

'THIS THEN IS THE SITUATION, as it stands,' I jotted in my notebook:

> *Fiyawena is, according to Peter, a day's walk 'at native speed'.*
>
> *My gut instinct is NOT to choose this option. Rather than walking out to Mount Kare with people I trust, I'd be putting my faith in a plane coming. This is all well and good in theory, but my own world has proved remarkably unreliable (c.f. Bisorio and Porgera) and trusting it is what I've successfully spent my working life NOT doing.*

I disobeyed my gut feeling. At Fiyawena, I already knew for certain there was an airstrip – and if no plane transpired, there must surely be a radio transmitter, just as Peter had said. The sensible alternative, walking out a safe way, would take seven days, and though I could easily find a means to phone from villages en route I would be exposed all that time to the risk of dengue fever – a low risk, but I was in no physical shape to take on an attack of such a potentially serious disease.

To reach Fiyawena for tomorrow, we would have to hurry on. We got to our feet, took a breath and raced off under the midday sun, led for a while by the goodly Peter, with his pearly teeth. At the river, a dozen youths were bent over the strange, livid water of the Laigap panning for gold.

'Come,' said Peter. 'They will try to waylay you.'

The men did indeed try. They shouted out whatever they thought would work. 'The chopper is coming! That man you are with is a liar! You must wait here! This is your best chance!' As I turned away, one of the men waved his shotgun contemptuously at me, holding it like a spear.

I refilled my water bottles at a side-stream and Peter wished me well, pointing up a near vertical path back into the forest and telling us to run if we wanted to catch the plane tomorrow.

The sun bore down and even under the cover of the trees there was little relief. After an hour I felt dizzy. I was having to pause repeatedly to catch my breath. *Something's wrong*, I thought. I slowed my pace. I drank more water. It did no good.

Still might be flu, I tried to reassure myself. *Or perhaps you're just too old now and packing up.*

To raise my blood-sugar level, I ripped open a packet of Milo, the chocolate drink, and swallowed it down like a dose of medicine.

We came upon a huntsman – or perhaps he was a robber – loitering on the path. It says something about my plight that even he, a disenchanted-looking character called Latinai, abandoned whatever he was up to and helped me over the worst of the slender poles that bridged gully after gully. I balanced with the aid of his shotgun – the stock held together by gaffer tape, the barrel a length of iron pipe. With him by my side, I staggered on, trying to believe in the plane that might take me out tomorrow.

People will say, 'He died doing what he loved,' I thought as I tramped along, flies pursuing me as if rotten meat, my brain increasingly gummed up and temples throbbing. *But I'm not loving this one bit.*

And then it was that the God in whom Peter so trusted chose to help me. The heavens opened. The rain tipped down and every leaf began dancing as the droplets struck. The air cooled, the flies departed.

I walked quickly on, squirting water with each step. I was being saved for something worse.

PART FOUR

PAYING THE FERRY MAN

I

Saturday, 11 November. Due to re-emerge in two days

Updating my notes in the early hours of the morning, I wrote, briefly:

Yesterday we came to a halt only at last light, having reached what is known as the Halfway Camp – unwisely positioned where a number of big trees are about to come down. Again, have a slight fever; I hope we are a lot more than halfway. I made the right choice?

We were gone long before daybreak, feeling our way through the diffuse dawn like water rats through the leaves. Sometimes, Latinai imitated the plane and tapped my watch. '*Yu hariap nau!*' You must hurry up!

Eventually, we descended – almost running, almost rolling – towards the mission station. Looking downslope through the forest now, I could see the end, a tidy segment of my world and all it represented – home, security, industrialisation – a stray section of my own post-modern culture marked with bollards. Viewed from among the greenery by someone sick, that small grass airstrip was very reassuring.

Samwell, Raimond, Soli and Alex were close behind and very soon I'd be saying an all-too-short farewell to them, these four people who had got me back to my people. Later, I would have a chat on the radio to Lenka and the children.

We kicked our way through a river, then up a steep bank, cutting footholds into the clay. At last we pelted through the garden plots and were at the runway of Fiyawena Mission Station.

'Praise be to the lamb of God!' exclaimed Latinai, dramatically uplifting his hands. He waited for his tip.

'Indeed,' I said, and gave him a bundle of small banknotes.

It was over. I smiled to see the windsock, signalling good order and intent from my own kind. I lay my bag down, waited for the residents of Fiyawena to appear. I began imagining conversations with the American evangelists. 'Oh, hello. My name is Benedict Allen . . .'

'Yes, we know exactly who you are,' would come the uneasy reply. 'You had rather a lot to say about our labours in Bisorio, did you not – in that TV programme about that character in the wheelchair?'

Or hopefully I might avoid that and get straight onto the plane.

One after another, members of our small expedition began assembling on the airstrip – Raimond, Soli . . .

The plane wouldn't have come yet – the cloud was only now parting – and we could afford to rest up on the cropped grass and begin saying a few goodbyes. Soon the journey would be behind me – and far too quickly, in some ways. I owed so much to so many people – and chiefly the Papuan people. Michael, who took me to Gibson, Gibson to Korsai, Korsai to Ashkai . . . I allowed myself again to think of those who were the focal point of the journey: Korsai, who was of the Yaifo past, and his boy Noah, who was of their future.

'You are a man of God?' yelled a swarthy local in wellington boots, approaching through the tall grass of the runway perimeter. He had a rough moustache and what sounded like worn-out vocal cords. He toyed with his bush knife as he strode, ready for what else might come out of the bushes.

'Not specifically,' I said.

'Well, I welcome you,' he said suspiciously.

'Thank you,' I said. 'We appreciate your welcome. Actually, we are here to catch the plane.'

'A plane is coming?' He was straining with his eyes, as if short-sighted – seeking to comprehend.

'Indeed it is!' I turned to Samwell, who was now plodding up behind. 'He doesn't seem to know about it . . .'

'The plane will come,' said Samwell, landing himself heavily on the runway. 'They are just out of date here.'

Alex arrived. Softly, he laid down his bag. He slipped on his flipflops. He breathed out contentedly. Time for a hard-earned rest.

A flock of children was creeping nearer, fingers in their mouths, and women too, straight from weeding their vegetable plots. Rich black soil was crumbling away from their hands; green plant juices marked their frocks.

'My name is Jokei,' the husky-voiced fellow said.

'And mine is Benedict. Might you very kindly introduce me to the missionaries here?' I got out my notebook and leafed through my list of contacts, pleased I could so readily come up with names so far off my intended route. 'Ah yes: Keith, Brian and, let's see, Scott.'

'They have gone away now.'

'Jonathan and Susan Kopf, then.'

'Gone away.'

'Or whoever it now is. And, if the plane is delayed, maybe someone might let me talk on the radio to Goroka or Hagen?'

Jokei said nothing. He cast another glance at the bushes, should anyone else come out.

I said, 'Er . . . you do have a radio, don't you?'

'Oh yes, we have a radio, of course.'

'Well, thank goodness for that,' I said. For a moment, Samwell and I chuckled together. 'We've walked a long way, as you can imagine!'

Jokei smiled, pleased that his visitors were happy. 'We will look after you, as best we can. We have some sweet potatoes most days, and bananas from time to time.'

'As I said, we're not staying, actually.'

'Ah yes,' said Jokei, and he looked at the empty sky. 'The plane that you talked about.'

Jokei escorted us to the mission buildings along a well-maintained path. A pet hornbill regarded us amiably from a fence post; trim hedges lined our way.

After so much dark forest, here was so much light – so much glory to God. A blue *Papilio* swallowtail looped through a bountiful maize crop; other butterfly wings flared dramatically in black and white as their owners settled to a chosen leaf. Ahead I spied a delightful orchard of avocados, lemons and oranges. 'Our beautiful patch, which Brian said is to remind us of the Garden of Eden,' explained Jokei.

Perhaps it was inevitable. Throughout my life I had pursued notions of Paradise, and even on this, my very last expedition, there seemed to be no getting away from it.

However, of Keith or Brian – or whoever was guardian of this praise-worthy acre of horticulture – there was no sign. We passed first one boarded-up mission house, then another and another. I began to get the picture. Fiyawena Mission Station was much like Bisorio – only, its abandonment was more recent.

'You had better stay the first night at Jonathan's house,' said Jokei, now escorting us along an avenue of mulberries. The hornbill manically pursued us in a series of bounds.

'Not necessary, though thank you anyway. As I said, a plane's due here.'

Jokei unlocked the front door of a robust, two-storey building armoured on all sides by weatherboards; towards the rear was a plastic water tub fed by a crafty system of gutters. Downstairs seemed to be a workshop, while upstairs must be the living quarters. These would afford the missionaries many splendid views – and, I suspected, much cherished privacy from the converts.

I was about to repeat again that I wouldn't be staying the night when up the path, advancing at full speed, ran a young Papuan with a handsome two-pronged beard. He was dressed in a dinner jacket.

'Seventh-day Adventist Church,' he said in English. 'I am Peter. Like the old one at Owaiee. You have met up with him?'

'Yes,' I said. 'We have. He told us there was going to be a plane.'

Peter smiled cheerfully. 'At ten o'clock! Precisely ten o'clock!'

'I must say,' I said, 'that comes as a relief! The thought of having to walk back three days, then to Mount Kare, skirting around any trouble at Porgera . . . Well, anyway, no need. Off in half an hour, then. Excellent.

But perhaps you can explain to Jokei here, because he seems to think we're staying quite a bit longer.'

'First things first,' said Peter, as Jokei relieved Samwell of my green rucksack and struggled with it like a decrepit bellboy up the stairs. 'May I say that I am glad you are come among us at Fiyawena.'

Peter shook hands with one and all, bestowing his congratulations. Expansively, with much walking about, he talked on in English – a language that only I spoke fluently – working his small audience as if a church congregation. 'It is God's plan above,' he said, 'that you are here. And if the plane does not arrive today—'

'Wait, wait. You said the plane *is* coming today. At precisely ten.'

'God willing, yes,' Peter said, touching the Bible cradled in his right arm.

'Good.'

'But it might be God's will that the plane comes on Tuesday.'

Already I had noticed that Peter had the habit of snapping his fingers to make a point. He did this again now, as he asked to be excused. He must ready himself for the arrival of the pastor's plane.

We ascended the stairs – *a fine bannister*, I thought, *tooled in a workshop far away* – and arrived in a space with chunky overly-varnished chairs arranged around a matching table on a dusty vinyl floor. To the left was a substantial stove with an elaborate surround of imported black slabs. To the right was a sofa, and above it three bookshelves – *Little House on the Prairie*, I noticed, *Adventures of Huckleberry Finn*, the Nancy Drew mysteries. Someone with a homely touch had painted blossoming roses around the hardboard alcoves. 'JESUS HAD COMPASSION ON THEM' read a little motif intertwined with the flowers. 'AN ANGEL IN EVERY ROOM' proclaimed another.

As Jokei looked on, the five of us pottered about, inspecting all that a very isolated and presumably very tight-knit American family had known and loved. Our voices, bare feet and boots sounded loud in the confined air, echoing off so many smooth, dry, manmade surfaces.

Adjoining the sitting room was a kitchen with an electric oven and sink. We examined the cupboards – already raided, though no one had wanted the garlic salt or Tabasco. Then to the storeroom, where the heights of two children, 'Micah' and 'Mikayla', had been marked off against a door frame. Their uneven progress was recorded in pencil, crayon and ballpoint through the years to adulthood. Micah had ended up at 5 feet 8 inches, on 1 October 2005.

I wondered when the house was last lived in. Two years ago? Two months ago? How long did it take wasps to unpick so much insulation from a ceiling?

'Jonathan and Susan went away at speed,' Jokei said, reading my thoughts. 'The Paielas cut up a man outside, where Micah played his basketball, and so all the white people left us. And many of us black people also left. Three hundred, maybe. Five hundred? They were troubled by the Paielas, so they went back into the trees. It's worse now.'

'But no more killing here?'

'Not so much here. A woman was also chopped down, but she was only a witch.'

'Even so . . .'

'It was very wrong of her,' Jokei stated firmly – and a bit harshly, I felt. 'She was spreading amongst us her measles.'*

Before I could enquire further, Samwell handed Jokei a pot of water to take away and heat up. 'We like to drink tea at this time of the day,' he said – for in this regard, he, like Jonny and Korsai before him, had become something of a Brit.

Alex found a broom. He swept the kitchen, wiped the grimy sink. Occasionally we looked up through the slat windows. But half an hour later there was still no sign of the plane, and while the others snoozed I rested my mug where a missionary called Jonathan must have done the same. I rocked in his too-thickly lacquered chair and thought about the wholesome books on the shelves – all of them well-thumbed. This simple life, the flowery motifs, this stove: this family wasn't just reading *Little House on the Prairie*, they were living the same nineteenth-century life.

Samwell, lounging on the sofa, opened an eye and said, 'The Adventist plane is not on time.'

---

* Jokei was probably referring to the recent killing of Misila, an ill-fated lady already saved by missionaries and police four months before. The 1971 Sorcery Act – which gave perpetrators of murder a reduced sentence if they believed the victim practised black magic – was repealed only in 2015.

I said, 'And now the clouds are rolling in.'

I noticed my hands were shaking again. And my forehead was soaking wet. *If no plane's coming, I should request one myself*, I thought. Otherwise, it'd be three days' walk back uphill to Minini – which was asking a lot of Samwell, or whoever might come with me. Also, it was asking a lot of me. From Minini it was, of course, another seven days to Mount Kare.

However, I fell asleep and now somehow it was mid-afternoon. Jokei had arrived with a balding dead cockerel. The rooster looked pitiful, hung like a broken old handbag from his arm. 'Twenty kina, please,' he said.

I paid up; an hour later, Peter from the Adventists arrived. He watched us chew through the bird.

'I have been praying for the plane to come,' he said, giving us an update. 'On Tuesday.'

'Couldn't you pray for it to come tomorrow?'

'Today is Saturday, which is the true Sabbath. It cannot come on Sunday, because that is the pilots' Sabbath. They take a day off on Monday, so that means Tuesday.'

Just then, Jokei came back again, bringing his tiny children so that they might see us tackling the leathery cockerel. They didn't understand English, but surely they did understand that Peter, as he talked on and on, was a man of faith unruffled by more immediate cares of the world. He trusted in the Lord, and I did not.

'And if it fails to come on Tuesday?'

'Then you talk to the missionaries at Yif-kei. They are good white peoples, like you. They will help.'

'I think I should establish radio contact with the MAF now. Or the airport in Hagen. Just to reassure my wife. Should be easy enough.'

'Benedik,' Peter said, addressing the entire room, 'through Jesus Christ all things are possible.'

'Absolutely. It is possible to talk on your radio, please?'

'It is not for us to understand the will of God, Benedik.'

'I think we're at cross-purposes. Can I use the radio?'

'Of course!' said Peter, and clicked his fingers. He calmly regarded us, his congregation. 'You have the parts?'

'No. No, I do not. Are you saying that you have a radio, but not a working radio?'

'Yes,' Peter said, triumphantly. 'Of course! A radio does not work when it is smashed up.'

'So, it's wait for your plane or go the whole way back?'

'The decision is yours. I cannot help any of you decide whether to trust to Jesus or not.'

The evangelist wished us all a peaceful night, reminding us we were in God's hands. We sprawled on the chairs or lay on the floor, appreciating the sudden tranquility. A small boy devotedly rocked Soli in his chair.

And that boy was soon eating my portion of chicken. I had no appetite. After so long out of doors I felt hidebound, held tight like the air within these four dead walls. We all did.

We pitched our mosquito nets between the chairs, as we might have in the forest, picking out convenient saplings. Jokei left us to sleep. He descended the stairway and, to be on the safe side, turned the key to lock us all in.

With that we were left alone in the dark, and personally I was left feeling not a bit comforted by the thought of everything being in God's hands, not ours.

I treated my worn-out feet, knowing that they were likely now to have to do more work. I wrote in my diary by torchlight:

> *But what the feet need is rest. The instep of both have been especially worked over by the leeches. The skin surface – a strange, liverish red – is patterned by a mass of small circles, like falling-away wall plaster subject to relentless drilling. I'm also running a temperature. My bones ache. Proper quaking too. Malaria or flu? A combination?*

All that I knew for certain that evening was that I was ill, that this would probably get worse, and that the day after tomorrow various people would notice I hadn't reappeared.

My best hope, as usual, lay with my companions, I felt. I must now begin to place them, and thereby myself, back in control.

II

Sunday, 12 November. Due to re-emerge in one day

From my diary:

> In twenty-four hours' time I am meant to reappear from the trees.
> Well, I have done just that already – only to find myslelf blocked by
> rampaging members of the Outside World.
>
> At daybreak, Jokei puckers his lips and blows. It's an
> extraordinary sight. He presses his wide mouth and moustache to a
> post horn – the sort of brass instrument you'd expect sounded from
> an eighteenth-century stagecoach rather than in the heart of New
> Guinea. Perhaps the missionaries thought the trumpeting suggested a
> company of angels.
>
> With half a dozen blasts around the Garden of Eden he announces
> the start of the morning church service, scaring the smaller dawn
> birds. And then it is that the dogs begin to howl . . .
>
> Peter, from the SDA Church, the other side of the landing strip,
> also has a brass horn. Not to be outdone, he too puckers his lips and
> blows. The birds stop calling there as well.
>
> And the dogs begin to howl, all over again.
>
> Meanwhile, Samwell and Alex, Soli and Raimond – the four men
> who are my best hope – sleep on.

10 a.m. I walked through the mission station, assessing my surroundings, seeing what resources are here. Then I attended the church service, slumped at the back with the only other attendant, Latinai. He left his homemade gun propped outside.

Through the service, sermonising only to us two strays, the preacher, Jokei, looked at me as he always does – with the compassion that I'm sure was once shown to him by the missionaries. What extraordinary confidence he has in the face of . . . everything. Even in a church that's empty, he yells to Jesus, giving him thanks and disturbing the dust.

After, he escorted me to his hut; Kaibum, his wife, brewed up water in my battered pot. NB Only ten tea bags and six sachets of coffee left.

While the water was boiling, a father lovingly applied an interesting grey paste to his child's leg sores. It turned out to be one of my sodden, discarded doxycycline capsules [for preventing and treating malaria].

Jokei handed over my pot and said he would ask around for sweet potatoes.

My existing food supplies must be allocated elsewhere: I have twelve kilos of rice, fifteen tins of fish – enough for six men for three days. If my companions are willing to head out on my behalf to find a radio – I have no doubt they are – it's important that each day they eat well and speed along.

But presently all four men are flat out on the living room floor. While three snore in unison, Samwell looks like he died some time ago. I'm so proud to have such friends. Soon they will respond: they will not pack up as a sat phone or GPS might pack up.

From time to time I find myself trying to recall those I've encountered through my life who, like me, seem to find it necessary to embark on journeys such as these – to put themselves deliberately, it would seem, in harm's way. Perhaps I need to justify the position I have got myself into, traipsing one last time into what we call the Middle of Nowhere. Perhaps, unable to address anyone from my own culture, I need to know that I'm not alone in my madness – if that is what this self-destructive urge is.

Wilfred Thesiger, I remember, at sundown viewing the plains of

Malalal, Kenya – still seeking things on the red skyline but now ageing fast. 'Is that a zebra, Benedict, or a mule? I don't seem to be able to see clearly out there these days. I don't think I could stand it, if I could not.'

Laurens Van der Post, alone with me among his bookshelves: 'The importance of the word. That is what compels me. I think words might be at the root of it all.'

Freya Stark, nattering in the New Map Room of the RGS about the horizon – a recurrent theme for her. 'This is nature's greatest wonder, I sometimes think – the far distance is like a lure to me.'

Jacques Cousteau, wearing his woolly red hat aboard the Calypso. 'All this talk that it is not possible to achieve such-and-such. All is possible for the human, if he burns with enough desire to go and do it.'

Thor Heyerdahl, aged around eighty at a Foyles Literary Luncheon. 'What more can I say about this? You are the type who understands this inside feeling – or you are not.'

Paddy Leigh Fermor, at home in Kardamyli, the Mani Peninsula. 'I was very young – and I was living. I don't think anything else mattered to me, whether I kipped the night in a haystack or a schloss.'

Whatever the question and whatever the cost to them, off they went, pounding the earth or being pounded by it.

I have been reviewing the photos of [my wife] Lenka and home – reaching out to where I belong, reminding myself of those who care. Come tomorrow, Lenka might expect the first news after three weeks – it's the date of my flight out of the highlands to POM [Port Moresby]. I won't be on it.

'I'm sure he's just stuck somewhere,' she will say to Natalya and Freddie. 'You know Daddy, he always finds a way out. He'll have made lots of friends in the jungle and he trusts them because they know a lot more than us. And that's what we like about the way Daddy does his exploring, isn't it? He'll be fine, just you see.' Nonetheless, he's never normally late.

Raimond is the first up. He has done his damnedest for me and now I must do my damnedest for him. I offer him the cherished pack of three (hotel) biscuits I've had tucked in my survival kit all this time, but he turns it down.

I notice that he is studying me, the woodman he is, as he might assess weakness in a tree. What does he see? The slowing sap. The rotted heartwood.

In the afternoon I pluck books from the shelves. Left Behind *by Tim LaHaye and Jerry B. Jenkins provides especially thought-provoking reading. This is a Christian horror story – set in the Last Days, when those few who are the true believers are instantly whisked to heaven at the time of the Rapture. Everyone else – e.g. pilotless passengers in planes – is left to their dismal end.*

I, too, will have a dismal end, at this rate. To prevent it, my friends will head out tomorrow in three different directions. Raimond and Alex will head east to Minini, then a bit further. Samwell will head west with Soli to Yipkei Mission. Both parties, and also a third party of two locals – names and details in my red field notebook – will do their best to find a radio transmitter or just a phone signal, and request a passing MAF aircraft. Standard procedure.

They will walk fast, with little to carry but the food I'm providing – and thus we shall together succeed in enacting my Plan B.

I will wait it out at Brian's 'Garden of Eden'. Sugarcane, guava, papaya, mango, avocado, orange, lemon . . . There are worse places to finish up . . .

Yet always the thought that somewhere near here lurks anger in the form of the dreaded Paielas. One of the mulberry trees has been ring-barked with an axe, to kill it off.

Monday, 13 November. Due to re-emerge today

My diary reads:

Raimond and Alex were the first to set out. We shook hands and Alex said, 'We do not wish to leave you, Benedik.' And I wished them luck and they wished me luck. They strode off into the trees, complete with axe and knitting.

Then Samwell, accompanied by Soli. Again, nothing much was said. 'Benedik, we will do our best,' mumbled Samwell. 'You know this.'

'I do know. Of course I know!' I thumped him in a matey way on the shoulder, and he looked into my face and smiled a small smile, before pulling down the rim of his floppy hat.

9 a.m.

Each morning (and evening!) the horns call us to church. The sounds of hallelujahs across the airstrip. NTM church had eight attendees today; all but me were naked infants. One of these received a thick ear from Jokei for making a sandpit right by the altar.

My aching feet. They are getting better – or not?

A fever this morning. What with the trumpeting sounds it's hard not to believe I'm already halfway to heaven.

Peter came for a visit. The polish of his face, his beard in two sophisticated points. 'I think you are lonesome,' he said.

'I'm fine. Really. But thank you.'

He sat down on the sofa, taking the Bible from under his arm. He introduced me to it, as if to a close acquaintance: 'And now may I present . . . the Revised International Version.' At the front was a historical chart marking the Flood at around 2300 BC.

Peter told me he'd given up on his education because his pastor had said the end of the world was coming and his protégé must spread the 'words of God' as quick as possible to people living 'out in the bushes'.

I watch Peter use his hands. They part the air in slick moves learnt not in the thick vegetation that surrounds us but somewhere more tarmac-ed and cemented; like borrowed tools, these effective hand motions come in use whenever there's no pulpit.

'When is the end of the world to happen?'

Peter was astounded that I should need to ask. It was all there in the Lord's book: the answer to my question.

He too needed to look up the answer, though – his version of the Bible has many such useful annotations.

The signs of the end of the world are:

1. America becoming a great power.
2. The Catholic Church adopting the sign of the Beast.

3. *All manner of sinning just as before the Flood.*

Peter shook his head, thinking of the sinning. 'The drinkings and the dancings. No one listened to Noah either!'

And I shook my head, thinking: if Samwell and the others don't manage to call a plane in, then I'll be relying on this man, who believes we're all about to die regardless.

Midday.
Even when I'm sick they come to me – the children, the adults. I am a 'white man' and they lay before me their hopes. They watch as I reveal money to pay for sweet potatoes from my varied secret stashes. The fascination in their eyes.

I told Peter that it saddens me: as I told Michael once, my life's no more valuable than anyone else's.

Peter said that this is of course true. 'Actually, we are all equal in God's mind.' And then he asked what I might do for his sick wife Eka. 'She needs tablets.'

He meant my malaria pills. I counted them out – though I am short myself. His eyes lit up, seeing the capsules in my hand. His faith was renewed. 'They are made in America?'

He dashed off with the white man's remedy – and I felt sadder than before his visit to cheer me up.

In a moment I'll again flick through Huckleberry Finn.

6.30 p.m.
Dusk; and Jokei has come to keep watch, because there are rumours of Paiela men sighted not far off. He sleeps on one of the crumbling foam mattresses and periodically stalks off to use the toilet that doesn't work. The house now reeks.

'Rats,' Jokei explained, blaming the innocent little rodents.

Tuesday, 14th
I'm awake in the night with a fever that's rendered me senseless. My thoughts fog in; they clear only slowly, along with the hill mist as the sun rises.

*This evokes memories of the cramping of my brain in the Amazon –
the first time. The night sweats, the fear, the shivery slip into delusion.
Is time up for me? I think not – but my great fear is that I won't be
able to think AT ALL soon.*

*The question is central: am I wrong? Have I been wrong all my life
in trusting to indigenous people?*

*I ask this question while I perch by the immense stove – dropped
here from the sky for one of my own sort, that he might, with his
family, further a dream, which is their idea of God's dream, in
greater comfort. The stove too is proud and rendered impotent.*

*Terrible to have it as company, the clock on the stove's impassive
steel face no longer ticking. At twelve minutes past six on a certain day
the power was turned off.*

Today is the day the 'plane from god' is to arrive.

*This morning I waited with Peter on the runway; the cloud lifted
as if reluctant.*

*Little boys showed off their handmade toy rifles. They were
fashioned from banana saplings, perfect in form and balance. Inspired
by the Paielas – the weapons they had when they hacked down one
man, ransacked the sickbay and destroyed the radio.*

*While the boys larked about, shooting each other dead, the little
girls collected grass seeds, and a couple of youths – dragooned by the
Adventist Church – swiped at the longer airstrip grass with their bush
knives.*

Then a young lady came and sat under her rainbow umbrella.

'She is fat,' Peter said, introducing his wife Eka with pride.

*While we waited in the sunshine for the plane that was never going
to come, Peter told me how God arranged for them to meet.*

*'I had a phone call. It was the wrong number. "Who are you?" I
said. "And who are you?" she said. We started talking and I liked the
sound of her. She said she liked the sound of me, too. So I said, would
you like to talk again? And, thanks God, we did.'*

'So you married. That's a lovely story.'

Joining us now was the other, older, Peter – here from Owaiee to greet the plane. He didn't exactly explain why the plane hadn't come on Saturday but listened with his sunny, honest eyes to the smoother, younger Peter. Sometimes he nodded agreeably.

Peter the Older can't click his fingers, I thought to myself. He lacks the sheen on his skin – he's someone content with this less prominent role in life: to provide a willing audience to those who, like his namesake, are in need of one. He wishes the world well – is content to help the general conversation onward.

'But,' Peter the Younger was saying, 'I found she was from Wabag. Not so easy! I walked over the hills and through the bushes and finally got to her and decided she was just about right. So, I asked her father for her, and he said she cost K20,000. I said that this was more than is regular. She should be K5,000. But the father said that for her hand in marriage it would be more than the usual. She wasn't smoking or dancing and she was properly fat so the total was K20,000. My pastor helped me out.'

'And now Eka's here. Perfect.'

'But here is too cold for her. So she's got malaria and now we need help to go to America, Benedik . . .'

The Adventist plane was taking a while to arrive. The Older Peter got to his feet, scythed through the airstrip grass, preparing the pastor's way.

The Younger Peter looked out at the sky and checked his substantial but cheap wristwatch; next, he joined Peter the Older in tackling the longer grass. He rolled his white trousers up and took a couple of swipes, not getting down low enough. After a minute or two he had very obviously not made much impression. 'Maybe I will start tomorrow,' he said, inspecting the blade.

'But your plane is due today,' I reminded him.

However, Peter's mind was elsewhere. 'I was going to marry a white woman once,' he said. 'But she refused and I don't know why.'

We sat it out on the airstrip, Peter the Younger blessed and cursed with an unassailable faith. The sun took itself higher, the colours of the rainbow umbrella paled in the intense light, and I wondered if I would ever journey anywhere again. I thought of Ecclesiastes: 'The eye never has enough of seeing, Nor the ear its fill of hearing.' And I thought too of those words scrawled by Robert Falcon Scott to his wife Kathleen, when his struggle onward through the snows became hopeless: '. . . but oh what a price to pay – to forfeit the sight of your dear dear face.'

Eka retreated. Peter and I waited some more while the boys played a game of pretend cards. Finally, feeling a bit faint, I left too. I went to unpack.

And here I am back at the mission house. I know I'll repack and unpack again, perhaps for days to come.

7 p.m.
I am weaker. They had better hurry, those who are meant to be flying in to collect me.

Odd: Samwell will have talked to the New Tribes Mission in Hagen by now.

Tonight, my speech at the RGS, Hong Kong.* I was also due for lunch yesterday with Steven Ballantyne [the Birds of Paradise expedition organiser] – of all people.

Steven has a clever head for strategy; he lives and breathes expeditions. Not for him a trip without a sat phone. Quickly in, quickly out.

Yet he will be sympathetic – I think. He too loves this country: knows it; trusts to it. The Papuans can get a friend out of the forest quicker than any foreign soldier, or any amount of our technology. He knows that too.

And, indeed, the friends that I made did indeed ensure that I got out. We are not talking about me being lost, deep in the unassailable forest. All I've asked for is a passing plane to drop in.

Feeling lonely – where now are Samwell with his pulled-down hat, Alex with his knitting? I went to the NTM church. The evening service always coincides with the cicadas, which screech at six o'clock right through Jokei's sermon. They stop only after half an hour – as if

---

* A branch of the Royal Geographical Society, which is based in Kensington Gore. I was a former Member of Council.

on condition that he stops. Which he then does.

Outside, I discovered a sparsely toothed lady in a black hair net. Instead of attending church she weeds the Garden of Paradise, wrenching with calloused hands at the herbage to keep the plot spick and span. This is her way, I think, of keeping faith with the missionaries and their vision of the kingdom of God.

But always that one chopped tree – the thought that someone like the First Man also felt the need to spoil Eden.

Wednesday, 15th

Dawn. The NTM trumpet blows and then the dogs howl.

What has gone wrong? Samwell, Alex, Raimond AND Soli gave up? I think not.

Or the missionaries are refusing me a plane, because I was too harsh [in comments I made on the TV programme] *about what has befallen the people of Bisorio? After all, the truth is that they've tried to be true friends to the people there, just as here; indeed, they have done a lot more than anyone to assist them.*

Peter the Younger and I went outside to inspect the cloud cover.

'My pastor is perhaps arriving today,' he said. I looked at the sky. It had never looked emptier.

The mist won't burn off – yet still the utter conviction of the evangelist. Though the Second Coming never comes, though the plane never comes . . .

Today, a practice walk. I must test my legs, test my head. I might yet have to do this by myself.

At 9.30, I took my pack, made my way out across the airstrip along the wiggly path created by countless bare feet.

I walked past Peter the Older, who was still slaving away with his bush knife. He too believes in a plane from God – although not his any more, but mine. He sent two small boys to tail me – they are Stanley and Magi. About eight years old, so the same age as Freddie.

They took my tripod, cut branches to help me across a gully. I stepped into the forest – and found it inviting.

How good it was to be in the company of trees again. I relished the familiarity of it all – my old friends the hectic flies, the fast-racing ants and pungent odours of warm bark. This noisy den that has over the years harboured me, provided for me. Also, almost killed me.

As I turned back, I knew I could make a reasonable bid to walk out alone – so long as I have a CLEAR HEAD. What I cannot do is navigate while sick. Latinai may accompany me a day or so but I cannot in all conscience allow anyone with me to cross the Lagaip river. It goes without saying I can't fend off men with guns.

Yet I must do this thing – walk out alone. Perhaps risk my originally intended route – much shorter. Because something in the outside world has gone wrong.

I am now as skinny and old as the cockerel we ate the first night. A fear that I too am being sacrificed.

11.30

I've done the piece-to-camera – the one I've put off.

The message to be first in Tok Pisin, I decided, then English.

'Mi gat wanpela bikpela toksave. I have an important thing to say. If you find this message I have probably died. Perhaps I have been robbed and killed by you. But listen: I am a father – maybe just like you. I have three young children and a wife. And they will worry. They will want to know what happened to me. So, if you find this, please take the camera or even only my papers to someone who'll get to the United Kingdom or Australian High Commission in Port Moresby – or to a policeman or an elder. My family will pay you – BIG TIME!'

I showed the viewer Freddie and Natalya, photographed tumbling towards me, jubilant in knee-deep snow, and another of Beatrice, aged two. Maybe her blonde curls will make the difference.

Then in English and Tok Pisin I described my proposed route, should anyone come looking for me.

I finished by repeating the names of my children: Natalya, Freddie, Beatrice . . . Enlisting sympathy – as someone might do before being taken outside to be shot.

*Mid-afternoon. Back to the mosquito net; the shivers. Thinking
about Porgera, the international mine just twenty miles away – the
envy and confusion it elicits. The gold-laden planes taking off: the
ancestral heritage being transported as if back to heaven. By people
like me.*

*There's something scratching at the door. Probably the rat – it too
wishes to take back control of its assets.*

5 p.m.

*It wasn't the rat but a mouse – a quiet but forthright little girl called
Mancina. Up the stairs she crept just as I wanted to lie down again.
She ran her hands over things. Showed me how she can drum her
fingers along her lower lip, making plopping sounds. Corrected me
sternly when I tried to copy and got it wrong – didn't do it with
smallest finger first. (NB The trust and confidence of the Fiyawena
children with me – the missionaries must have been very gentle with
them.)*

*She toyed with the chair cover zip, examined it as it glided,
splitting open the material like a knife. I gave her a hotel biscuit.
Have just the two left.*

*Seeing Mancina's success, Stanley and Magi also visited. They
drank from the dusty cups using the one working tap. Mainly as an
experiment, rather than for water.*

*They had brought me a pineapple. It was unripe and, I think,
stolen. As they were about to cut it for me a plane passed overhead. I
raced outside. I waved. The plane flew off.*

*'I'll be all right,' I said to my camera. 'Just as long as I don't
have malaria.' Which is evidence that my mind isn't straight. I have
malaria already, surely. Need to forego the remaining daily tablets to
whack the disease dead in one go. Or it's dengue fever – the one
obvious risk that I can't mitigate. This was my fear all along, of course.*

*This evening in church Jokei knelt behind the high altar – it's like
an auction house desk. But what is he auctioning?*

*He prayed in the fine dirt, kneeling sideways. He didn't pray for
Peter's Adventist plane but asked aloud – only me and Latinai in the*

congregation – where my plane was. It's blatant now: he's appealing for me to be saved. All in his smoker's gruff voice.

Back at the mission house, I deliberately scared myself by looking at the pic of my children as they were about to bombard me with snow.

I must do what I would not – in normal circumstances – think advisable: walk out alone along my first intended route.

This seems the Least Worst Option. I give myself an 80–85 per cent chance – which sounds acceptable, but is a false estimate, because it's assuming I do not go down with a fever. I have more like a 0–15 per cent chance if I do. Humans can do great things – but only if they are able to envisage a better tomorrow. What if they can't – because they can't even see where to put the next foot?

An acceptable risk? I went over to the window – it felt like I was playing for time – where there was a large trapped cricket. The cricket leaped at the netting and kicked at my fingers as I caught it. 'I am actually your saviour,' I said, releasing the creature outside – and wondered where was mine.

By the front door, Mancina was waiting to show me her new game: with her other diminutive friends, she takes a strand of purple taro skin and swings a ball of clay on it, like a pendulum. The boys do the same, fashioning their own – but for use as a weapon.

Today is my last day here. I cannot wait for the outside world – I have never had faith in it, and that lack of faith seems ever more justified.

Even the Hewa think the white men have given up on one of their own, though like me they can't think why.

Jokei came after dark. He demanded I got up and have kaikai [food] *to gain strength before I set out. I felt obliged. And even more so when I found he'd given me such a generous chunk, the tender meat along the pig's spine. Speared through the neck, he said, and then waited as one might over a sick child, till it has had its medicine. (What a fine man he has turned out to be.) I ate only what I could. The meat was part raw. Jokei went to the unworkable toilet a lot in the night.*

Thursday, 16th

There was no church – the horn failed to cry out. The dogs did not howl.

And all because of Jokei's suffering stomach; he's now having a lie-in. I don't suppose it matters. The sermon today would have been the same as yesterday – and the same as next week. It's from Matthew, chap. 24.

'Yumi ino save wanem taim bai Jesus kam bek . . . *We don't know when Jesus will come. In the afternoon, dead of night. We must be ready all the time. No good you drink, sleep with this or that wife . . . Noah heeded the warning. He was ready for the flood when it came.'*

Fever: I am not up to walking out. Not today. Though I had a better night. That is, I didn't have to wring out the sweat from my shirt. I tossed and turned, thinking of Lenka not sleeping either. Has she told the children? Or chosen not to worry them. Not yet.

I now feel I know every aspect of this house. The left tap that is dry, the right tap that coughs and spews; the maggoty reek of the toilet; the comings and goings of the bachelor rat; the scraping sound of the chair feet as I place them to hang the corners of my mosquito net.

Much like in the highlands, when I was mist-bound with the film crew at Ambua Lodge, wondering whether Frank would be be allowed to see his bird of paradise, so it is with me here. I'm held as if in a waiting room by St Peter. He'll make time to see me at the Pearly Gates – or he's too busy with more worthy cases and will not.

And in that waiting room I am given time to think back on what I could have done better.

I write these notes in a school exercise book, complete with a child's doodles – a jungle fowl, a bird of paradise and a machine gun.

It has begun to seem like purgatory. Marooned, now lapsing into fever.

As if, after so many narrow escapes through three decades, I am at last about to pay for my 'damnable desire for knowledge beyond all bounds'.*

---

* It seems that in my mind I had ended up in Dante's eighth Circle of Hell, a ditch of false

Friday, 17th
6 a.m.
Last night the sky cleared and for the first time on this entire journey
I saw the twinkling heavens. The skies had opened up, as if to tell me
something; the clouds had curled back. To what can this be
attributed?

This was such a strange phenomenon, it's tempting to see it as not
natural but supernatural, the hand of a Greater Power. After so many
days of skies obscured by branches or cloud, the heavens open – and I
am released.

A premonition? A foretelling? Put it down to dengue fever.

Nonetheless, an odd sense that something extraordinary is about to
happen. Am I about to be taken out of here? Or am I simply about
to begin the process of ending my life here?

But you don't need to be a seer to know what's going to happen next
– my last attempt to take my destiny back into my own hands.

Is Lenka very upset? She'll have shared her fears now with Natalya,
Freddie and even tiny Beatrice.

Last thoughts.
Outside, they're very kindly praying for me.

Normally the ladies at least wait till dawn – each day a little more
fervent, and each day a little more high-pitched. The mist ascends, the
birds of paradise open their wings in a shower of vanilla and gold,
and up go the screeching pleas to heaven.

Last night Jokei lay on guard beside me, curled on his side, bush
knife to hand. Now, though, my only companion is the moth that
remains silent on the windowsill. Foxy brown and lightly furry, it
lives on, like me. The difference is, all but the head, half a thorax and
wings have been removed, gutted by the ants.

Time to say goodbye to my sanctuary, then: the dirtied window
slats from which I hang my socks to dry, the motifs lovingly painted on
the wall – 'Jesus Had Compassion On Them' – and the blue vinyl

---

councillors, for misusing like Ulysses my gift of reason.

floor where American missionaries once held hands in prayer but where I sweat out my fevers.

On a separate page I have set out my intended route. I'm writing these last words here in case something else occurs.

Already I've checked the medicines and bandaged up my feet. I have thought through the usual protocols, everything that will help me stay alive over the next few days. There's little else to do now than study the map, tick off another checklist and say things to reassure myself. At such a moment it's hard not to think back – to times I might have died but didn't. To the life I've lived – and the life I haven't.

I will take up my rucksack at around 8 a.m.

III

I rolled my mosquito net into a bundle, returned the chairs to where they had waited for their owners before.

Next, as usual, I placed my green rucksack and yellow scarf on the airstrip as a signal to anyone looking that I was here and began asking among the Hewa for any sweet potatoes they might spare.

In the distance I could hear the sounds of the church service getting underway – the trumpeting, then the mournful howling. And I listened with a new fondness. This would be the last time. Things were coming to a close.

I checked my watch: it was approaching 8.15 and I should be gone – but instead I stood listening to the lesser birds of paradise as they called to each other, disporting themselves among the upper foliage as they do from that hour. *Frank would have enjoyed this*, I thought. *The congregation calling, the birds calling.*

I went along to the rival church to say goodbye to Peter the Younger. The Seventh-day Adventists had a table in place of an altar, and Peter had spread his Bible on it and was alone, absorbed in what it had to advise. Beside him was a blackboard upon which was sketched a child-like angel and this put me in mind of Benedik, the girl named after me. On impulse I said a quick, silent prayer for her. Whatever happened to me in the next few days, I wanted the 'new Benedik' – who knows, she might be a much improved version of me, for all her skin problems – to stay safe up there with the clouds on her mountain peak.

I approached Peter and told him that I couldn't afford to wait longer.

'But my wife wants to go in your plane! She needs to go in your plane!'

'Peter . . .' I said. I needed him to know the truth now. 'The plane is not coming. Not your plane, not my plane. They have let us down.'

'We must pray together,' Peter said, following me back to the mission house.

But we did not pray together. We just waited together, powerless, like the two tramps in *Waiting for Godot*: 'I should go now,' I kept saying. But neither of us moved.

I looked at the stove – the two hands of the clock that had no ability to move either. And waited a few minutes more. Even at this stage I was hoping I wouldn't have to walk out.

Then we did move, slowly at first. We'd heard a distant noise – but not a noise from anything that belonged here. It came and went through the skies to the south-east, a thumping, steady beat – pulsating, creating echoes.

'It is only a helicopter from the Porgera mining hole,' Peter said. 'He is lost.'

We looked through the windows to where the sound rattled on and off the clouds. It was getting louder – not something lost but something purposeful.

I found myself outside, running between the mulberry trees. I was aware of villagers coming from different directions, springing out of the gardens and racing to the airstrip, calling 'Hallelujah, hallelujah!' and waving at the sky. Jokei was fast coming up behind me; Peter too. I could hear his jubilation – his valediction. 'We have been answered!'

The helicopter was occasionally visible now, circling, banking sharply – like a bumble bee as it buzzed at us and hovered. The pilot seemed to be assessing the wisdom of descending to the frenzied mob below. And the more the pilot hesitated, the more everyone on the airstrip flapped their hands and bush knives, shrieking.

Then all became strangely calm. There we were together – the ladies leaping about with their cutlasses, me feeling faint, unsteady on my feet

– and a sort of stillness overcame us. We gazed up, as the Yaifo had once gazed up, and the sight of the chopper hovering above us – so alien and disturbing, so loud and metal as it thrashed the sky – for a moment was something mesmorising.

Thwak, thwak, thwak . . . the rotor blades turned through the air like wands casting a spell over us, down here among the trees.

For an age, it seemed, we stared up and still the helicopter hesitated over our heads – almost like something guilty, I began to feel.

But now the craft was descending, the crowds around me drawing back. We waited in a circle, like puny earthlings observing a spaceship as it came to be amongst us. Next the violent wind was diminishing, the engine quietening. Slowing, the blades became visible, were made solid before our eyes.

There was a pause – and I was suddenly remembering how it was when I was aged nine, gathered with Mum, Dad, Katie and Stew around our black and white screen. The eagle had landed, and now we must wait for the astronauts in the lunar module to emerge.

A door opened, tentatively. As if the astronauts were assessing their surroundings for signs of friendly life. The two men who stepped out were in bright garments that were freshly laundered. One of the pair was for some reason feeling the need to take a great deal of photographs. The other was walking forward now, grinning uneasily. He seemed to wish to address me. I noticed that his companion was dashing into position, raising his camera to capture the moment.

It was only now, seeing that urgency of the photographer – the value of what would happen next – that I understood that this visitation was no accident. And whoever our guests were, I was beginning to realise that they weren't the missionary pilots I'd asked for, nor the people the Hewa had been praying for. Inadvertently, we had called in something else from the outside world.

With that realisation came another. I was the sole objective: the prize. Here it was, then, made simple for everyone to see. Over the course of thirty-five years I had proclaimed to people who dwelt in woods or among the dust or out on the ice that I was no more valuable than they – and I was shown to be lying.

It simply wasn't right – the high price tag placed on us, not them. And for their part the Papuans knew it all along, of course. They even accepted it – or else tried to become one of us. And who could blame them? Peter – close by in his long-sleeved shirt, white office trousers held on to him by means of a plastic belt – was better dressed as a white man than me.

However, now the fast-approaching stranger was going to say something of importance. Those around us quietened; they looked on, to see what would happen.

Perhaps my wariness showed. The man smiled to reassure me, and again I thought of how it must have been for the Yaifo, and all the millions before. 'And they believed that we had come from the heavens,' concluded Columbus, regarding his arrival in the New World.

It seemed to me that our own visitor was now attempting a joke: 'Dr Livingstone, I presume . . .' And though he went on to say more words, I was still weak from hurrying here and all I registered was that the speaker was courteous and affable. He was also careful, word-perfect. He had rehearsed this encounter. *He's from the New Tribes Mission,* I thought, not understanding. *They're collecting evidence – hence the photographer – because I'm again making a nuisance of myself on their land. Or more likely from the Foreign Office, sent by Simon, the High Commissioner – the one who served Frank and me Earl Grey on his balcony.* My brain was working hard, but making all manner of misconnections. Ten minutes ago, I'd been about to step into the trees with my survival kit, attempting to save my own life. Now I was expected to delay things, converse pleasantly with whoever this was.

'Your wife has been very worried,' he was saying. I vaguely noted that our guest was English.

'She's okay?'

'*She's* fine,' he said, and laughed lightly. 'She's more worried about you. She says that you're to come home!'

Home; a very distant place.

The man introduced himself properly. I said, 'Sorry, could you say that again? I'm having trouble taking this in . . .'

'Your son Freddie misses you too. He said we'd get you out in five days. And that's today. He's exactly right!'

But I'd have got out sooner, I thought. *Had I not trusted to the outside world.*

'I have a daughter called Natalya and a toddler as well,' I said. And then I thought, *But wait: this man already knows. He knows all about me.*

I looked at him closer, saw that his blue shirt matched the newly opened sky. He smelt faintly of soap. 'Who are you again?'

'Sam, the chief reporter. And he' – Sam looked at the figure who was circling us, squinting through his lens even as he waved with one hand – 'is our very lovely staff photographer, Jamie.'

'He's from a newspaper,' I said to myself, and I began to walk around in circles too. 'I think that's what he said.'

It swirled around me, this cloud of confusion I was enveloped in. The Hewa, I saw, were seated all around. They watched our antics, how I was to be taken back to my people. It was an interesting process, how we – so faded in colour, so plausibly the ancestral dead – assisted each other in this way from the opaque heavens.

'I'm not well,' I tried to explain. 'You see, to me you are something like angels. Something extraordinary come down from above.'

Sam smiled, made a note. He had a little ruled book to hand and I now noticed that all I was saying, all that I was doing, was being set down.

I attempted again to accommodate these new circumstances. An hour ago I'd been going from house to house with my pot of water because at around 8 a.m., after hoeing their gardens, the Hewas were in the habit of shoving a couple of sweet potatoes in the embers – and at that time I stood the best chance of an act of kindness. Back then, before my world changed, these had been my thoughts: *Will I get so much as a banana to eat today? If I set out now, will I lose consciousness? Will I be shot?* And all the while the Hewa children had trailed behind me, tittering; often they had a sweet potato to hand and wrenched a bit off as they peered up at my sickly face.

I had been someone steeling himself: gathering my last strength, steadily cutting out distractions (the test pilot cross-checking his flight deck) to focus on the daunting mission ahead. But now? Now, I might be spared the whole thing. I need only wave goodbye to the Hewas and hand myself over to our two unexpected callers, 'Sam' and 'Jamie'.

But not so fast. Was this monumental effort by me, and by everyone here, to be discarded so readily? Even now the woman with the black hair net was laying sweet potatoes at my feet – her contribution.

Sam, I expect, saw my confusion, my spread loyalties. Until now, he had talked on happily, with his likeable, disarming voice, but he was also a professional. He knew what he was here for – and hadn't got the top job by being the slowest in the pack.

Quickly, he sought a way to my heart. 'Would you like to speak to your wife?' I sensed that this call was as important to the nice journalist as it was meant to be for me.

He was already dialling the number. I looked at the phone, this thing that I had rejected until now. Slick and black, battery at 61 per cent, the device wasn't reassuring in the slightest. 'Lenka? Sam here.' The familiarity of his tone was striking. He had been talking a lot to my spouse in the last few days. I, not he, was the outsider, the excluded one. 'Sorry to wake you. I've got someone here who'd very much like to talk to you . . .'

This was being made very personal: about to speak to me was someone who, without equivocation, without any complicated agenda, cared for me.

'Is that really you?' Lenka said to me from somewhere far away.

I remember little else of that conversation. Later, people wrote that I apologised for the worry I'd caused. I hope I did not apologise for the beliefs I held – the beliefs I was now about to betray.

IV

It was done quickly, my betrayal.

But first I took Sam on a tour.

'Might we see where you've been staying?' he asked, and I was happy to take a final look. The Garden of Eden, *Huckleberry Finn*, my mosquito net tomb. It seemed important to say goodbye properly to these things; they too had stuck by me.

Sam took particular interest in the last of my food supplies – three portions of coffee, one of oats and the remaining powdered milk scattered with the dust on the floor.

Back at the helicopter, I found that Peter had embedded himself among my bags with Eka.

'Don't worry,' I said. 'I'm not going anywhere without you both.'

Sam looked up from his notebook. He exchanged a glance with Jamie. 'Er . . . will that be all right, Craig?'

Craig seemed to be the pilot. A big, tired-out sort of man, he leant on his chopper – large, baggy fingers intertwined across his high-visibility jacket, the startling yellows of which were a source of great wonder to the Hewa children.

'No skin off my nose,' he muttered, begrudgingly.

'And my cassowary?' said Peter.

'He's made a special container for it,' I said. The young bird popped its head out enthusiastically from a box of missionary plywood.

'No. And that's my final word. No cassowaries.'

'Probably the thing will be happier here anyway,' said Sam thoughtfully, trying to console Peter.

I raced around, shaking hands. 'Make it quick,' Craig said – and informed Eka that she wouldn't be taking her walking stick either.

'But it is a very nice stick!' said Peter.

'It is indeed,' Craig said, and the fat of his chin rose as he smiled, indulgently. 'And too long.'

Peter broke the stick in half. The crowd watched it snap – and juddered. The stick had to be broken because the white man said it had to be broken.

I embraced Jokei, and then looked at who and what else I was leaving here: the assembled people, the assembled trees.

'Funny,' said Jamie, 'we thought we might be out here three weeks, searching. We came equipped for everything and anything.' I nodded, casting an eye over their solitary olive-green backpack, still with its price tag. 'Our main concern was you might choose to stay out here. Refuse to come back with us!'

But what choice was there? I thought. *I'm a dad.*

I was strapped in, then Peter, then Eka holding her two bits of walking stick. The Hewa were ordered to stand clear. The downwash swept over them.

And it was all over, so I thought. The journey had begun as a desire to reach back into the past. It was a handshake, the sealing of a contract made long ago. And we had done this, Korsai and I – briefly held hands. It was a matter for two friends – of little interest to anyone else. No one much would be any the wiser.

———

The Hewa were now lost behind us, and from a right-hand seat I was looking upon all that I had been spared: the dispassionate trees, the landslips, the furious bees, an angry people called the Paiela. In precisely eleven minutes the helicopter delivered me from the Central Range, saving me the walk that I'd been dreading – but perhaps had needed to do.

As we flew onwards, and Eka unaccountably regained her appetite, gobbling her way through the four snack boxes, I wondered what lay in store in place of that walk. Already it was evident that this personal act of mine had been made a very public one. Somehow my absence had become a centre of media fascination – though as a physical feat the trek hadn't to me seemed so very remarkable. The journey wasn't even a complete one; it had been interrupted. Already I knew a part of me would need to come back.

Occasionally, Jamie took a picture of the trees cascading down slopes, or Sam pointed at his phone. 'From *The Times* . . .' he would say, and Jamie would read the headline and raise an eyebrow or grimace. Or 'That. From him . . . Fairly typical.' And both would check I wasn't listening. 'Sour grapes,' said Sam. 'Pure sour grapes . . .'

I was powerless. Already the narrative was set – even in my disorientated condition I could see that. This, I began to realise, was a story that everyone might savour, something refreshingly distant from our everyday concerns, yet resonant of them. The appeal was global and timeless: the archetypical hero who sets forth to undergo epic trials. I had listened to many such accounts myself through the years, crouched around firesides in lands as far apart as the Orinoco, Siberia and Borneo.

To the European mindset, though, I was a wayfarer whose imagined ordeals brought with them an age-old resonance of *The Odyssey*, *The Song of Roland*, *The Nibelungenlied* – tales that had once, in far-off times, like the Icelandic sagas or tales of Prester John, spoken of who we had once looked to and who we had been. I was another Fawcett seeking his jungle city, a Franklin wedged in his Arctic ice, or a Livingstone on his knees. Here was a hearthside yarn – a pause for thought, a cautionary tale: no matter that I felt I was something more complicated than a leftover from yesteryear.*

From an imposing building off High Street, Kensington, a national newspaper had dispatched, in the manner of H.M. Stanley sent to find

---

* Having introduced the self-filming of expeditions to television, I could also find placed at my door blame for being the first to popularise that most contemporary of phenomena, the video selfie.

Livingstone, their best man ('I shall not give up the chase,' Stanley had written to Gordon Bennett, editor of the *New York Herald*, some one hundred and fifty years ago. 'If alive, you shall hear what he has to say. If dead, I will find him and bring his bones to you.'). This time round, it would not be Africa but New Guinea – which was the same, for all practical purposes. That day a rival newspaper under the same ownership, but at a different end of the building, sent a stringer from Hong Kong to overtake him.* The race was on. Not knowing what I was doing out there or why, others piled in with their own contribution: some saw that I was white and male and needed me to be an imperialist; some saw me as white and male and needed me to be their champion. And for some it mattered not who or what I was, as long as I was waylaid by savages in another *Heart of Darkness*.

As we whirled onward – Enga Province, Western Highlands Province – over the forests and through the skies, my compatriots tried gently to get me up to speed. Both were decent men, genuinely concerned for me. I can see now. But I didn't want to listen. The more that I heard of the world out there (which was my world), the more it imposed – and the more the home that I'd constructed in New Guinea fell apart.

Sometimes Jamie took photos of me as I stared out. Did he notice that I was looking not with relief but anguish? All I wanted to do was get back to the airstrip – as if I had left behind something important.

Perhaps I felt this only because of the shock of having my fate so abruptly wrenched from my hands. Or perhaps because of the strangeness of it: a people of a distant place had become close to me, and those nearest to me become remote. Whatever the reason, I'd been reminded of what had always made me feel so alive. But too late, I was to be taken away.

Throughout the whole business, Sam and Jamie were utterly gentlemanly. They helped see Peter and Eka safely on their way and in Port Moresby sat with me at the hospital.

Then, while I convalesced back at the hotel, they went snorkelling.

---

* The journalist gave his version in an article for the *South China Post* in an article entitled 'Like a Caper from *Scoop*'.

And I shut the curtains and sweated some more, thinking through the friends across New Guinea who had come together to bring about this journey and friends from home who, it would now seem, had come together to fetch me safely back.

I didn't read the news stories – though there was no avoiding the headlines over previous and subsequent days:

'Explorer Vanishes Searching for Lost Tribe of Headhunters', *The Sun*.

'Rescued from Remote Forest', *New York Times*.

'Privileged Fool or Intrepid Adventurer?' *The Telegraph*.

None of this was about me, of course. In a sense, it was about everyone except me.

In a world conditioned to instant answers – any information you wanted just a click or two away – I provided none. The planet had been fully explored, so they repeatedly said, but I had disappeared – and with hardly a word of explanation. For less than four weeks I was 'off the grid', but I might as well have been the navigator John Cabot sailing off the map. Here, just as in the fifteenth century, was a big blank that we might fill with monsters and imagined deeds.

In my younger years, when I was out of touch for months at a time, my absence had been accepted. Since then, great changes had taken place – but not within the forests and icefields, which had merely been decimated. The greater change was in us.

We were ever more connected with ourselves – and ever more disconnected from our surroundings. That was the price of our progress – and the consensus seemed to be that it was worth paying. We would not let go from what we knew as reassuringly familiar.

It seemed to me, in my befuddled state, that this made it more important than ever that a few of us disconnect, risk freeing ourselves to connect with elsewhere. In this, an Age of Information – so much of which was false information – we were in danger of losing sight of what was real.

On 21 November I landed before dawn at Heathrow airport and was shuffled through Arrivals by a friend who had a black belt in karate and an ability to blend with a crowd.

I was disorientated, still suffering from what transpired to be both malaria and dengue fever, but perhaps nothing could have prepared me for the fascination caused around the world by my brief absence from it.

'Some of these tribes are infamous for cannibalism,' pronounced *The Day*. 'The White Man Blunders of "Explorer" Feed Racist Myths,' shrieked *The Guardian*.

Before the sun was up, I was back at my dear friend Susanna's house in West London. There, as the day broke, I was interviewed live by Frank Gardner, the one person I could rely on to give a reasonably fair and informed interrogation. There were others yet more famous who interviewed me, after. I didn't know who they were. I confirmed that it was true, I did not believe in taking a phone. No, this was not a publicity stunt. Yes, I had been gravely ill.

I flew back to my family in Prague, embraced my wife and children, and for a while tried to disappear all over again. I read *The Secret Garden* with Natalya, constructed a Lego rocket with Freddie. Beatrice I took to the park, where there was a sandpit.

On a late autumn morning I watched the toddlers around me as they constructed castles or excavated tunnels. A boy surveyed the playground from his heap, like a conquistador upon a peak in Darien. Then a little girl came along and trampled the lot – 'I'm the king of the castle!' – and everything had to be rebuilt.

This was the way of us all, I thought. Some felt the urge to wander, some the need to vent their frustration – to kick out, 'do their own thing'.

But there were other children also, unnoticed in the corner of the sandpit. These were of a quieter disposition. Running the sand through their small hands, contemplating the structure of the grains, they too were explorers, among them no doubt our future scientists, the people who might do more than anyone to push back the boundaries of our knowledge. Yet they would never be sufficient for the job of scrutinising our ravaged planet – just as scanning the earth's surface in ever increasing detail would never bring us the entire truth. The point was this: the human being at heart remains a poet; it's not enough to establish bald facts about our world. We need to experience, with each fresh generation to taste and smell and touch.

You could choose to think of our exploring instinct as acquisitive – a means by which our forefathers gained ground – or as something that opens opportunities, enables us to bring about a better tomorrow. In New Guinea, I had been reminded that exploration lay not in the past but now, and did not stem from a capacity within the likes of me, or Sir Francis Drake, or the irrepressible Mary Kingsley with her thick skirts, but a capacity within the Niowra, the Yaifo – and us all.

I did try to explain to *The Guardian*, a paper I particularly valued for its environmental coverage. As I understood it, the journalist – who had felt it fitting to hold this conversation with an extraordinary explorer relic in the faintly antiquated, Old World setting of the Savoy – would be none other than Stephen Moss, a naturalist and writer I very much admired. It was not the same Stephen Moss who turned up . . .

———

Of course, all this lay ahead of me that morning at Fiyawena Mission as I prepared to walk out – light-headed, the odds not particularly favourable, but knowing that I had held true to my ideals.

Then the helicopter came and suddenly behind was the journey that had come so close to claiming me, and ahead lay my own world – also wishing to claim me. As we flew from the Central Range, I felt confused, despairing, euphoric. I was homeward bound – and I should be thankful, I began to see, for having been spared, when Fawcett, Livingstone, Bering and Cook were not.

I was to live, not die. And I might look back with gratitude – and some amazement – that, however anyone else understood my experience, the journey had met with an unlikely success. I had found Korsai; I had been allowed to see so much that I'd thought already gone. The forest had held firm – clacking, sizzling, smothering – and the Yaifo had not sold their birthright for a dream of Paradise. They had managed to find accommodation with our world – even as so many of us were consumed by it.

There was more: a sense of completion. A long time ago now, my father had inspired me to take off. And when, shortly after in the Amazon,

I had proved ill-prepared for what seemed to be my function in life, I had acquired a second father – Jonny Gowi, of Kandengei village, by the River Sepik. His people had shown me that I could not succeed alone. That this was the commonality of humans: we must stand like the trees together.

Had I been right, in my more headstrong years, to claim that those we call 'explorers' were imperialists – with their flags, with their imposing ideas, with their booted feet? Was the European inherently someone who must seek control and lay claim?

Many would say so. One need only think of Cortés laying waste to the Aztecs. And, of course, the tendency of the European to spread their influence afield was long-standing. 'Help me to journey beyond the familiar and into the unknown,' are words attributed to St Brendan in the sixth century. 'Give me the faith to leave old ways and break fresh ground with you.' These days we broke fresh ground not just on earth but in the heavens. The most famous imprint of all was on the moon – the tread of Buzz Aldrin's space boots, snapped by Armstrong as his travelling companion disturbed the Sea of Tranquillity. 'We came in peace for all mankind,' they said, and we marvelled at what they had accomplished on our behalf, putting aside the matter of the Space Race and that flag.

But to proclaim there is a simple correlation between the white man's adventures and imperialism would be lazy. As aggravating and unjust as it might be that we did a lot of colonising, and the Brits in particular – that early Industrial Revolution, that need of a small seafaring nation to out-trade its more powerful neighbours – the central, embarrassing truth was missed by many.

And here was that central truth: the varied races of humanity are not so very different. Yes, the amount of resulting destruction has differed, and shockingly so, but to a greater and lesser degree we share the same desire to find out, to set forth.

One and a half million years before Armstrong had tramped on the moon, *Homo erectus* made his mark in the sediments of Ileret, northern Kenya. A giant step for proto-mankind: the hominid placing the ball of his foot to the clay, then pressing down, declaring himself present.

And again and again, determinedly proceeding over the hills. This was the act of a bipedal creature who had left his hands free for tools – the flints and sticks with which he would order his existence. And so off they toddled: Adam and Eve beginning to appreciate the wider possibilities of their Fall – the world of drudgery but also possibility into which we had been cast. Through wise use of our new Knowledge, things might yet turn out all right.

Communicating this heartening message too was the job of the explorer. They were our envoys, stronger or more expendable cavemen than the rest. They waved farewell to their loved ones and passed over the craggy horizon, promising to bring news of wonders – driven onward by something implacable, a 'calling', a madness. Like Sisyphus of the Ancient Greek tale, doomed to perpetually roll a stone up the hill, they pressed on regardless, empowered by a totally unrealistic sense of expectation.

Nor was the impulse unique to hominids. Rather, it was hot-wired into every living thing – from the crusty lichen advancing through the seasons across its boulder to the microbe that seeks beyond its petri dish. Chucked out of Eden, Adam was sentenced to 'till the ground from whence he was taken', but the punishment of toil was inflicted on every other species too. Each bat was forced to try its canines, every mosquito to probe with her snout. I'd seen as much, closeted with the teeming species of New Guinea. From now on, it would be like this: cease to explore and you ceased to keep up with the living. You stood still, then you died out.

I reflected on all these things, peering down through the clouds with a quiet excitement, suddenly realising that out there in the forests I had reignited the flame – small, insistent, exquisite – of my yearning to investigate our wider surroundings. I thought of Tennyson's 'Ulysses', whose hero insists on pushing onwards to the western stars, 'made weak by time and fate but strong in will'. And I remembered again how it was at the beginning: a little boy looks up into the sky. What he sees is magnificent – ascending, dipping its wings, flaunting its power.

That boy was me, a child looking up with wonder as his dad manoeuvred his plane towards somewhere far away.

AFTERWORD

A year after the events recalled here, I took up my green rucksack, the one carried much of the way by Samwell, and saved up some money to check on people I had known elsewhere. My first destination was the Amazon, the forests which had almost done away with me as a rash twenty-three-year-old. Full of foreboding (not for myself, but for the people I had known; wasn't it asking too much to find another community for whom things had worked out?) I went in search of the Matsés family I had lived with on the Upper Yavari. Somewhat to my amazement, I found the drug gangsters who had once threatened them evicted, the loggers chased off too. Meanwhile, of course, the children who long ago had walked with me through the undergrowth, teaching me how to snare a mouse, use bark for medicine and weave a shelter of leaves, had grown up. Their own children liked nothing more than to kick a football about, but here's the thing: the members of this next generation, too, were proud of their heritage. They were no longer nomads who wandered in amongst the trees, but broadly they were in charge of their own destiny.

I went next to northern Mongolia, where among the reindeer herds, larch and spruce I tracked down Gana, another of those who had, more than twenty years before, helped me on my way. 'We never forgot you in all this time,' he cried out, as I approached. 'And now I see that you did not forget us!'

Papua New Guinea, a country which had provided a fresh start for me as a young man – in a manner, it provided a nest so that I might again launch out – a generation later had again come to my aid. And I'd not been chastened by the experience of that gruelling return journey, rather the opposite: I understood now that I'd wasted precious time, that disappearing into unfamiliar worlds was my field of expertise – and that I should never have stopped.

Afterwards, even as I readied myself to leave once more, friends again insisted I took a phone. They did this with the best intentions, but I saw now that they would never quite understand me – as those of a church-going persuasion must feel, discovering they are seated in a pew among those of a quite different creed. My prophets were not their prophets; the laws which governed my universe were not theirs. To go somewhere, it was necessary to leave somewhere, so it had always seemed to me – not be impeded or necessarily even advantaged by your place of origin. There were risks involved, as there were for my dad as a test pilot and for the astronauts of Apollo 11 rocketing into space. Taking those risks was important, too.

My expeditions, like all expeditions perhaps, at heart had always been about casting off from safe shores. I notice the word 'safe' crops up repeatedly through the pages of this manuscript: my brother Stewart, 'who had always kept me safe'; my attempts to 'safeguard' a people's past; the 'safety briefings' from Os the medic. For me, though, safety matters in PNG boiled down to this: once again, thanks to some people in a faraway place, I had been kept just safe enough, until it was time to get back to my own kind. Thanks to them also, I was never lost – just as I was never found.

As for why no missionary dropped by for me, the reasons to this day remain unclear. An unfortunate series of mechanical failures? An overloaded roster? We do know that the New Tribes Mission, informed of my location by Samwell and the two youths I recruited from Fiyawena, were besieged by the world's news outlets.* When no less

---

* 'The phone went hot!' Keith Copley, the coordinating director in PNG, later explained to me from Goroka. 'We had to take it off the hook!' I expect the missionaries, themselves subject to so many spurious tales through the years, knew only too well how this story would play out. This didn't stop Keith's efforts to enlist help. As time went by, his concern was that I would head off into the fighting zone – 'criminal activity in that area is very high', he wrote to an anxious friend – as indeed I was just about to do.

than two newspapers declared they were sending their best man, and both were equally determined to do the honours, the missionaries must have smiled, knowingly. This was an irony that Evelyn Waugh would have appreciated. Such was the desire of so many caring people to rescue me, I became in need of rescue.

More journeys will follow – while my health holds out, while my family allows me leave of absence. Perhaps one night in the Amazon forest, when I am old, I'll meet an equally old and toothless jaguar or, like Tony Last in *A Handful of Dust* I'll end my days held captive in a Brazilian clearing, doomed forevermore to read aloud the complete works of Dickens. Until then, once more my children Natalya, Freddie and Beatrice will do what they like to do on my safe return: conclude proceedings by pulling my large green rucksack out of the hall. Only then do we know the mission is done, except for the sharing of it. I might think of where to go next.

Whatever ideas emerge from these future expeditions, it seems to me now, having set down this account, that they will be unlikely to come together as they did in New Guinea. Far from being the chaotic enterprise that many depicted, there was something remarkably coherent about the themes that overtook me along the trail. I didn't need to force them. The most obvious was the reoccurring notion of being lost – there were children adrift in the mist, an explorer and societies mislaid. Similarly, Frank sought birds of paradise, and I sought places that in my childhood had seemed so perfect – and finished up semi-delirious beside a homemade Garden of Eden. Likewise, in the world from which I had come nature everywhere had been 'fenced out', yet the Niowra fenced in their young. The Sepik created wounds, but there was a healing to be done of a greater wound. And the coupled, overarching theme: I suffered psychological trauma in the Amazon, yet we were all in trauma.

Looking back, it strikes me that a pivotal hero of this tale is not Korsai or Frank, or the people I most wanted it to be – the string of Papuans who had helped foreigners like me – but the unlikely figure of the Typist. Although she was always at risk of being portrayed as a figure of passing amusement, I included her to illustrate the power of social constraint in a more traditional community. As someone in my twenties, I'd needed to escape from not her but it. Now, however, I see that she carries more significance than as another downtrodden female, a means of social entrapment. For it is just her daring kind – awkward, unquieted, everywhere breaking the taboos – who will feel a way forward for her community.

Sometimes, I even mention the Typist when invited to talk about my experiences at primary schools: I want girls, especially, to believe they can be – indeed, are – explorers. Shepherded by their forebearing teachers, the excitable members of each class file into the sports hall for morning assembly, they sit cross-legged and sometimes they sing 'All Things Bright and Beautiful'. Then I'm introduced: 'This morning, girls and boys, we are really, really lucky to have with us a real-life modern-day explorer!' And I do what I can to engender the sense of wonder that I felt at their age, by telling the stories I think they most want to hear: the shootings, the distrustful camels, the loyal huskies, the seal eyeballs that you might eat raw. 'But don't you ever have fun?' a younger child once asked, in the unfiltered way younger children have. I thought of a line from *The Mayor of Casterbridge*: 'Happiness was but the occasional episode in a general drama of pain.' And this reminded me that I should also convey why it is that some people choose to put themselves through such unpleasantness. So these days, when asked, I might liken myself to a mountaineer who finds in a sheer rock face not only an exhilarating challenge but also a moment where life is made beautifully clear.* But usually everyone but the outdoor activities teacher looks nonplussed, in which case I go on to tell my patient audience it's the same for any one of them who plays football or the flute; there are rewards to be had when you've achieved something for which you've trained so hard. And I conclude by putting it to the pupils straight: the time of the classic, romantic type of traveller is gone; there's no longer any necessary reason – not a geographical one, anyway – to march to the Poles or to follow the course of a mountain range or river

---

* 'On mountains everything is made so simple. You descend the mountain, or you die.' From *Into the Abyss*, my book discussing what keeps adventurers going in the face of adversity.

– and I remember that Thesiger was harsher still, dismissing such terrific physical feats as 'stunts'.

Where, then, do we stand as explorers of our globe? Somewhere not at the end but near the beginning. For that reason I'm always sure to remind my own offspring what great challenges await – the Mariana Trench, the volcanic plumes in our oceans, the many species that we do not understand, which include every one of the 8.7 million that we have named, and the other millions that we will ever name, including our own.

The antics of many of today's adventurers would seem, at first sight, irrelevant, a distraction from more important matters; and worse, by a strange perversity, rather than add knowledge, many 'explorers' have not revealed for us more of the planet but rather reinforced age-old myths, thereby keeping narrow our world view. Rather than bringing us closer to the Other, they have ended up highlighting our differences; rather than allowing alternative ways of living to be a useful counterpoint to our own lives, they reassure us in our prejudices, that we may stay safe in our secluded lagoons and on our mountainsides.

But we are not any more safe; it's not so easy to hide away. The coronavirus that, as I write, is sweeping around the planet, threatening to lay our species low, has been a useful reminder of that. Perhaps, then, it is as well that the story of the explorers of today is not the story of a breed apart. The world is found to be small – we all now have access to it. And we might all play our part – scientists, artists, computer programmers, novelists and, yes, occasionally even those that undertake glorious, seemingly pointless ventures too, because these strong-willed women and men may be foolhardy, but they inspire us onward.

There is a star called Icarus* – official designation MACS J1149+2223 Lensed Star 1 – that is nine billion light years away, harboured in a spiralled galaxy. This is the most distant object we know of, as of now – and I suppose we shall never reach it. But you can bet this will not stop explorers of the next millennia trying their best to get as far as they can. Should we dismiss the moon landing as a stunt? Its value – rather

---

* According to NASA. 'Hubble Uncovers the Farthest Star Ever Seen', 2 April, 2018, Nasa.gov.

than the winning of the Space Race or building of three thousand hospitals* – was a fresh unleashing of the human imagination. And this imagination of ours seems to know no bounds. It's the quality that powers us on. Call it a lunacy, call it a miracle, the 'optimism bias' referred to by psychologists. All this stems from the particular arrogance of the pioneer: a type of blasphemy. Daring to think all things are possible means daring to think that we are God.

Once, back in 1969, a man stuck up a flag; to assist in conditions of low gravity, wires were strung along the banner to make it hang better. The astronauts left it behind, having staked their claim like goldminers – or as a dog might, signposting its territory. As a child, though, I needn't have worried. When the module blasted off, back to Michael Collins and thence home, Buzz Aldrin saw it pitch over, consumed in an inferno of dust.

Yet the achievement stands. The flag was a mere marker, a reminder of a step made along the way. Unless we press on, we are no more living than that lunar dust – or, put another way, the clay that God fashioned us from in Genesis. And perhaps we understood that all along, as our ancestors marked with their feet their passage out of Africa, already equipped with our stone axe and imagination to explore the horizons of elsewhere.

---

* The original bill for the Apollo project was $28 billion, according to the Planetary Society. In today's money, $300 billion – and a hospital might cost $100 million.

AN ACKNOWLEDGEMENT

In the days and weeks after my return to the UK I began to understand that a huge number of people had tried to come to my rescue – to save me from the 'jungle', and perhaps save me from myself. 'Let's hope he's learned his lesson!' wrote a relative on his Christmas card to my sister Katie, but this wasn't typical.

During the time I was 'lost' they did their best to counter the worse prejudices about the world's more isolated communities, about Papua New Guinea – and about me. They put out the word on Papuan social media, they rang round the missionaries, and they alerted the Australian special forces, who considered whether finding me might be incorporated into a training exercise. Friends, but also complete strangers, chipped in with ideas, or sought to explain 'the explorer mindset'. Some of my stoutest defenders were just the type of adventurers whom I'd been so rude about over the years.

It was no good. Soon there would be nothing left of my journey, so I said little to anyone by way of thanks and instead held on to what I had in PNG, hoping that those who knew me would understand and forgive. Deep down they would appreciate that I had somehow (as usual) got by through the good will and abilities of the men, women and children I'd made friends with out there. I believed in the Papuans, just as I believed in the Matses who had enabled me to cross the Amazon Basin and in the Chukchis who had prepared me for a lone journey into the Bering Strait with sledge-dogs. That was just the way it was, and always would be.

In addition to the debt I owe to the *bikmen* of Kandengei and to those in the village with whom I've had allegiances and friendships over thirty-five years, and the people of Bisorio, Hanamata, Wilifa, Fiyawena and other settlements along the way, I'd like to acknowledge the support I received from my own world. For the most part, these people intervened for no other reason than they worried for me. I had gone in search of a friend called Korsai, but they too had done their level best, reaching out to me as I had done to him.

I'm particularly grateful to the following: my dear friends Susanna White, Catherine Marsh and Charles and Fiona Robinson, also James and Georgie Riley in Hong Kong, and Rupert McCowan and the forbearing Hong Kong branch of the Royal Geographical Society. At the New Tribes Mission Keith Copley, and the two couples who launched me out from Bisorio on the first occasion, Bob and Noby Kennell and George and Harriett Walker. Those instrumental to my initial return visit, to make *Birds of Paradise: The Ultimate Quest*, included Kim Shillinglaw and Jamie Balment at the BBC, and, at Tigress Productions in Bristol, Dick Colthurst, Sarah Swingler and Anne Varley, and the patient members of the TV crew: Simon Davies, Steven Ballantyne, David 'Os' Osborne, Mark Roberts, Nick Allinson, Ralph Bower, Caspar Dama and Felix. It was Sarah Hubbard who encouraged me to get back in touch with Frank Gardner, as Dick Colthurst suggested, to make the BBC film.

The extent of my debt to Frank I hope is obvious from this story; in addition, I'd like to mention the further support given me before and after the final trek, particularly by Steven Ballantyne, who leapt into action when I failed to re-appear, also Os, Charles Blackmore and John Perry and dozens not mentioned by name in the book, including Lawrence Postgate – the mysterious friend who slipped me through Arrivals at Heathrow.

Among those who bolstered me during the lonely days before I departed were Giles and Alexandra Milton and daughters, Cathy and Frank Arne Sandsund and, at October Films, Matt Dewar, Jos Cushing and meticulous tech man Martin Long, as well as 'Angus' of Niugini Helicopters.

Among the many who worked to get me home, foremost were the indefatigable Jo Sarsby, who with Haley Miles and Steven Ballantyne and my lovely, uncomplaining sister Katie Pestille, did everything in their power to assist me from far away – and assist Lenka, my wife, on the 'home front'. I should underline again here how thoughtful, generous and caring were Sam Greenhill and Jamie Wiseman of the *Daily Mail*, the paper that came all the way around the world to save me. Robert Beverton tracked down my likely whereabouts from his laptop in a Costa Coffee outlet in Prague; Harriet Fennell, Larissa Petryca, Roger Boyd and the hard-working staff at the British High Commission each pursued different avenues, from combating the silliest of the surrounding publicity, to marshalling contacts civilian and military.

I would like to add a special word of thanks to Harry Marshall, Walter Donohue, Vivien Green, Nicola Spooner and Nic Fleming and Denise Cook, who I always knew would be willing me on, with Suzie Allen, my wider family and so many others who had been good enough to take an interest in my books and programmes over the years.

Finally, to my agent Victoria Hobbs at A.M. Heath, and Jamie Byng and all at Canongate – most obviously my editor Simon Thorogood, but as well Leila Cruickshank, Vicki Rutherford, Melissa Tombere and Debs Warner for their careful work on the manuscript, Mehr Husain for her thoughtful comments, Guy and Binky Sellers for theirs, to Lucy Zhou in Publicity and Martin Hartley, David 'Os' Osborne and Richard Baker for the use of their photos.

This book is compiled from memories and a combination of three sets of field notebooks and diaries. In addition, I drew in particular from the following books and articles, most of them alluded to, or cited, in the text:

Allen, Benedict, *Into the Abyss: explorers on the edge of survival*, Faber and Faber: London, 2006

Allen, Benedict, *Into the Crocodile Nest: a journey inside New Guinea*, Macmillan: London, 1987

Allen, Benedict, *Last of the Medicine Men*, BBC: London, 2000

Allen, Benedict, *Mad White Giant: a journey to the heart of the Amazon Jungle*, Macmillan: London, 1985

Allen, Benedict, *The Faber Book of Exploration: an anthology of worlds revealed by explorers through the ages*, Faber and Faber: London, 2002.

Allen, Benedict, *The Proving Grounds: a journey through the interior of New Guinea and Australia*, HarperCollins: London, 1991

Allen, Benedict, *The Skeleton Coast: a journey through the Namib Desert*, BBC: London, 1997

Allison, A, 'Introduction to the Fauna of Papua', *The Ecology of Papua*, eds. Andrew J. Marshal and Bruce McP Beehler, Periplus Editions: Singapore, 2007

Anon., 'Papua New Guinea Earthquake: tens of thousands need urgent aid', BBC Online, 4 March 2018

Bashō, Matsuo, *The Narrow Road to the Interior, Classical Japanese Prose: an anthology*, ed. and trans. Helen Craig McCullough, Stanford University Press: Redwood City, 1990

Bashō, Matsuo, *The Narrow Road to Oku*, trans. Donald Keene, Penguin Books: Australia, 2017.

Bateson, Gregory, *Naven*, Stanford University Press: Redwood City, 1958

Berry, Wendell, *The World-Ending Fire: The Essential Wendell Berry*, Penguin Books: London, 2018

Bonington, Chris, *Quest for Adventure*, Hodder and Stoughton: London, 1987

Breeden, David, ed, *The Adventures of Beowulf*, CreateSpace Independent Publishing Platform, 2011

Brody, Hugh, *The Other Side of Eden: Hunter-gatherers, Farmers and the Shaping of the World*, Faber and Faber: London, 2002

Burton, Richard Francis, *Explorations of the Highlands of Brazil: with a full account of the gold and diamond mines*, Tinsley Brothers: London, 1869

Carrington, Damian, Niko Kommenda, Pablo Gutiérrez and Cath Levett, 'One football pitch of forest lost every second in 2017' *The Guardian*, 27 June 2018

Chagnon, Napoleon A., *Yanomamö: the Last Days of Eden*, Harvest Books: San Diego,1992

Chase, Allison and Gordon Brown, 'The Man Who Knocked the Bastard Off', *Outside* Magazine, 1 Oct 1999

Cook, James, *The Journals of Captain James Cook on his Voyages of Discovery*, J.C. Beaglehole, J.C. ed., Cambridge University Press: Cambridge, 1955

Dangerfield, J.M. and Mark Hassall, 'Phenotypic variation in the breeding phenology of the woodlouse *Amadillidium vulgare*', *Oecologia*, Volume 89, pp. 140–6, 1992

AN ACKNOWLEDGEMENT

De las Casas, Bartolomé, *The Diario of Christopher Columbus's First Voyage to America, 1492–1493*, University of Oklahoma Press: Norman, 1989

Dowie, Mark, *Conservation Refugees: The Hundred Year Conflict between Global Conservation and Native Peoples*, The MIT Press: Cambridge, Massachusetts, 2011

Du Soutoy, Marcus, *What We Cannot Know: explorations at the edge of knowledge*, 4th Estate: London, 2016

Duguid, Julian, *Green Hell: adventures in the mysterious jungles of Eastern Bolivia*, The Century Co.: New York, 1931

Fiennes, Ranulph, *Mad, Bad, Dangerous to Know*, Hodder and Stoughton: London, 2019

Fiennes, Ranulph, *Beyond the Limits: the Lessons Learned from a Lifetime's Adventurers*, Little, Brown and Co.: London, 2000

Global Witness Report, 'A Major Liability: Illegal logging in Papua New Guinea threatens China's timber sector and global reputation', 30 July 2018

Greenslade, Rob, *What's Going On Downriver*, Xulon Press: Camarillo, 2010

Hadow, Pen, *Solo: The North Pole, alone and unsupported*, Michael Joseph: London, 2004

Hanbury-Tenison, Robin, *Finding Eden: a journey into the heart of Borneo*, Bloomsbury: London, 2017

Hutchinson, Alex, 'Why We Wish for the Wilderness', *NY Daily*, *The New York Review of Books*, 11 June 2019

Ibn Battuta, Abdullah Muhammad, *The Travels of Ibn Battuta to Central Asia* trans. Ibrahimov Nematulla Ibrahimovich, Ithaca Press: New York, 1999

Jubber, Nicholas, *Epic Continent: Adventures in the Great Stories of Europe*, John Murray: London, 2019

Kingsley, Mary, *Travels in West Africa*, Macmillan and Co.: London, 1897

Laman, Tim and Edwin Scholes, *Birds of Paradise: Revealing the World's Most Extraordinary Birds*, National Geographic Society: Washington D.C., 2012

Madge, Tim, *The Last Hero, A Biography of the Explorer*, The Mountaineers Books: Seattle, 1995

Murphy, Dervla, 'Older Travellers are now more intrepid than their young', *The Telegraph*, 23 September 2015

Noyce, Wilfred, *The Springs of Adventure*, John Murray: London, 1958

Parry, Simon, 'Like a Caper from Scoop', *Post* Magazine (*South China Post*), 27 Dec 2017

Pascoe, Bruce, *Convincing Ground: Learning to Fall in Love with Your Country*, Aboriginal Studies Press: Canberra, 2007

Planetary Society, *How much did the Apollo Program Cost?* 14 June 2019

Polo, Marco, *The Travels*, trans. Ronald Latham, Penguin Classics: London, 1958

Raleigh, Walter, *The Discoverie of the Large, Rich and Bewtiful Empyre of Guiana*, Argonaut Press: London, 1928

Scott, Doug, *Himalayan Climber: a Lifetime's Quest to the World's Greater Ranges*, Sierra Club Books: San Francisco, 1992

Scott, Ernest, *Australian Discovery*, J.M. Dent and Sons: London, 1929

Simpson, Colin, *Adam in Plumes,* Angus and Robertson: Perth, 1954

Simpson, Colin, *Adam With Arrows: Inside New Guinea*, Angus and Robertson: Perth, 1954

Stanley, Richard and Alan Neame, eds., *The Exploration Diaries of H.M. Stanley*, Vanguard Press: New York, 1961

Van Linschoten, Jan Huygen, *The Voyage of John Huyghen van Linschoten to the East Indies*, Elibron Classics, Hakluyt Society: London, 2005

Wallace, Alfred Russel, *The Malay Archipelago: The Land of the Orang-utan, and the Bird of Paradise. A Narrative of Travel, with Studies of Man and Nature*, Macmillan and Co.: London, 1869

Weir, James, *In Search of Eden: the Course of an Obsession,* Haus Publishing: London, 2007

Whymper, Edward, *Scrambles Amongst the Alps in the Years 1860–69,* John Murray: London, 1871

William Wills, ed., *A Successful Exploration through the Interior of Australia, from Melbourne to the Gulf of Carpentaria, from the Journals and Letters of William John Wills*, Richard Bentley: London, 1863